THE BOOK ON FLIPPING HOUSES

PRAISE FOR
THE BOOK ON
FLIPPING HOUSES

"Learn the step-by-step process of house flipping from the best in the business. This book is the perfect blend of fix-and-flip concepts, tactics and real-world examples."
> – Joe Fairless, author of *Best Ever Apartment Syndication Book*

"This book is not about motivating you and then leaving you hanging. Instead, it is packed with real-world advice and is written honestly with both the good and the bad. If you are looking for all of the things you need to know, whether you are starting your first flip or your hundredth, this book is THE Book on Flipping Houses!"
> – Brian Burke, President/CEO of Praxis Capital Inc., has flipped over 500 homes

"J Scott is one of the premier real estate investing writers in the industry. He has a knack for delivering top-notch content in a way that is easily understood by everyone. This book is one of the best ever written on the subject of flipping houses. Highly recommended!"
> – Mark Ferguson, Flipper, Landlord, Creator of InvestFourMore.com

"When it comes to the house flipping business, there are only a few people I trust and J Scott is one of them. The Book on Flipping Houses is an excellent guide that can help you understand the inner workings of a very complex and lucrative business."
> – Seth Williams, Founder of RETipster.com

THE BOOK ON
FLIPPING HOUSES

How to Buy, Rehab, and Resell Residential Properties

REVISED EDITION

J SCOTT

BiggerPockets®
PUBLISHING

The Book on Flipping Houses, Second Edition
J Scott

Published by BiggerPockets Publishing LLC, Denver, CO
Copyright © 2019 by ScottBuilt, LLC.
All Rights Reserved.

Publisher's Cataloging-in-Publication Data

Names: Scott, J. author.
Title: The Book on flipping houses : how to buy , rehab , and resell residential properties, revised edition / J. Scott.
Description: Denver, CO: BiggerPockets Publishing, LLC, 2019.
Identifiers: LCCN 2018957762 | ISBN 9781947200104 (pbk.) | 9781947200111 (ebook)
Subjects: LCSH Flipping (Real estate investment) | Real estate investment--United States. | House buying. | House selling. | Dwellings--Remodeling. | BISAC BUSINESS &ECONOMICS / Real Estate / General | BUSINESS & ECONOMICS / Real Estate / Buying & Selling Homes
Classification: LCC HD255 .S37 2019 | DDC 333.33/83--dc23

Second Edition

Published in the United States of America
10 9 8 7 6 5

To my amazing wifey, without whom I never would have had the inspiration to embark on this crazy and wonderful journey. There's nobody I'd rather be doing this with.

Thank you from the bottom of my heart.

J Scott

TABLE OF CONTENTS

Foreword by Scott Trench 14

Introduction 17
    Why I've Written This Book 17
    20 Steps to Your First Rehab. 18

CHAPTER 1 | First Concepts 25
    House Flipping Defined 25
    Does Flipping Still Work in Today's Market? 27
    How Much You Can Earn Flipping Houses 27
    The Truth About Taxes. 28
    Are You a Contractor or an Investor?. 29
    Controlling Your Deals 31
    Part-Time House Flipping 34

CHAPTER 2 | Prepare Your Financing 35
    First, the Bad News. 36
    Types of Real Estate Financing 37
    Summary of Financing Options 44
    Your Financial Resume. 45
    No Cash or Credit? No Experience? Know This!. 48
    Final Thoughts on Financing. 49

CHAPTER 3 | Find Your Agent(s) 52
    The Types of Agents You Need. 52
    Becoming Your Own Agent 56
    Your License as a Secondary Income Stream 61

CHAPTER 4 | Where You Should Buy 62
Determining Your Farm Area 62
Analyzing Potential Markets 63
My Farm Area...70

CHAPTER 5 | What You Should Buy.......................75
Distressed Properties 75
Retail Properties 77
The Foreclosure Process...................................79
Property Criteria..81
Level of Renovation 85

CHAPTER 6 | Who to Buy From 88
Purchasing from Owners with Equity 88
Purchasing from Absentee Owners with Equity 92
Purchasing from Owners Without Equity 94
Purchasing Bank Owned Foreclosures (REO) 97
Purchasing Foreclosures at Auction (Trustee Sales).............. 100
Finding the Seller Who's Right for You........................101

CHAPTER 7 | How You'll Find Deals 103
The Acquisition/Marketing Grid.............................. 104
The MLS 105
Online and Auctions...................................... 108
Direct Marketing 112
Advertising...123
Wholesalers...127
On-Site (Trustee Sales)...................................128
Other Marketing Techniques 128

CHAPTER 8 | The Flip Formula 129
The Flip Formula 130
Determining Sales Price.....................................131
Calculating Fixed Costs 140
Your Profit...144
Estimating Rehab Costs.....................................145

CHAPTER 9 | Looking at Properties 156
The 100 House Rule 156
Start Looking for Deals 158
Deciding to Make an Offer..................................165

CHAPTER 10 | Making Offers 168
State Contract vs. Custom Contract 169
The 5 Major Contract Components...........................170
Negotiating Tips 182

CHAPTER 11 | Your Due Diligence 186
A Cautionary Tale 186
Due Diligence Tasks 188
Run the Numbers Again 190
If the Numbers Don't Work.................................191
Purchase Checklists 192

CHAPTER 12 | Create Your SOW 196
Determining How Much Renovation You Need.................197
Over-Rehabbing 198
Under-Rehabbing 199
The 25 Renovation Components.............................200
Scope of Work: The Demo House 201

CHAPTER 13 | Create Your Budget 216
Building Our Budget 216
Budget: The Demo House 216

CHAPTER 14 | Create Your Schedule 223
Scheduling Components 224
Scheduling Rules of Thumb 237
Schedule: The Demo House 239

CHAPTER 15 | Hiring Contractors 244
The Spectrum of Contractors 245
The Value of a Great Handyman 249
Creating Your Rehab Team 249
Finding Your Contractors 255
Better, Faster, Cheaper 258
Your Contractor Paperwork 259
Employee or Independent Contractor? 262

CHAPTER 16 | Managing Your Rehab 265
Don't Lose Days 266
Plan Your Schedules Upfront 267
Prepare for Dependencies 268
Know Who Supplies What Materials 269
Never Pay Ahead of the Work That's Been Completed 270
Make Sure You Visit the Jobsite 271
At First Sign of Trouble, Don't Hesitate to Fire a Contractor 272

CHAPTER 17 | Agent or FSBO? 273
The Value of a Good Agent 273
When to Consider "For Sale by Owner" 279
Flat Fee Listings 280

CHAPTER 18 | Staging 282
Deciding Whether to Buy or Rent Furniture. 283
Top 16 Staging Tips. 284

CHAPTER 19 | Buyer Due Diligence 293
Preparing for the Buyer's Inspection 293
Dealing with Inspection Issues. 296
Handling Appraisals 297
Beware of Buyer Financing Traps. 300

CHAPTER 20 | The Closing 302
The Closing Process 302
10 Tips to Improve Your Closing Success 306

Final Thoughts 309

Acknowledgements 311

About the Author 312

FOREWORD BY SCOTT TRENCH

President, BiggerPockets

The Book on Flipping Houses and its companion, *The Book on Estimating Rehab Costs*, were the first two books ever released by BiggerPockets Publishing. It's no stretch to say that they validated a business model and laid a foundation that has allowed our company to build what is now one of the largest independent book publishers in the country, with works that have reached millions of readers and changed countless lives.

What I hope to communicate to you in this foreword is just how *uniquely* qualified J Scott is to bring these books to aspiring and growing real estate investors. In 2013, as a first-time author, J produced not one but two complete, publication-ready, professional works. They've gone on to sell more than 115,000 copies and are almost universally accepted as foundational books in the flipping and rehabbing houses industry. His accomplishments with these works are the result of two qualities that he firmly possesses: a relentless drive towards business and operational effectiveness, as well as a generosity of spirit.

It will be obvious to you as you read this book just how well he understands the business of flipping and rehabbing properties. You'll have the privilege of peering into his mind as he breaks down the business step-by-step, in a manner designed to help you understand all of the challenges and opportunities this business has to offer.

J has completed over 150 single-family projects since 2008 (I write this towards the end of 2018). He has documented his journey perhaps more completely and publicly than any other investor operating at a similar scale. You can follow much of his journey through his decade of forum contributions on BiggerPockets.com, which are freely accessible to the public.

While his business credentials and experience are impeccable and speak for themselves, it's his spirit of generosity that truly sets him and his work apart. J has poured his heart and his mind into the BiggerPockets forums. His contributions have provided value not only to tens of thousands of people with whom he has directly engaged through these posts, but also the millions more who have benefited from viewing the discussions.

The cumulative effect of his giving spirit is astounding—he has literally posted to our forums more than *17,000 times* over the course of the last decade. After tens of thousands of discussions (often with intelligent, lively debate and pushback from other smart investors in the community), J Scott has had the chance to hone his perspective in a way that is not replicable through any other form of study or experience. He's seen what resonates with people—a nd what doesn't—a cross thousands of discussions. By his own admission, he's been wrong more times than he can count and constantly uses his forum interactions to tweak his knowledge and teaching style. All of this makes him a better investor. It also makes him a better writer.

J understands the typical investor who is attempting to get started or to scale their flipping business. He's perhaps more aware of the problems that arise with rehabbing than any other ordinary house flipper. A great business author lives his business, but he also writes in a way that conveys his expertise. J Scott does both of these things in spades.

He knows how to write to you. And for you.

There is no substitute for experience. There is no substitute for the learning that comes through debate with other intelligent minds. There is no substitute for the ability to articulate complicated business concepts simply. J Scott has demonstrated these qualities and worked tirelessly to improve in all of these areas for the past ten years.

You will come across few people in this world who have devoted so much time and energy to mastering their craft, let alone with equal passion who engage one-on-one with their audience.

Make room on your bookshelf. If you are a real estate investor, flipper or not, these books will be a staple of your collection and give you an incredibly detailed, realistic, and accessible lens into the world of buying, rehabbing, and selling investment property in a repeatable and scalable fashion.

Scott Trench, President of BiggerPockets.com

INTRODUCTION

Why I've Written This Book

I've spent years watching real estate "gurus" rip-off eager new investors with high-priced seminars and training programs. I've seen the late-night infomercials that lead starry-eyed newcomers to believe making money in real estate is as easy as making a phone call, buying a system, and waiting for the money to roll in. I've spent many years in this business talking to up-and-coming investors who have paid thousands (or even tens of thousands) of dollars to these scam artists hawking their courses.

Unfortunately, what these gurus don't tell wannabe investors is that becoming successful at real estate takes more than buying a system or listening to a motivational speaker. Typically, these "teachers" and "coaches" are more about motivation than they are about education. They get their students excited about making lots of money and becoming financially independent, but they don't provide the knowledge and tools necessary to do it.

In other words, while they may get their students jumping up and down with excitement—and at that same time get them to spend more money on more training—most of these so-called mentors don't do anything to help their students start investing. In fact, the vast majority of people who consider getting into real estate **never close their first deal!**

It's not that real estate investing is tremendously difficult. And—despite what the gurus and infomercials would lead you to believe—it's not that there are "secret" ways to make money in real estate that only the experts know. In fact, there are hundreds of different ways to make money in real estate. Even one small investing niche—like flipping houses—provides endless opportunities for the creative investor to be successful and earn large profits. But, while these endless opportunities might be great for established investors who are looking for new ways to earn a fortune, they can become daunting challenges for up-and-coming real estate investors looking to break into the business.

Experienced investors often throw around the term "analysis paralysis" to refer to those new investors who really want to get the ball rolling with their first property but can't seem to get past the "research" phase. Either because they are scared of the unknown or because they don't feel like they have enough information to be successful, these new investors never feel ready to jump into the game.

This book is for those up-and-coming investors who want to flip houses, but don't want to entrust their education (and their money) to gurus or scam artists. It's for those who already have the motivation to become a rehabber and an investor, but just don't know where to start. It's for those who need that little extra push to help get past their fear and over that hump of completing their first deal.

If you're ready to start flipping houses, this book is for you. My goal with this book is to help get you past your fear of the unknown and to provide all the information necessary to give you the confidence to take that first big step of completing your first—or next—deal.

20 Steps to Your First Rehab

Before I go any further, let's get a few things out of the way right upfront:

- I'm not a real estate "guru."
- You won't find any "secrets" in this book that haven't been published elsewhere.
- I can't teach you how to get rich overnight flipping houses.

If any of those things surprise or disappoint you, you'll want to close this book right now.

Still reading? Great! Then let's get started...

If you're anything like me, you hate picking up a book like this, reading it cover-to-cover and then trying to figure out what you should do next. Too many of these types of books are more motivational than educational, and by the time you're done reading them, you're tremendously excited but no closer to actually acting. I don't want you to finish this book and not know what the next steps are—in fact, on the contrary, I want you to start acting *while* you're working your way through the book.

In other words, I want you to treat this book as a *road map*, with each step clearly defined and explained. And just so you know that I'm serious about the idea of this book being a step-by-step guide. In this first chapter I'm going to lay out all the steps you should follow to flip your first house. The goal of this chapter is to provide a 50,000-foot overview of the flipping process and create a guide to the rest of the book. My hope is that you'll occasionally return to this chapter to help remind yourself of the big picture.

If you're already an experienced rehabber and are just looking for some tips and tricks to take your business to the next level, feel free to use this chapter as a guide to each of the steps with which you're already familiar, and then jump to those chapters where you think your business could use some improvement or optimization.

With that said, here are the 20 steps to profiting on your first (or next) flip:

Step #1: Make Sure You Really Want to Do This

Before you get too far into the book, it's important for you to decide if rehabbing houses is a challenge you really want to undertake. Chapter 1 will cover all the things you should know before you take the plunge—for example, what exactly is house flipping? How much money can you make doing it? What type of personality do you need to be successful?

Step #2: Get Your Financing in Order

For many investors, finding the money is the biggest thing standing between them and success. Now is the time—early in the process—to figure out where you're going to get the money to do that first deal. Chapter 2 will talk about all the different avenues available to get your deals financed and will even provide you an "ace in the hole" if you find that traditional financing methods aren't an option for you.

Step #3: Find (or Become) a Great Real Estate Agent

It's time to find your first (and for the time being, your most important) team member—a great real estate agent. He or she can help you define your business strategy and research your market, making the difference between success and failure. In Chapter 3, I'll discuss what a great agent can do for you, how to find a great agent, and if your best option may be to become your own agent.

Step #4: Determine WHERE You Will Buy Your Properties

While rehabbing will work in many locations, it won't work everywhere. And it will certainly work better in some places than others. You need to be confident you're purchasing a house in a location that supports rehabbing and flipping, and if it doesn't, it's better to know upfront so you can start looking elsewhere. In Chapter 4, I'll reveal how you can quantitatively assess different locations to determine which ones are candidates for making money flipping houses. The information in this chapter can make or break your investing career, so read it carefully.

Step #5: Determine WHAT Types of Property You Will Buy

Now that you know *where* you want to buy houses, it's time to determine *what types* of houses you want to buy and *from whom* you plan to buy them. Are you going to buy run-down, single-story ranch houses or large, move-in-ready McMansions? How many bedrooms and bathrooms should you be buying? Will you buy in subdivisions or along back roads? Will you be buying houses with pools or without? There are many different types of houses, and you need to determine where you will focus your time and effort. Chapter 5 will help you decide what your target property looks like.

Step #6: Determine WHO You Will Buy Properties From

By now, you know where you'll be buying and what types of properties you'll be looking for—it's time to figure out from whom you'll be buying them. Will you be buying from overworked landlords looking to dump their properties at a discount? Will you be buying from homeowners underwater on their mortgages? Will you be buying from the banks, either at the courthouse steps or after foreclosure? There's no right or wrong answer to this question, but before you decide from whom you'll be buying, it's important to understand the different challenges you'll be facing. Chapter 6 will discuss all the different opportunities for flipping houses and the benefits and downsides for each.

Step #7: Determine HOW You Will Find Your Properties

We're making progress—you now know where you'll be buying, what types of properties you'll be looking for, and from whom you'll be buying them. But how exactly are you going to generate leads to find these properties? Will you be buying off the Multiple Listings Service (MLS)? Direct mail marketing? Internet marketing? Bandit signs? Other investors? There are many options, and Chapter 7 will discuss them and help you clarify which acquisition strategies are right for you.

Step #8: Learn How to Analyze a Deal

Once you've figured out what types of properties you'll be looking for, where you'll be looking for them and from whom you'll be looking to buy them, it's time to dig into the numbers. Without knowing what a good deal looks like, you can look at 1,000 houses and still have no idea what you're doing. That's the purpose of Chapter 8—to teach you everything you need to know in order to recognize a potentially good deal when you see it.

Step #9: Search for Properties

It's taken us some work to get here, but now it's time to put all our planning into action and start looking for that first (or next) deal. You'll be looking at lots of houses, and if your plan is to be marketing or advertising for deals, now's the time to put your marketing hat on and start generating some leads. Chapter 9 will walk you through the process of getting the leads flowing, looking at potential deals, talking to sellers, and deciding when it's right to move forward with an offer.

Step #10: Make Offers

By now, you've found a property or even ten properties you think would make great deals, and it's time to make some offers and try to buy one of them. Chapter 10 will go into the basics of real estate contracts, how to make offers, what to include in your offers, and how to give yourself the best chance of getting your offers accepted.

Step #11: Complete Your Due Diligence

Congratulations—you have an accepted offer! For the first time in your real estate career, there is now some time pressure. You need to decide if you really want to go through with this deal, which means verifying that there's a profit to be made and putting together your plan for getting to that profit. Chapter 11 will help you get through your due diligence by providing checklists, goals, and strategies for completing your inspections and other due diligence tasks that you must complete in the days following your accepted offer.

Step #12: Create Your Scope of Work (SOW)

As part of your due diligence, you're going to need to come up with a precise estimate for how much the renovation will cost. But there's no way to know how much it will cost if you don't know exactly what work you're planning to do! In Chapter 12, we'll introduce our example property—The Demo House—and I'll walk you through the step-by-step process of creating a detailed scope of work ("SOW") that you can use to create your budget and that you will use as your roadmap to the renovation.

Step #13: Create Your Budget

Now that you have your detailed scope of work, it's time to use that to generate a detailed budget estimate for the project. You'll need this renovation estimate to complete your due diligence efforts and help you decide whether it makes sense to move forward with the project. In Chapter 13, we'll use our scope of work to create a detailed renovation estimate for The Demo House.

Step #14: Create Your Schedule

You've now completed your due diligence, decided to move forward with the project, and have your SOW and budget in place. It's time to get working on the rehab. But before you begin renovating, you're going to want to create a schedule for both you and your contractors. Without one, you risk having the project drag out for far too long. Chapter 14 will teach you how to order your rehab work and create an optimal schedule. As an example, we'll create a renovation schedule for The Demo House.

Step #15: Build Your Rehab Team

You're ready to get to work on your renovation, but before you can start, you need to assemble your crack team of contractors. If only it were that easy! With all the different types of contractors, finding a strong crew and preparing the paperwork is going to be a major undertaking. Chapter 15 will help you navigate the world of contractors, put together a strong team, and help you protect yourself with the proper paperwork.

Step #16: Get Your Rehab Done

Most people think that completing the rehab is the hardest part of the job. And they're not wrong! But if you've done all your preparation—created a detailed SOW, a detailed budget, and a realistic schedule, and put together a great crew of contractors—the actual renovation should be a lot easier than you've been told. Chapter 16 will tell you what to watch out for during the renovation, how to keep things moving along, and what to do if you run into issues.

Step #17: Build Your Selling Team

While your crew is completing the renovations, it's time to start thinking about the most important component of the project—getting it sold! Of course, this involves building another team, but by now, you've gotten the hang of that. Chapter 17 will lay out the members of your selling team, what each of their roles will be and how you'll find and select these team members.

Step #18: Get It Staged and Listed

The renovations are complete, and your selling team is ready to get moving. Time to get the house looking its best and listed for sale. Chapter 18 will tell you what you need to know about staging, working with your agent to get it listed, and handling potential buyers.

Step #19: Get Through Buyer Inspections and Appraisals

You have an offer! Unfortunately, for many investors this is where things start to get difficult. The buyer is going to be required to jump through many hoops by his agent and lender, and that means he's going to make you jump through hoops as well. However, if you're prepared, you can ensure that the whole process goes easily and smoothly. Chapter 19 will tell you how to prepare and how to deal with difficult situations, and most importantly, will teach you how you can ensure that if problems do arise, you have the best chance of keeping the deal together and moving forward.

Step #20: Get to the Closing Table

After all the hard work and effort you've put in, now is the best part—getting to the closing table and getting your check! There are many little things that will need to take place before closing day, and while a good real estate agent will take care of the bulk of them, you're going to want to make sure that you have plenty of control over the process so that it doesn't stall. Chapter 20 will help you navigate the closing process and get you your paycheck.

CHAPTER 1
FIRST CONCEPTS

House Flipping Defined

The business model behind house flipping is simple:

Flipping is the act of purchasing a property with the intent of reselling it at a profit.

As you might guess, there are a couple different strategies for flipping houses, each with its own benefits and drawbacks, and each providing savvy investors the opportunity to not only make some extra cash but also build a profitable long-term business, if that's their goal.

Specifically, there are two specific types of house flipping you'll hear real estate investors discuss:

Wholesaling

Wholesaling involves purchasing a property and immediately (oftentimes the same day or even at the same closing table) reselling it to another investor for a profit. Wholesaling doesn't require the house flipper to do any repair or maintenance work on the house, and sometimes doesn't even require the house flipper to put up the money for the house.

Because a wholesaler is simply reselling the exact same product he or she bought—but at a higher price!—the successful wholesaler must be a strong negotiator. He must be able to convince property sellers to sell well *below* market value, and then convince property buyers to buy for *close to* market value. The better a wholesaler negotiates, the larger the "spread" between the price they buy the property for and the price they sell it for—meaning a larger profit in their pocket.

Additionally, great wholesalers are tenacious marketers. Wholesalers look for a property that's very inexpensive relative to other properties in the area, either because it is distressed and in need of major repair or because the owner of the property is desperate to sell (for example, going through a divorce, leaving town for a new job, or having financial difficulties). This often requires the wholesaler to spend hours sending letters, making phone calls, knocking on doors, or putting up signs, looking for that "needle in a haystack" property that can be bought low and sold high.

Rehabbing

Rehabbing involves buying a property in a state of disrepair, adding value by fixing it up, and then reselling the property, either to a homebuyer who plans to live in it or another investor who plans to keep it as an investment.

Some rehabbers will look for houses that only need minor cosmetic repairs (often referred to as "paint and carpet" rehabs), while others would prefer to tackle larger projects, such as properties with structural problems, properties with fire or water damage, or properties requiring building additions and adding square footage.

In some cases, the rehabber will even move into the house while it's being rehabbed. This is called a "live-in flip," and not only might this strategy provide the flipper a place to live for a period of time but can also provide tax advantages when done correctly.

Successful rehabbers have great teams behind them, including skilled contractors who can renovate properties quickly and cost-effectively, and knowledgeable real estate agents who can market and sell the newly renovated property to a prospective homeowner. Additionally, they have the business and management sense to keep projects on schedule and on budget, and the design sense to make the proper renovation decisions.

While there are certainly other methods to flipping houses besides wholesaling and rehabbing, these are by far the two most common. And while wholesaling is a fantastic way to earn cash and bootstrap your real estate investing career, a great rehabber has a lot more options that will generate a lot more opportunity for profit. As such, the remainder of this book will focus on the rehabbing side of flipping, and I will be using the terms "rehabber" and "flipper" interchangeably throughout the text.

Does Flipping Still Work in Today's Market?

Both in good and bad markets (and everything in between), I invariably get the questions, "Is now a good time to flip houses? Does it still work in this market?"

To answer that question, here is what you must understand:

In real estate, there's never a great time to be both buying and selling real estate. In a typical up-market, houses are easy to sell (there are plenty of motivated buyers), but it's difficult to find a great deal when buying. In a typical down-market, houses are easy to buy (there are plenty of motivated sellers), but it's difficult to turn around and find lots of demand to resell your properties.

If flipping required both a great market to buy and a great market to sell *at the same time*, there would never be a great time to flip houses. Luckily, that's not the case.

For a great flipping market, you either need to be able to *buy* property at a massive discount or you need to be able *sell* property at a good premium—you don't need both. In fact, when I wrote the first edition of this book during the Great Recession, around much of the country houses were very easy to buy and very difficult to sell; as of the writing of this second edition, it's become much more difficult to find great deals, but much easier to sell them once you've completed your renovation.

Depending on when you're reading this book—and what specific market you're in—you may find it challenging to find deals or you may find it challenging to sell your completed projects. But neither is impossible in any market. The key to making money in this business is to buy the right properties at the right price, fix them up to appeal to the widest possible group of end buyers, and then market and sell them better than your competition. I plan to spend the entirety of this book focusing on exactly those things, and pretty soon you'll see why flipping in any market is not only possible but really not that tough.

How Much You Can Earn Flipping Houses

Not surprisingly, the biggest question on the minds of most prospective investors is, "How much money can I make flipping houses?"

First, there is no one correct answer to that question. Obviously, part-time flippers are going to be hard-pressed to make as much money as full-time flippers. In addition, someone living in California may be able to make $300,000 (or more!) on a typical flip compared to someone in rural Nebraska who may only be able to average $30,000 per flip (not accounting for the differences in cost and risk, as well).

However, because this is an important question, let me give you an idea of what a typical flipping business might look like. In fact, let's take my business as an example, as I live in a fairly typical real estate market, and focus on the types of houses many house flippers target.

Before I started hiring employees, I found that it wasn't very difficult to manage one or two flips per month on my own, with just the help of a real estate agent to find and resell the properties. On average, I earned about $30,000 in profit on each flip. Therefore, over the course of a year, I could average anywhere from $360,000 to $720,000 in profit, without any employees to manage!

Other than myself, I now have two full-time employees in my business. One is my wife, who has her real estate license, and is responsible for all the marketing and real estate agent tasks. The other is a project manager responsible for hiring and managing the contractors and ensuring that the projects stay on schedule and on budget.

Between the two of them and a personal assistant, they handle about 90 percent of the day-to-day work required by the business, while I handle the other 10 percent and focus on our future strategy and growth. Between us, the business could potentially handle up to five flips per month, creating a gross yearly profit of more than $1 million!

Even a part-time house flipper who has a full-time job can easily flip between two and four houses a year. With an average profit of $25,000–$35,000 per flip, there's no excuse why an average person shouldn't be able to make an extra $50,000–$150,000 per year flipping houses in their spare time.

The Truth About Taxes

Now that I have you excited about all the money you can earn by flipping houses, it's the right time to break the bad news: You're going to pay taxes on your profits.

Your profits are whatever is left from the sale of the house after you subtract out your rehab costs (labor and material), your fixed costs (commissions, fees, closing costs, loan costs, taxes, insurance, utilities, etc.), and any other costs directly related to buying, fixing up, and selling the house.

You may have heard that investment income is taxed more favorably than other business income, but unfortunately, the money earned from flipping houses is not considered investment income. As a house flipper, you are buying and selling a commodity—no different than if you were buying and selling shoes, furniture, cars, or food. As such, you'll likely be paying the same percentage in taxes as you would if that income were coming from any other type of business or even from a full-time job. In addition to income taxes, on at least part of the income you'll also likely have to pay another 15 percent in self-employment taxes.

I'm not going to lie: Taxes will significantly eat into your profits. But it's better to earn a lot and have to pay taxes on it than to not earn much in the first place. All that said, if you plan to do more than one or two flips per year, there *are* some ways to structure and manage your business that can potentially shield you from part of your tax burden.

I highly recommend that once you make the decision you're serious about being in the house flipping business (either part time or full time), you consult a qualified accountant or CPA who can help you structure your business in a way that will allow you to pay the least amount of taxes possible.

For more on this topic, I highly recommend the BiggerPockets book, *The Book on Tax Strategies for the Savvy Real Estate Investor.*

Are You a Contractor or an Investor?

When you start out flipping houses, one of the first questions you'll ask yourself is, "What parts of the rehab work will I be doing myself, and what parts of the work will I be hiring out to contractors?"

For those who decide to use professional contractors to get the work done, invariably they will eventually think to themselves, "Why the heck am I planning to hire expensive contractors instead of just doing it myself or hiring cheap day labor, and saving thousands of dollars?"

While there is no right or wrong answer to the question of "do-it-yourself vs. hire-it-out," I would like to give you some perspective on what it takes to turn house flipping from a hobby into a serious business that will allow you to make serious money!

For the house flipper whose goal is to make a substantial part of his or her living from flipping houses, the goal can't be to focus lots of time and energy on rehabbing houses; the goal must be to focus lots of time and energy on the parts of the business that generate the real profits: finding deals and finding money to do those deals! While your business may involve flipping houses, that little fact is relatively unimportant.

Many business owners believe that what the *business* does should affect what ***they*** do; they confuse their business with their job. That's not how successful business owners think.

Successful business owners realize that their goal is to create systems and processes around doing something profitable. They then use those systems and processes to replicate and scale that profitable effort over and over and over again.

In this case, the business is all about rehabbing and selling houses. However, your job as a business owner has nothing to do with rehabbing and selling houses. Your job has to do with creating systems and processes to allow your business to rehab and sell more houses.

For example, you could spend three months doing all the rehab work yourself on your first house and save $15,000 in contractor costs. If you spent 40 hours a week for those three months working on this particular rehab, that extra $15,000 would equal about $30/hour in extra profit in your pocket. But what if you instead took those three months and focused your time on finding three more houses (one per month), each of which generated $30,000 in profit?

That's an extra $90,000 in profit over that period of time, or $200/hour! That's not bad, but...

What if you spent those three months streamlining your process around buying, rehabbing, and selling houses, and got to the point where you could do it 12 times in three months (once per week)? That's an extra $360,000 in profit, or $750/hour.

Where would you rather be focusing your time—saving $30/hour by doing your own construction work or earning several hundred dollars per hour by doing more deals?

Along the same lines, I know many investors who choose to save a few hundred bucks here and there by hiring unskilled labor—those guys standing outside of Home Depot who work their butts off but need to be told what to do. If you do this, you run into the same trap. Those guys require a lot more oversight, and babysitting contractors is just another $10/hour job. Wouldn't you rather hire the contractor who costs twice as much, but whom you know can be trusted to get the job done on schedule, on budget, and with a high degree of quality to free you up to focus on replicating and scaling your business?

In the time you save by not having to babysit contractors, if you're able to pick up even one more house, that expensive contractor will pay for him or herself many times over. Moreover, if you spend that time figuring out how to scale your business and buy even more houses, that expensive contractor has now become invaluable.

By the way, while rehabbing 50 or 80 or even 100 houses a year might seem far-fetched, there are many people who are successfully doing it. But they don't do it by spending time caulking showers, laying tile, or any other $15/hour task. They do it by focusing on the processes that allow them to replicate and scale. Everything from having a vast network of supporting team members (attorneys, CPAs, agents, brokers, contractors, etc.) to having well-documented systems for getting the work done (things like creating a list of materials used in *every* house and training contractors how to replicate the same finishing touches in every house).

Doing your own rehab work (i.e., being your own general contractor) is no different than trying to be your own lawyer or your own CPA. While you could give it a try, you'd rather let your lawyer do what he or she is good at, let your CPA do what he or she is good at, and let your contractors do what they're good at.

Meanwhile, you can focus on figuring out ways to help all of them work faster, smarter, and more efficiently, which will lead to being able to rehab more houses and make more money for both you and for the great team of people you have helping you.

Isn't that the goal?

Controlling Your Deals

One of the hardest things to drill into a new investor's head is the importance of controlling all aspects of every deal you do. In fact, I tell my team, "If something goes wrong, it's always my fault." And I mean it—the buck stops with me!

Some investors who can't get their deals done will blame their buyers:

"He wasn't serious about buying and wasted my time!"

Some will blame their contractors: "My GC didn't show up on time all week, and now we're behind schedule!"

Some will blame the lender: "He said he could push the loan through, but he couldn't!"

Or the agent: "She said the paperwork was completed, but it turns out she was so excited to go on vacation that she forgot to get all the signatures!"

In fact, I used to be guilty of this mindset myself. Here is an excerpt from a blog post I wrote a couple months after I started flipping houses:

> "The Second Chance House has been under contract for nearly six weeks now, and we're about three weeks past the original closing date. The main reason for the schedule slip is that the mortgage broker forgot to order the second appraisal on the house until nearly two weeks after the first appraisal (and after the original closing date). When we called him out on the mistake, he got very defensive, made up a horrible excuse for why it took two weeks to get the second appraisal, and said, "I don't really care what you think, I'll schedule the closing for whenever I feel like it."
>
> Well, it pissed us off, but given that we thought we'd close the following week, we didn't want to do anything drastic, and let it be.
>
> Once the second appraisal was completed, the broker sent the information to the Department of Transportation to have it processed so they could cut the buyers a check (the buyers were getting their down payment from DOT because of some weird eminent domain situation).
>
> A week passed, and the buyer still hadn't received a check from the Department of Transportation. We called the broker to find out what was going on, and he again said, "I don't know, I don't care, leave me alone and I'll schedule the closing whenever I feel like it." It appeared he was still pissed that we had called him out on his mistake and was now just trying to piss us off.
>
> When we didn't hear anything on Monday, we called the broker, only to have his answering service tell us that he was out of town for the week. We left a message for the guy in his office who was supposedly covering for him, but he didn't call us back. We drove to their office, but it was just a storefront and nobody was there.

We called the closing attorney, and he told us that he was ready to close but was just waiting for the broker to send him the loan package (he had talked to the broker a few days earlier but hadn't heard from him since). The broker was not answering the buyer's agent calls either.

Just as most sellers would do, I spent this entire blog post ranting about the incompetence of the buyer's mortgage broker. After lamenting about my experience to some investor friends I continued to complain for several weeks throughout the entire ordeal, which ended with the buyers not getting a loan and us having to put the house back on the market.

In retrospect, the only thing I should have been complaining about was my own lack of foresight into the potential pitfalls of allowing my buyer to use an unknown lender!

After that, I made the conscious decision to start taking full control of my deals. For example, to avoid situations like the one above, I started requiring that potential buyers for my houses get a pre-approval letter from **our** mortgage broker. Not my buyer's broker, but one with whom I work very closely and who will provide me all the details about the buyer's credit, including his exact credit score and exactly what bills he's been delinquent on, not just a pre-approval letter that may or may not mean anything.

In addition, we started to "encourage" our buyers to use our broker to actually apply for the loan, so we would know the status of the loan and any issues that might come up. Moreover, we never have to worry about our broker giving us an attitude or deciding not to return our phone calls!

Of course, some buyers insist on using their own lender (for whatever reason), and when that happens, we require a much larger non-refundable earnest money deposit; this way, if the loan falls through or if the buyer's mortgage broker flakes on us, we at least get some repayment for our time and effort.

As the business owners, it's our job to foresee issues, keep them from happening, and mitigate the impact they'll have. At the very least, we must make sure we're compensated if issues do occur.

In summary, there are always a million things on which to blame your lack of success, but in reality, every one of these things is within your control and you have the power to mitigate all these issues by being proactive and always knowing what your worst-case scenario is. It takes some extra work, and it certainly requires a proactive mindset, but for the diligent investor, there is no reason why any part of your deals should be out of your control.

Part-Time House Flipping

It's safe to say that many of you who are reading this right now aren't planning to venture into full-time house flipping, at least not at first. For you part-time house flippers, keep in mind the two discussions above, as they're even more important when you only have limited time to devote to your investing.

In terms of treating flipping like a business and pulling yourself out of the day-to-day rehab work, this may be the only way you'll find the time and energy necessary to undertake your rehab projects. If you plan to hold down a full-time job while also doing your own renovations, you'll quickly find yourself tired, frustrated, and ready to give up. By hiring responsible contractors to handle the day-to-day process of renovation on your homes, you can focus your energies on your full-time job when necessary, and spend your extra time performing the important aspects of flipping houses—planning, managing and marketing.

And, in terms of controlling your deals, when you only have a small part of the day to devote to your flips, it's even more important that you don't have to spend a lot of time cleaning up other people's messes. Remember, nobody cares about your deals as much as you do, and if you think you can trust your contractors, your agents, your lenders, etc., to always do what's in your best interest, you will end up sorely disappointed. This is why you must strive to maintain full control over all aspects of your deals; otherwise, you'll find your deals spinning out of control while you're working your day-job.

We'll have plenty more tips throughout this book for part-time flippers, but for now, remember this: As a part-time investor, you must take extra care to manage your business like a business and to control your deals as if you're the only one who can.

CHAPTER 2
PREPARE YOUR FINANCING

In the simplest terms, there are two ways to buy a house:

1. You bring your own cash to the closing table;
2. You borrow someone else's cash and bring that to the closing table.

In both of these scenarios, you (the buyer) come to the closing table with all the funds to purchase the property and the seller receives the full amount of the sale price in cash, minus whatever is needed to pay off mortgages and loans against the property. While many people who have never bought or sold a house don't realize it, when you get a bank loan to buy a house, the bank is actually bringing certified funds (e.g., cash) to the closing. Therefore, while you are paying the house off on a monthly basis (paying your mortgage) the seller is getting their full lump sum at the time of sale.

As an investor, you eventually want to get to the point where you can pay for your deals in cash. (I'm not saying you should *always* pay cash, but you want to get to the point where you have the ability to.) This could involve saving up the entire purchase price of the house you want to buy, or pulling cash out of the equity you have in other assets, such as your personal residence. Most investors won't have the option to do either of these things on their first couple of deals, though hopefully after completing a few successful flips, bringing your own cash to closing will be a viable option.

Assuming you won't be bringing your own cash to the closing table on those first few deals, that means you will have to bring someone else's cash to the closing table. This is called "financing" the deal, which is another way of saying that you're borrowing the money.

There are many ways to borrow money for real estate deals, and in this chapter, we'll discuss many of them.

First, the Bad News

You'll hear the late-night gurus (and even many daytime gurus) talking about getting rich in real estate without any of your own cash and without even having good credit. While I'm not going to dismiss the possibility of bootstrapping your real estate business without cash or credit, I will say that if you don't have cash or credit (or at least access to it), flipping is going to be a tough place to start.

While it's true that if you can find a good enough investment deal, you may be able to find a lender who will lend 100 percent of the purchase and rehab costs on the property, allowing you to do your flip with none of your own cash invested. However, these amazing deals are few and far between, and the number of lenders who are willing to accept 100 percent of the risk on a deal are even fewer and farther between. Most lenders want to know that you have "skin in the game." These days, even with a great deal and the most reasonable of lenders, you're going to need to bring *at least* 15 percent to 20 percent of the total costs for your project. So, if you're planning to buy a $75,000 house that needs $25,000 in renovations, be prepared to find at least $15,000 to $20,000 in cash to contribute to the deal.

Once you get some experience and build up a reputation as someone who knows how to successfully buy and sell real estate for a profit, you'll get to the point where lenders may be willing to finance the full price of your deals. Ironically, at that point you likely won't need the extra financing, as you'll have built up a nest egg from your previous rehab projects.

While I'd love to be able to tell motivated new investors that all it takes is hard work to be successful in real estate, the reality is, you're going to need to have access to at least some cash to get started. This can be your own cash or cash that you borrow from friends and family who aren't requiring you to use the real estate you purchase as collateral.

Throughout my investing career, I've spent hundreds of hours talking to lenders and potential financiers of my deals. With all the different types of loans and equity financing available these days, it's important to have a good understanding of the benefits and drawbacks of each, so you can choose the most appropriate financing option for your particular needs.

Throughout the rest of this chapter, I'll discuss the most common methods of getting your rehabs funded and will go into more detail about where rehabbers should be looking for money and some tips on dealing with lenders. And, while it won't be easy, there will be some methods that may allow you to bootstrap with no cash. Also keep in mind that there are, of course, more ways of financing real estate investments than I lay out below, though most are a derivative—or combination—of the six types I will discuss.

Types of Real Estate Financing

1. Conventional Financing

Conventional financing is done through a mortgage broker or bank, and the lender may be a large banking institution or a quasi-government institution (Freddie Mac, Fannie Mae, etc.). The requirements to qualify for a loan are based strictly on the borrower's current financial situation—credit score, income, assets, and debt. If you don't have good credit, reasonable income, and a low debt-to-income ratio (where you earn a lot compared to your monthly obligations), you likely won't qualify for traditional financing.

Since traditional financing isn't a great option for most investors, I won't spend a lot of time discussing it here, but for completeness sake, I do want to mention some of the biggest benefits and drawbacks of traditional financing.

Benefits: The benefits of traditional financing are low interest rates (between 4–5 percent at the time of this writing), low loan costs (or "points"), and long loan durations (up to 30 years). If you can qualify for traditional financing, it's a great choice. However, when buying investment property, it's a long shot.

Drawbacks: There are drawbacks to traditional financing for investors, and some of them are major:

- The biggest reason it may be difficult to get traditional financing for your investment project is that large banks won't lend against a property that isn't in move-in-ready condition. For example, a house I closed on with traditional financing almost fell through because the lender wouldn't make the loan to me until the hot water heater in the property was working. As an investor, it's common that I'll buy houses with broken hot water heaters (and often much, much worse defects), and I can't expect the seller to fix these things for me just so I can get my loan. In my situation, in order to get my loan, I had to replace the hot water heater before I even owned the house, which is not a risk I want to do on a regular basis.

- Traditional lenders take their time when it comes to appraisals and pushing loans through their process. It's best to allow for at least 21 days—and often longer—between contract acceptance and close. As an investor, you want to incentivize the seller to accept your offer by offering to close quickly; with traditional lending, that can often be impossible.

- If the lender will be financing through Freddie Mac or Fannie Mae (and most will), there will be a limit to the number of loans you can have at one time. Currently, that limit is either four or ten loans (depending on the specific bank you work through), so if you plan to be an active investor going after more than five or ten properties simultaneously, you'll eventually run into this problem with traditional lending.

- There are very few traditional loans that will cover the cost of rehab in the loan; those that will are difficult to get through underwriting, can take a long time to get approved, and are generally more trouble than they are worth. If you plan to buy a $100,000 property and spend $30,000 in rehab costs, expect that $30,000 will have to come out of your pocket; the lender won't put that money into the loan. In fact, as you get more experience, you may find yourself buying properties where the rehab is more expensive than the property itself!

2. Portfolio/Investor Loans

As opposed to getting the money from a large bank that works with Freddie, Fannie, or some other major institution, some smaller banks will lend their own money. These banks are referred to as "portfolio lenders" and they have the ability to define their own lending criteria; in other words, they have the option to lend to anyone they want, regardless of financial situation. That said, while most portfolio lenders will still care about your financial situation (they won't want to see a bankruptcy, foreclosure, or large unpaid debts on your credit), they'll also take into consideration your real estate experience and the specific deal you're looking to get financed.

Because many portfolio lenders have the expertise to evaluate investment deals, if they are confident that the investment is solid, they will be a bit less concerned about the borrower defaulting on the loan, because they have already verified that the property value will cover the balance of the loan. That said, portfolio lenders aren't in the business of foreclosing on real estate, so they aren't hoping for the borrower to default; given that, they do care that the borrower has at least decent credit, good income, and/or cash reserves.

I have used portfolio lenders on several occasions and highly recommend this type of financing if it's available to you. Your biggest challenge may be finding the banks that actually provide this type of financing, as they have become scarce over the past decade.

When looking for a portfolio lender, you want to focus on the small, local banks. By "small" and "local," I mean focusing on banks that have no more than three to five branches in total. (You will be surprised by how many of these types of banks exist.) And because most of these banks lend only to local investors, focus on banks that are within an hour's drive of where you plan to invest. If you want to find a list of banks in your area that have these qualifications, check out the FDIC website: www.fdic.gov

Benefits: As mentioned, the major benefit of portfolio lending is that (sometimes) the financial requirements on the borrower can be relaxed a bit, allowing borrowers with less than stellar credit or low income to qualify for loans. Here are some other benefits:

- Some portfolio lenders will offer "rehab loans" that will roll the rehab costs into the loan, allowing the investor to cover the entire cost of the rehab through the loan, with a down payment based on the full amount.
- Portfolio lenders will verify that the investment the borrower wants to make is a sound one. This provides an extra layer of checks and balances to the investor about whether the deal they are pursuing is a good one. For new investors, this can be a very good thing!
- Portfolio lenders are used to dealing with investors and can often close loans in ten days or less, especially with investors with whom they're familiar and they trust.
- If you are able to build a good relationship with a portfolio lender and can qualify financially, there is typically no limit to the number

of deals they'll fund simultaneously.

Drawbacks: Of course, there are some drawbacks to portfolio loans as well:

- Some portfolio loans are short term—even as short as 6 or 12 months. If you get short-term financing, you need to either be confident that you can turn around and sell the property in that amount of time, or you need to be confident that you can refinance to get out of the loan prior to its expiration.
- Portfolio loans generally have higher interest rates than conventional loans and "points" (upfront loan costs) associated with them. It's not uncommon for portfolio loans to run from 6–9 percent interest and 1–3 percent of the total loan amount in points.
- Portfolio lenders may seriously scrutinize your deals, and if you are trying to put together a deal where the value is obvious to you but not your lender, you may find yourself in a situation where they won't give you the money.
- Because portfolio lenders care about the success of the deal, they often want to see that the borrower has real estate experience. If you go to a lender with no experience, you might find yourself paying higher rates, more points, or having to provide additional personal guarantees. That said, once you prove yourself to the lender by selling a couple of houses and repaying a couple of loans, things will get a lot easier.

3. Private Investors

Private investors are typically well-off professionals who have money to invest (either cash or retirement funds) and are looking for better returns than what they can achieve from the stock market or other investing avenues. These days, it's not uncommon for real estate investors to work with doctors, lawyers, or business professionals they know who are looking to lend out part of their retirement savings in return for a decent rate of return—typically somewhere in the 8–12 percent range.

Normally, private lenders are people in your network of family, friends, and acquaintances whom you can approach and personally discuss the option of having them invest in your projects. If you can find these people and convince them that your deals are more lucrative than, and equally as secure as, their current investments, you could be well on your way to getting access to hundreds of thousands of dollars without too much paperwork or overhead.

I both borrow from private lenders and personally lend out part of my retirement savings in this very fashion, so I know first-hand how well these relationships can work. The key is to provide a level of confidence to the private lender that the money will be secure in your hands and will also provide a decent return to the lender.

Benefits: There are several benefits to using private investors to fund your deals. First, with interest rates so low (at the time of this writing), well-off professionals with cash are itching to find opportunities where they can get high single-digit or even double-digit returns. Second, if you can prove your ability to find and execute on real estate deals, these investors may very well not care at all about your creditworthiness, as their funds are secured by the underlying properties you buy. Additionally, these types of potential investors are everywhere—you can start by asking the professionals in your family as well as your doctor, your dentist, or your attorney if they'd like to invest.

Drawbacks: The biggest drawback to working with private investors is convincing these people—who likely have little experience with real estate—to trust you with their money. Of course, this is where a good business plan can help, as well as a track record of having a good work ethic and being trustworthy in the eyes of these professionals. Another thing to keep in mind is that those investors who want to lend from their retirement funds will have to move retirement money to a special account—called a Self-Directed IRA (SDIRA)—allowing them to make private loans. If you go this route, do some research on setting up and using SDIRAs, as you'll want to make the process as simple as possible for your lenders.

4. Crowdfunding

Over the past several years, technology has been catching up to the real estate financing business. Not only are lenders starting to take their businesses online, but some unique solutions have emerged that take advantage of both technology and those who use it.

Specifically, the idea of crowdfunding has emerged and started to thrive. Crowdfunding is the idea of raising small amounts of money from a large group of people, typically over the internet. This allows investors to finance deals without having to find a single lender that can provide all the funds.

For example, a house flipper who needs to raise $200,000 may find it easier to get 20 people to each lend (or invest) an average of $10,000, as opposed to raising the full amount from a single lender. Several online crowdfunding businesses have emerged in the past few years, including popular sites like FundThatFlip.com, RealtyShares.com and FundRise.com.

Benefits: The biggest benefit of crowdfunding websites is that the site will already have a network of lenders looking for deals in which to invest their cash. Instead of the house flipper having to seek out the individual lenders themselves, the crowdfunding site handles much of the marketing. They also handle all of the legal and regulatory issues.

The house flipper will need to provide the details of the deal looking to be funded—this information will be used by potential investors to evaluate the deal—as well as information about their experience and track record. But if you have a good deal and can justify why you're the right person to execute on that deal, crowdfunding is a great way to raise money even if fundraising isn't your forte.

Drawbacks: While there are no big drawbacks to crowdfunding, there are a bunch of smaller concerns that potential borrowers should be familiar with before heading down the crowdfunding road:

- Because the funding is coming from many "mom-and-pop" lenders as opposed to one bigger lender, the amount of time it takes to complete a funding raise is typically longer than when dealing with a single lender, like a bank or private lender. You'll typically want to plan for at least three to six weeks to raise and receive your funds.
- There is a risk that you won't be able to attract enough lenders to complete your entire raise, and it may take several weeks before you realize that your fundraising won't be successful. For deals that are time-sensitive, this lack of certainty may be a problem.
- The cost of borrowing from a crowdfunding site is typically on the higher end of what you'd expect from private lenders. At the time of this writing, most crowdfunding loans charge 10–13 percent, plus 1–3 percent of the loan in upfront fees.

5. Hard Money Lenders (HML)

Hard money is so called because the loan is provided more against the "hard asset" (in this case the underlying property) than it is against the borrower. Hard money lenders often pool funds from wealthy business people (either investors themselves, or professionals such as doctors and lawyers who are looking for a good return on their saved cash) and then lend at high rates.

Hard money lenders generally don't care about the financial situation of the borrower as much as banks do, as long as they are confident that the loan is being used to finance a great deal. If the deal is great and the borrower has the experience to execute, hard money lenders will often lend to those with poor credit, no income, and even high debt. That said, the worse the financial situation of the borrower, the better the deal needs to be.

Because of the high interest rates and upfront fees, hard money loans are often considered a last resort, which is why new investors without much cash and with little experience will often go down this road. While it's quite possible to put together successful deals using hard money loans, you must be extra careful to factor in the loan costs and the monthly mortgage payments into your deal analysis, as these high payments can quickly eat through any potential profit from the deal.

Benefits: The obvious benefit of hard money is that even if you have a distressed financial situation, you may be able to get a loan. Again, the loan is more against the property than it is against the dealmaker.

A second benefit of hard money is that hard money lenders can often make quick lending decisions, providing turn-around times of just a couple of days on loans.

Lastly, hard money lenders—because they are lending their own money—have the option to finance higher loan percentages if they think it makes sense; while not common these days, some HMLs have been known to lend up to 100 percent of the purchase and rehab costs for a deal.

Drawbacks: As you can imagine, hard money isn't always the magic bullet for investors with bad finances. Because hard money is often a last resort for borrowers who can't qualify for other types of loans, hard money lenders will often impose very high costs on their loans. Interest rates up to and exceeding 15 percent are not uncommon, and the upfront fees can often total 4–7 percent of the entire loan amount (five to seven points). This makes hard money very expensive, and unless the deal is fantastic, hard money can easily eat much of your profit before the deal is even made.

6. Equity Investors

Equity investor is just a fancy name for "partner with cash." An equity investor will provide you money in return for some fixed percentage of the eventual profit. A common scenario is that the investor will front all the money for the deal but do none of the work. The borrower (you, in this case) will do 100 percent of the work, and at the end, the lender and the borrower will split the profit 50/50. Sometimes the equity investor will be involved in the actual deal, and sometimes the split isn't 50/50, but the gist of the equity investment is the same—a partner injects money to get a portion of the profits.

Benefits: The biggest benefit to an equity investor is that there are no legal requirements that the borrower needs to fulfill to get funding. If the partner has the cash and chooses to invest, they can do so. Oftentimes, the equity investor is a friend or family member, and the deal is more a partnership in the eyes of both parties, as opposed to a formal lender-borrower relationship.

Drawbacks: There are two drawbacks to equity partnerships:

- Equity partners are generally entitled to a piece of the profits, sometimes even 50 percent or more. While the investor doesn't need to pay anything upfront (or any interest on the money), they will have to fork over a large percentage of the profits to the partner. This can mean even smaller profits than if the investor went with hard money or some other type of high-interest loan.
- Equity partners may want to play an active role in the investment. While this can be a good thing if the partner is experienced and has the same vision as the investor, when that's not the case, this can be a recipe for disaster.

Summary of Financing Options

In the sections above, we discussed the six major types of financing available to real estate investors. Here is a breakdown of those financing types in an easy-to-read format:

	CONVENTIONAL	PORTFOLIO	PRIVATE	CROWDFUNDING	HARD MONEY	EQUITY
COST OF MONEY	CHEAP 4-6%	IN-BETWEEN 6-9% + 1-3 POINTS	IN-BETWEEN 8-12%	IN-BETWEEN 10-13% + 1-3 POINTS	EXPENSIVE 12-18% + 4-7 POINTS	EXPENSIVE 50% OF DEAL
LEAD TIME	3-5 WEEKS	2-3 WEEKS	0-2 WEEKS	3-6 WEEKS	1-3 WEEKS	0-3 WEEKS
PROPERTY CONDITION	MOVE IN READY	REHAB OKAY	REHAB OKAY	REHAB OKAY	REHAB OKAY	REHAB OKAY
LENGTH OF LOAN	UP TO 30 YEARS	6-36 MONTHS	NEGOTIABLE	6-24 MONTHS	6-24 MONTHS	NEGOTIABLE
FINANCIAL STRENGTH	GREAT CREDIT VERIFIED INCOME	GOOD CREDIT INCOME HELPS	NEGOTIABLE	GOOD CREDIT INCOME HELPS	NEGOTIABLE	NEGOTIABLE
DEAL QUALITY	DOESN'T MATTER	MUST BE GOOD	NEGOTIABLE	MUST BE GOOD	MUST BE GOOD	NEGOTIABLE
EXPERIENCE	DOESN'T MATTER	HELPFUL, BUT NOT REQUIRED	NEGOTIABLE	HELPFUL, BUT NOT REQUIRED	HELPFUL, BUT NOT REQUIRED	NEGOTIABLE

Your Financial Resume

Now that we've discussed the generic types of financing you'll find, let's talk more about the specific financing vehicles that may be available to you.

If you were to apply for a high-paying job, you wouldn't even think about going into an interview without your resume prepared, would you? Likewise, if you plan to start asking people for money to back your investments, you need to put together your *financial resume*. While you don't necessarily have to write it down on a piece of paper, there are several key components to your financial situation that you must be prepared to discuss with anyone who may be a financial backer of your investments.

It is these financial components (again, your financial resume) that will determine the types of financing available to you, so it's important that you realistically take stock of your situation before you start asking for money from lenders, partners, or family members.

Specifically, there are five key components of your financial resume that lenders will care about:

Credit History/Credit Score: Do you know your credit history and your credit score? You should! As an investor, strong credit is of critical importance to your getting funding for your deals. If you don't know what your credit history looks like or what your credit score is, visit www.AnnualCreditReport.com to receive a free copy of your credit report, and spend some time looking over it. Many lenders will start their underwriting process by looking at your credit score, and if it's not very good (at least 680 is where you should strive to be), they will immediately dismiss any consideration for giving you financing. This isn't to say you won't have other options, but by focusing on building a strong history and credit score, you will present yourself with the greatest number of financing options available.

Income: The next most important component of your financial situation is income. Do you have a job that is generating recurring income? Do you have investments that are paying interest or dividends? Do you have rental property that is generating cash on a monthly basis? All of these things will combine to provide lenders with an idea of what position you will be in to repay any loans or lines of credit they provide you. The more income you have—and the longer your history of having it—the more comfortable lenders will be giving you money. From their perspective, if you have considerable income in addition to your investing, you'll likely be able to repay any loans even if your investments are not successful. Like credit score, if you don't have any income, there are still options available to you; they're just not as plentiful.

Assets: The next component of your financial situation that lenders will consider is any assets you might have. Do you have cash in the bank? Do you have stocks, bonds, or large retirement accounts? Do you own your home or have substantial equity in investment properties? Are there any other assets you might have that will provide lenders confidence that—in the worst-case—you'll be able to repay a loan should the investment fail? Oftentimes, lenders will consider lending you money if you have assets that you're willing to "collateralize" against the loan. This means that you promise the asset in return for the loan; if you can't repay the loan, the lender gets the asset instead. For example, if you have substantial equity in your personal residence, a lender might ask that you put the house up as collateral in exchange for investment loans. If for some reason you can't repay your loans, the lender gets your house.

Debt: The more debt you currently have, the more difficult it will be for you to get financing. Unfortunately, that's a simple fact that real estate investors—even the successful ones—must face. While there are different types of debt—some better than others—any existing debt is going to inhibit your ability to repay additional loans and is going to hurt your chances of getting financing for your projects. Specifically, lenders are going to look at the ratio of debt you have to the income you make. If your debt payments—including things like rent, mortgage, and monthly bills—are very small compared to your income (low debt-to-income ratio), this means you have a lot of money left over at the end of every month, and you're a lower risk to default on your loan. If your debt payments are a substantial chunk of your income (high debt-to-income ratio), you're probably having trouble paying your bills already, and additional loans are likely to not get repaid. Lenders will calculate your debt-to-income ratio as a percentage, and they want to see low numbers (lower than 30 percent, ideally).

Investing Experience: Lastly, some lenders are going to be very concerned with your investing experience. An investor with a long history of successful investments is much less of a risk than an investor who has no experience whatsoever. We'll discuss it in more detail in an upcoming section, but in many cases, a strong business plan will prove to be a good substitute for investing experience. Lenders are often willing to overlook lack of experience in someone who has a well thought-out plan and clear direction. As you gain experience, your financing options will open up tremendously; in the meantime, ensure that you at least have a strong business plan and clear idea of your goals and how you will achieve them.

These five components make up your financial resume and will have a significant impact on your ability to find financing for your deals.

Of course, if you have strong credit, high income, lots of assets, low debt, and lots of experience, you should have no problem finding financing. But very few beginners have that type of financial resume, so it's important to figure out what aspects of your financial situation are strongest and focus on leveraging those.

With strong credit and income, bank financing (portfolio lenders) and crowdfunding may be a great way to get capital for your first investments. As you build experience and achieve some investing success, you will quickly attract financing from private lenders or others who are interested in partnering with you. In fact, as you build your investing bankroll, you'll find that raising money becomes easier and easier: Money is always easier to raise when you don't need it!

But, what if your entire financial resume is a mess? What if you have no experience, your credit score is shot, you don't have a job, and you have lots of debt?

Is there any hope for finding financing for your deals?

Luckily, there's *one* other important piece of the financing puzzle that might help you...

No Cash or Credit? No Experience? Know This!

In the beginning of this chapter, I mentioned the two most common ways of buying a house: bringing your own cash to the closing table or bringing someone else's cash to the closing table. But, there's actually a *third* way to buy a house that smart investors will attempt to use as often as they can.

This is to convince the seller of the property to contribute some or all of his equity to the deal.

This type of financing is often referred to as "seller financing," and involves getting the seller of the property to allow you to buy or control the property in return for regular future payments. Seller financing is one of the best ways to buy property with little or no money, and also one of the best ways to generate large returns in real estate.

For example, imagine you find a seller who owns his or her home outright. The house is worth $100,000, and the owner has no mortgage or loans against the property. Instead of handing the seller $100,000 at the time you purchase the house, you convince the seller to agree to hold off making you pay for the property until some point in the future. In return for you not having to come up with the bulk of the purchase price upfront, you may be able to offer the seller a higher purchase price or interest on the loan—a win/win for both sides.

For example, you give the seller a $10,000 down payment at the time of purchase, and then make monthly interest payments at an agreed-upon rate while you're renovating the property. Once you resell the property, you pay off the seller using the proceeds from your resale.

Think about it—had you gone a bank or hard money lender, you probably would have been required to put down a larger down payment, and your interest rate may have been higher. Plus, if you do a good job of negotiating with the seller, he may not care that you have no income, bad credit, or no real estate experience.

These types of deals are much more common than a lot of new investors realize—personally, I've purchased several houses using this method, with little or no money out of my pocket. In fact, I once purchased a 38-unit apartment complex where the seller financed 90 percent of the purchase price with his equity!

Why would a homeowner do this? There are two common reasons:

- The owner is not desperate for cash right now and is more concerned with getting the property sold. For example, if the seller is older and is moving in with family, or if someone who inherits a property simply doesn't want to deal with upkeep any longer but doesn't need the sale proceeds immediately.

- You offer the owner a better deal for the property than he would get if he sold the property to a buyer who was using an alternate type of financing. If a cash buyer were to come along, he would likely expect the owner to sell at a discount in return for the cash purchase. Another investor getting a hard money loan will pay high upfront costs and high monthly payments with a hard money loan, reducing their profits and forcing their purchase price lower. And if the property were in distressed condition, traditional banks likely wouldn't want to finance the deal, leaving many traditional buyers in a position where they couldn't afford to buy the property at all. When the owner is willing to finance the deal himself, he can often sell the property for a premium over any other type of financed sale.

Want to learn more about seller financing and other creative ways of acquiring property? Check out the following two BiggerPockets books:
The Book on Investing in Real Estate with No (and Low) Money Down
The Book on Negotiating Real Estate

Final Thoughts on Financing

Financing for inexperienced real estate investors is never easy. Many new investors will find that getting the money to do their first deal is the most difficult part of getting into this business. But some of the most successful investors I've met have started in this business in a tough financial position.

There is a saying in real estate:

If the deal is good enough, the money will find you!

In other words, if you can find a fantastic deal—one that is so great it would be difficult to not make easy money—you should be able to find the cash you need, regardless of your financial situation.

Once you find that awesome deal, here are two suggestions on where you can find the money...

Find Another Investor to Partner with

For most rehabbers I know, the hardest part of the business is finding great deals. This is why most rehabbers are happy to pay wholesalers and bird-dogs to bring them a house. When you find that great deal you can't afford, I highly recommend approaching a seasoned investor with the deal—but not as a wholesaler or bird-dog.

Instead, let the investor know that you want to partner on the deal, in exchange for two things:

1. Being allowed to shadow the project from beginning to end. It doesn't need to be a mentorship (that's a bigger commitment than most rehabbers want to take on), but they'll allow you to watch the project, ask some questions and get an idea of how the business is run. Consider it your first hands-on experience in rehabbing.
2. Giving you between 10 percent and 20 percent of the profits. If the deal is truly great, a smart rehabber should be happy to give up 10–20 percent of the profits, as they know there will still be plenty left for themselves.

Lastly, you should ask the rehabber if they'd be willing to consider the same arrangement should you continue to bring them deals. Think about it—if you can get 20 percent of the profits on five deals, that's equivalent to doing an entire deal yourself, and will probably give you enough working capital (and enough experience!) to find your own financing.

Find a Smart Hard Money or Private Lender

Now, let's say you don't know any other successful rehabbers, or you just really don't want to have to partner on the great deal you've found. While it's true that most hard money and private lenders will require that you have some skin in the game—that is, some of your own cash invested—there is one other component they are even more concerned with: the deal itself.

In a situation where the deal is great, you should also be able to convince a smart hard money or private lender to loan you money or to partner with you on the deal. Remember, lenders are most concerned about not losing money, but if—for example—you find a house worth $100,000 that you can buy for $30,000, there is almost no risk to the lender by financing this deal or partnering with you on it.

Think about it from the lender's point of view:

The best-case scenario is that you borrow the money, purchase the property, rehab and resell it for a nice profit, and repay the loan. The worst-case scenario is that you default on the loan and the lender is out $30,000, but now has a property worth $100,000. While not an optimal situation for the lender (who presumably doesn't want to have to deal with the property), he can turn around and sell it for more than $30,000 to another investor and get his money back and then some!

Remember, even if your financial resume is a complete mess, there is still hope for financing your deals. You just need to ensure that your deals are spectacular, at which point other investors, hard-money lenders, and private-money lenders will be banging down your door to get a piece of the action.

CHAPTER 3
FIND YOUR AGENT(S)

In this chapter, I want to have the first discussion (of many in this book) about finding members of your team. When thinking about your team members, I want you to keep this old saying in mind: "Always use the right tool for the job."

Throughout the process of building your strategy and completing your first deal, you are going talk to many potential team members, and I promise you that every single one of them will over-represent their strengths and abilities. Your contractors will tell you they can do any renovation job, mortgage brokers will tell you they can handle any type of loan, and agents will tell you they can handle any aspect of buying or selling. Unfortunately, that is usually not the case.

Most contractors are good at one or two things; most mortgage brokers specialize in one or two types of loans; and most real estate agents are either good on the buying side or good on the selling side, not both. It's up to you to determine where each team member's strengths and weaknesses lie, and to ensure that you always have the right person for the job, even if that means having to bring in more people and having to manage a bigger team.

The Types of Agents You Need

At this point in the process, it's time to find a real estate agent. However, as I said above, not all agents can do all things, and over the course of a single deal, you may work with several different agents in different capacities.

In general, there are two types of agents you'll come across in the real estate world:

1. **Buyer's Agent:** This is the agent who specializes in helping you analyze the local market and who can help you find and buy properties. The best buyer's agents are the ones who focus 100 percent of their time working with buyers and don't spend any of their time listing properties (working with sellers). A great buyer's agent is not only intimately knowledgeable about their local market, but they are ruthless about protecting buyers and getting them great deals. In addition, the best buyer's agent for an aspiring real estate investor should also have some experience working with investors, or even investing themselves.

2. **Listing Agent:** This is the agent who specializes in marketing and selling properties. The best listing agents are the ones who focus 100 percent of their time working with sellers and don't spend any of their time representing buyers as a buyer's agent. A great listing agent understands current market values, pricing, and sales trends, and is an expert at marketing. The best listing agent for a real estate investor should specialize in selling renovated and vacant houses.

Some agents will claim to be highly skilled as both a buyer's agent and a listing agent. They are likely not skilled at either.

At this point in the process, you will want to find your buyer's agent. Depending on your property acquisition strategy (which we'll discuss more in Chapter 7), you may need that agent to help you search for and find properties. This is especially going to be true if you're planning to purchase homeowner properties off the MLS or if you're considering purchasing bank-owned foreclosures.

But even if you don't need a buyer's agent to help you with your property search, there are still many services a great buyer's agent can provide.

Specifically, a buyer's agent should be able to help you with all the following:

- Provide insight into local markets and help define a "farm area"—a specific geographical area or market demographic where you'll be looking for deals.
- Provide current and historic property sales data.
- Provide access to properties on the MLS.

- Submit offers, help negotiate, and help navigate the due diligence and the closing process for any MLS listed properties.

While there are many great buyer's agents out there who specialize in working with buyers, things are unfortunately a little bit more complicated because most buyer's agents aren't accustomed to working with investors. Moreover, if the agent doesn't understand the goals, the needs, and the process of the investor, the agent will quickly get frustrated... as will the investor.

The Investor-Friendly Buyer's Agent

Just as some agents will tell you they are great at being both a buyer's agent and listing agent, there are plenty of agents who will tell you that they are great at representing both retail buyers (homeowners) and investors. Again, this means they're probably not great at either.

Homeowners look for a property that they can emotionally connect with, that meets their family's needs and that will serve them far into the future. An investor is looking for something that will generate a profit. These are very different goals, and it's unlikely that one agent will specialize in handling the needs of these very different types of buyers.

There aren't too many agents out there who specialize in working with investors, and most of those that do aren't very good at it. However, they're out there, and you need to find one; never settle for less.

Finding Your Investor-Friendly Buyer's Agent

The best way to find these agents is through referral. Successful investors in your area have been successful in large part because they've built a strong team, and that usually includes a great buyer's agent. You need to find the agents that other investors are using and do whatever it takes to get one (or more) of those agents to work with you as well.

Keep in mind that the agents who specialize in working with investors will want to evaluate you as well and will need to be confident that you are worth working with. They will want to know that you are serious about actually buying properties (they aren't paid until you buy!), have the ability to purchase with cash or financing in place, and will not be wasting more of their time than necessary.

Just as most real estate agents aren't very good at their jobs, most new investors are just tire-kickers who will waste the agent's time and effort. For the relationship to work, both sides must be competent and motivated.

Evaluating Your Investor-Friendly Buyer's Agent

Let's say you've found an agent who gets good references from other investors and you're ready to speak with him or her. The first step is to invite them to coffee or lunch. Make it somewhere casual, inexpensive and quick—good agents are busy, and they'll be trying to determine from the very beginning if you're going to be respectful of their time.

Start by saying something along the lines of the following: "I got your number from Jane Doe, an investor friend of mine. I'm an aspiring real estate investor, I'm almost ready to start buying, I have my financing approved, and now I'm just looking for a great buyer's agent to work with. I know you're probably very busy, but I was hoping I could buy you a quick lunch and see if we might be able to work together?"

When you meet, here are the questions you'll want to ask. Don't make it seem like an interview, and be prepared to answer plenty of the agent's questions as well:

1. How long have you been an agent in this area? (Do they know the area well?)
2. How long have you been working with investors? (You only care about their experience with investors, not homeowners.)
3. Do you own any investment property yourself? (The best agents are also investors.)
4. How many investor buyers do you currently work with? (The more buyers they work with, the worse the situation for you, as you'll be competing with a lot of other investors for any deals the agent brings.)
5. Do you have time to take on another client? (You don't want an agent who is too busy to actually help you out.)
6. What types of deals do you specialize in? (You want to know if they have experience with short sales, bank-owned [REO] properties, etc.)
7. Do you help with many REO purchases? (If you go the REO route, you'll want an agent who understands this process, which can oftentimes be complicated.)
8. Are you willing to list and negotiate short sales that I find on my own? (If you go the short sale route, you'll want an agent who can do these for you.)

9. Will you be able to help me analyze the local market to determine where I should be looking for properties, in addition to helping me find deals? (You want an agent who's willing to help you grow a successful business, not just sell you a property now and then.)
10. I'm serious about buying; will you have time to show me a potential deal the day it hits the market? (This tells them that you're serious and sets the expectation that you expect them to be as well.)

What Your Buyer's Agent Can't Do

While it would be nice if your agent had the ability to bring you all the deals you could ever want, the reality is this: Not only do agents often-times have difficulty finding great deals (especially in a hot market), but there are many types of deals that real estate agents won't get involved in and won't be able to help you with.

Buyer's agents specialize in helping to buy off the MLS, meaning they can help you purchase directly from homeowners who have listed their property for sale, they can help you purchase bank-owned foreclosures (REOs), and they can help you purchase short-sale properties. However-er, with other types of transactions—for example, "For Sale by Owner" properties and other properties that aren't listed on the MLS—they likely won't be able to help you.

We'll discuss all these types of deals in Chapter 6, but for now, keep in mind that, depending on what types of deals you choose to focus on, your buyer's agent may or may not be able to help you.

Becoming Your Own Agent

If you can't find a great investor-friendly buyer's agent—and even if you can—there *is* another alternative:

GET YOUR REAL ESTATE LICENSE!

Yes, I did mean for that to be capitalized and in bold. I'm a big believer that getting your real estate license will provide opportunities and control that you can't get otherwise. While you certainly don't have to get your license to be successful at rehabbing houses—in fact, there are many investors who would actually disagree with me and recommend *against* getting it—I believe it increases a new investor's chances of being successful.

Below, I describe all the pros and cons of getting your license so that you can decide whether it's right for you and your business. However, before I do that, let me give you the two biggest reasons why I recommend that all new investors seriously consider going this route:

1. Once you go through the process, the time and effort you will have invested will solidify your commitment to real estate. The process of getting your license is tedious and drawn-out—it takes about up to 150 hours' worth of study and work—but after doing all that work it will be much more difficult for you to get discouraged and give up on your dreams of being a successful investor.

2. Once you have your license, you now have the potential to generate a new income stream as a real estate agent. While I'm not recommending that you ever become a traditional real estate agent, as you start to build momentum with your investing, you'll find that opportunities to represent buyers and sellers often appear out of nowhere, and by having your license, you'll have the ability to seize those opportunities for some extra cash flow and experience. Consider it a "backup" plan while you're getting your investing business off the ground.

Getting licensed was one of the best things we ever did for our business. Right after our third rehab, my wife got her license because we were getting frustrated with our real estate agents and we felt as if we had very little control over our deals. I got my license several years later, and currently we're both licensed. Given our experiences, I couldn't imagine being a full-time real estate investor and not having someone in our business who had their license.

So, should *you* get your license? Here are some pros and cons so you can decide what's right for you.

Benefits of Getting Your Real Estate License

There are lots of benefits to getting your real estate license. Among them:

- **Access to MLS.** First and foremost, having your license means getting access to the local Multiple Listing Service (MLS). While there are certainly other ways to get access to the MLS, having your license will allow you access without having to rely on other agents, friends, or colleagues. This means you don't have to worry about it going away, and you don't have to worry about anyone getting in trouble if they're giving you access to their account illegally.

When we first decided that my wife would get her license, this was the impetus. We wanted access to the MLS not just to be able to run search queries and find candidate properties, but because we wanted access to the wealth of historical data that the MLS provides. I have spent hundreds of hours on the MLS mining data to determine which locations to focus on (discussed in Chapter 4), which types of buyers to target (discussed in Chapter 4), which types of houses to buy (discussed in Chapter 5), and which types of deals to go after (discussed in Chapter 6).

I credit this research with much of our early success in this business, and I never would have had access to this data without access to the MLS.

- **Make more money.** Many investors realize that every time they sell a house through another agent, they are spending about 6 percent of the sale price in agent commissions. What they don't realize is that when they buy property, their agent is also collecting up to 3 percent for facilitating the transaction.

  This means that on a typical purchase and sale of a property, an investor could have access to as much as 9 percent of the total sale price of the property in extra profit but has to give that money to his agent. For example, if you buy a property for $50,000 and sell it for $100,000, that's between $4,500 and $7,500 in additional profit (depending on whether your buyer had his own agent) that you could earn by being your own agent on the purchase and sale of that deal! Doing just four deals per year, having your real estate license could save or earn you an extra $30,000.

  In most years, we save or earn nearly $50,000 in extra income by not having to use another agent. Even with the brokerage fees we pay (about $5,000 per year given our volume), we still net an extra $45,000 or so in our business *each year* by having a real estate license. It makes the extra paperwork well worth it.

- **Controlling our deals.** Being our own agents for our purchases and sales allows us full control over our deals. We can submit offers to and negotiate directly with listing agents. We deal directly with the lenders, the appraisers, the inspectors, the closing attorneys, and all other parties involved in the closing of our transactions, both on the buy and sell side. We control our marketing, our sales, and the showing of our properties to prospective buyers.

While there is certainly overhead involved in being the agent for your own deals, that headache is far outweighed by the fact that you have full control over every aspect of every transaction. Will your agent drive to your property before every showing, turn on the lights, open the windows, and put out fresh cookies? Will your agent follow up with everyone who has viewed your property to get feedback and recommendations? Will your agent send marketing materials to renters in the neighborhood who might be looking for a house to buy? Will your agent be at the house with the appraisers to ensure that they get a favorable viewing of the property?

Probably not. But, because all aspects of the transaction go through us, we can—and do—do all these things. It's a good part of why our typical property is sold in far less time than what is average for the market.

- **Access to properties.** When you aren't a licensed real estate agent, the only ways to legally gain access to a property that you might be interested in purchasing is to either have your own buyer's agent or to contact the listing agent representing the seller. The agent will coordinate a showing, and you can schedule a time to view the property.

While there is nothing wrong with this process, it can be tedious and time consuming. Oftentimes, an agent isn't available to meet you at the property to unlock the door—and monitor your actions—for several hours or days. In that time, another buyer might swoop in and scoop up the deal, never giving you an opportunity to even make an offer!

But when you have your license, you have far more control over your ability to gain access to properties. If you are driving down the street and see a "for sale" sign on a property you want to take a look at, you can simply contact the listing agent yourself and ask when the property is available for showing. In many cases, the listing agent will tell you that the property is ready to show immediately, and you can simply let yourself into the property right then and there!

An added benefit is that not only can you easily get access to properties you might want to purchase, you can also get easy access to properties that are your competition—other properties for sale that have already been rehabbed or don't need rehabbing. Because these aren't properties you're interested in buying, an agent isn't going to want to waste time helping you gain access to these houses; but when you have your own license, you can view these houses any time you want.

The Drawbacks of a Real Estate License for Investors

While there are many benefits to having your real estate license, as I mentioned above, there are some drawbacks as well.

Among them:

- **Getting your license.** First, you need to actually get your license. This often requires an investment of several hundred dollars, and then 100–150 hours in coursework, studying, and taking exams to qualify to get your license. In addition, once you have your license, you need to find a broker to work under, and that may involve some additional fees and responsibilities.

  For example, you'll typically pay a broker to be affiliated with their brokerage and to assist in each transaction. You will likely pay a monthly or quarterly fee to get access to the MLS. And to keep your license, you will likely need to take continuing education courses—expect about ten hours per year, on average. If you're a part-time investor, the cost and time commitment required to get—and keep—your license may be prohibitive.

- **Paperwork.** If you do a lot of deals, you'll end up doing a lot of paperwork. In my opinion, this is the most annoying part of having your license. You'll be responsible for writing your own offers, submitting forms to attorneys, agents, brokers, and the MLS.

  Depending on the requirements for your state and your specific broker, each transaction can result in several hours of paperwork. In years where we've done 30 or 40 flips, we easily spend five to ten hours per week doing paperwork. That said, there are people who can handle most of the paperwork for you (for a fee), so there are ways to get around the paperwork if that's something you want to avoid. Regardless, part-time investors may find the paperwork requirements a bit daunting in terms of time commitment.

- **Disclosures.** When you have your real estate license, you are held to a higher standard by both your state real estate commission and the law. You must disclose to buyers and sellers that you are a licensed agent; you can't knowingly take advantage of a buyer or seller; etc. Some investors feel that having to make these disclosures and being held to this higher standard negatively affects their business, and that is why they don't want to get their license.

  While I can't speak for other investors, I haven't had a circumstance—and can't imagine one—where I would have any issue disclosing to a buyer or seller that my wife is licensed. In fact, in my experience, this has been a selling point for those buyers who are untrusting, and now feel more confident that they are dealing with someone who is licensed and knowledgeable. But it remains a concern for some investors.

Your License as a Secondary Income Stream

While I touched on this earlier, I wanted to spend a little more time discussing a side benefit of having your real estate license, should you decide to go that route. Having your real estate license can provide you a consistent secondary stream of income when you represent other investors in their deals.

In the course of my business, I meet a lot of successful investors who rely on real estate agents to both bring them deals and sell their deals. Most of these investors don't particularly like the agents they work with, but the lack of great investor-focused agents means they have to settle for what they can find. I've discovered that as an investor and real estate agent myself, I'm better than 90 percent of the agents they'll ever work with.

While I don't advertise my services as a buyer's agent or as a listing agent, many investors ask me if I can help them find and sell their properties. In any given year, it wouldn't be very difficult for me to earn as much money representing other investors in their deals as I earn from my own deals. In other words, if I wanted or needed the extra cash, I could probably double my annual income just by putting my real estate license to work.

Again, I'm not suggesting that you become a typical real estate agent, and, in fact, I rarely do work for other investors unless they happen to be good friends, or the work is exceptionally easy. But for an up-and-coming investor who is looking to hone their skills, learn their farm area, expand their network, and start to build their cash reserves, representing other investors as their buying or listing agent is a tremendous opportunity.

When a new investor comes to me and asks how to break into this business with no experience and no cash, the first thing I will tell them is to get their real estate license. In my opinion, it's a great way to start building up both the experience and the cash needed to succeed in this business.

CHAPTER 4
WHERE YOU SHOULD BUY

One of the biggest decisions most new investors struggle with is where to invest. An investor's buying area is often referred to as their "farm area," and farm areas can be as small as a neighborhood or two or as large as an entire metro area. Obviously, the smaller the farm area, the better you will get to know it and the houses in it, but conversely, the larger the farm area, the more opportunity you'll have to find great deals.

For most new investors, I would recommend a farm area that includes one or two reasonably sized zip codes—the size of a small city. You don't want an area too much bigger than five or ten square miles, and no more than a population of about 25,000 (which would be about 5,000 households in most places). If this seems daunting, start with an even smaller area—you can always expand later.

Determining Your Farm Area

I mentioned above that deciding where to invest is often a difficult decision for a new investor. Ironically, this should be one of the easiest decisions you'll need to make. The secret to real estate investing is to invest where you know, and for most people, that's right in their backyard.

When starting out, the best place to invest is often your own neighborhood, your own town, or your own city. If you've lived in the same place for several years, you probably have a good handle on which neighborhoods are "good" and which are "not so good." You may know which areas have held their property values and which have had wild fluctuations.

You probably know where new residential construction is taking place and the neighborhoods that are starting to get a bit run down.

There are other benefits to investing in your own backyard: You won't have to drive far to view properties when you're looking to buy, you won't have to drive far to monitor your property during renovations, and you won't have to drive far to check on the property while it's listed for sale. When I first started investing in the suburbs of Atlanta, I defined my farm area as "within ten minutes driving distance of my personal residence." That actually served me well for several years.

Now, it might not always be possible to build a rehabbing career where you live, but if you're going to start evaluating areas for your business, you might as well start where you know. If you later determine that—for some reason—investing in your own area isn't feasible, then you can start to branch out to other areas. Unfortunately, you may find that you don't live anywhere near a profitable investing area, in which case you may need to make some hard decisions, such as whether you're willing to move to focus on your real estate goals.

For example, I have several friends who live in tremendously expensive parts of California. For them to invest in real estate, they'd need $500,000 or more just to get in the game. This is a show-stopper for many of them, and they recognize that if they want to invest in real estate, they either need to move somewhere with lower property values or they need to spend a lot of time and energy trying to invest far from home. (We'll discuss that later.)

Analyzing Potential Markets

Determining how well a market can support flipping houses is as much art as it is science. Unfortunately, I can't give you a short checklist of things to look for that will decisively tell you whether a particular farm area will allow you to be successful as a rehabber. However, I can give you some general principles that you can use to evaluate whether your area is suited for profitable rehabbing.

Here are six guiding principles you can and should use to start evaluating and deciding on your farm area. The criteria will encompass a combination of quantitative data and some good old-fashioned driving around and seeing for yourself what the area is like. For the quantitative aspects of this analysis, this is where having a reliable buyer's agent—or having your own real estate license and access to the MLS—will come in very handy.

1. Price Ratios Between Distressed and Retail Sales

This ratio between what distressed properties in an area are selling for and what retail properties (meaning move-in-ready houses) are selling for is going to be a key factor in how well an area supports rehabbing. In an area where distressed houses are selling for much, much less than what retail houses are selling for, there is going to be more opportunity to make a profit than in areas where distressed properties are selling for nearly as much as retail properties.

As a general rule of thumb, what you want to see is distressed properties (REOs and short sales) selling for 50 percent or less of what similar retail properties are selling for. For example, if in your area, an average move-in-ready house that was built in the early 1990s and has four bedrooms and two bathrooms is selling for $200,000, and similar run-down houses in the same area are selling for less than $100,000, you may have a great opportunity to make money rehabbing those types of houses.

It's important to keep in mind that we're talking about averages, and not about the highest and lowest sales in an area. It's not uncommon that the *lowest* priced house will sell for less than 50 percent of what the *most expensive* similar house will sell for, but if the *averages* are at 50 percent, that's a very good sign. Also, keep in mind that the similar houses must be within a small distance from one another and in similar neighborhoods. The goal is to try to get an apples-to-apples comparison of the selling prices, where the only difference between the properties is the fact that they are being sold as "distressed" sales vs. move-in-ready houses.

2. Are There Buyers in the Area?

A second key determination of whether your area will support a rehabbing business is whether houses in your area are selling in general. While this is less of an issue in hot markets (like we've seen in much of the country between 2015 and 2019), this isn't always the case. For example, in many parts of the country between 2008-2011, there were practically no homeowner property sales in some areas. This was because with so many houses to choose from at ridiculously low prices, the few qualified buyers were focusing only on areas with the best schools and the areas where the bulk of people really wanted to live. In other, less desirable areas, buyers were few and far between, and even the high-end houses listed at bargain prices weren't getting any interest from buyers.

Therefore, you need to determine if your area is one where buyers are currently looking to buy houses. The key metric I use here is whether at least 60 percent of all retail listings in the area eventually sell, as opposed to being pulled off the market prior to selling. If you find that the majority of retail houses in your area are eventually finding buyers, you know that there is a reasonably sized pool of buyers interested in the area and who will be interested in your properties when you turn around to resell them.

If you're finding that the majority of retail sales in your area are expiring without ever being sold, are being leased instead of sold, or are being foreclosed on because they can't be sold, you may want to seriously consider looking at a different market to be rehabbing houses.

3. How Much Real Estate Supply Does the Area Have?

You'll often hear real estate agents talking about how vibrant their market is in terms of how many months of supply is available. By this they mean, how long it should theoretically take to sell all of the houses currently listed for sale given the current rate of sales in the area. If the number of months of supply is large, this indicates that there are relatively few sales for the given number of sellers. This is often referred to as a *buyer's market* because buyers have many houses to choose from. If the number of months of supply is small, this indicates that houses are selling quickly, and inventory will stay low. This is a *seller's market* because buyers are competing for the small number of houses available.

While it's possible to be successful rehabbing houses in either a buyer's or a seller's market, most new investors will find that working in a seller's market provides a lot less uncertainty and stress. While it might be a little more difficult to find great deals, once you have something purchased and rehabbed, you will be much more likely to sell it at your anticipated asking price.

Determining the number of months of supply is easy:

1. Determine the current number of houses actively listed for retail sale in your area;
2. Determine how many retail houses were sold in that same area in the past 30 days;
3. Divide the number of actively listed houses by the number of sold houses to get your supply.

As an example, let's say that there are 50 houses currently listed for retail sale in your farm area right now. In addition, let's say that in that same area, six retail houses have sold in the past month. Dividing 50 by 6 gives you 8.3, the number of months of supply currently in that area. That means it should theoretically take about 8 months to sell all the houses currently listed for sale in your area.

You should be looking to rehab in areas that have less than 12 months' supply of inventory. In a hot market, this is rarely an issue; but in slower markets—like what was seen in much of the country between 2008-2011—it's not uncommon to see inventory well above 12 months' supply.

4. Are There Other Investors Active in the Area?
While this isn't going to be the most reliable of benchmarks, knowing that there are other investors active—and successful—in the area should give you some additional confidence that the market will support your efforts.

A few years back, I partnered with a successful investor from Phoenix, Arizona and we started looking for new markets to break into together. After talking to several analysts and doing lots of research, we decided to give Milwaukee, Wisconsin, a try. Before flying up there for the first time, I jumped online and checked out the Milwaukee Real Estate Investors Association (Milwaukee REIA) website to see if there were many local investors. What I found surprised me—not only was the membership small, but the website showed little activity over the previous few years.

Upon arriving in Milwaukee, we started talking to real estate agents, closing attorneys, and other industry insiders. Our big question to each of them was, "Is there a lot of rehab investment activity in the area?" Almost unanimously, we were told there were very few rehab investors in the Milwaukee area. Even after several months of working on our first project, interviewing contractors and networking with other real estate professionals in the area, we were hard-pressed to find more than a couple of other serious investors in that relatively large city!

It turned out that there were some pockets in the Milwaukee suburbs that were ripe for finding great rehab deals, but the lack of investor activity at the time was a great indication that the deals were probably less plentiful than we were originally assuming. I don't recommend that you use this metric by itself; sometimes there are few investors in an area simply because the market is on the cusp of improving, while sometimes a lot of investors in an area is an indication that the market is saturated, and the deals are few and far between.

One more thing to keep in mind: Even if you are lucky enough to find a great untapped market, it probably won't stay that way for long. Other investors will see that you are being successful, and they will follow your lead. We spent about two years in the Milwaukee market and did about 50 flips, and by the time we stopped flipping in that market, it was saturated with investors. My belief about untapped markets not lasting very long was certainly true with Milwaukee. So, if you happen to find one of these markets, take advantage of it while you can!

5. Market Indicators and Trends

Generally speaking, market indicators and trends will give you an idea of the long-term prospects for real estate in a given area. While familiarizing yourself with these data and trends is going to be much more important when you're planning to hold property for the long term as opposed to when you plan to resell your property within a few months, there are still some very good reasons to be familiar with your area's trends even as a rehabber.

For example, if you plan to be working in your farm area for several years into the future, it's advantageous to recognize whether the area seems a likely candidate for long-term success. Also, if you ever find yourself having to decide whether you want to hold on to one of your properties for a long time, knowing the longer-term market trends can help you with that decision. Not to mention, familiarity with the long-term real estate outlook for your farm area may open up additional opportunities within and outside the world of rehabbing.

Here are the four indicators and trends that will tend to define your real estate market:

POPULATION TRENDS

Population growth or contraction is perhaps the strongest influencer of long-term real estate strength. When populations grow, the demand for housing can quickly outpace the existing supply, creating a seller's market. This increased demand for housing causes housing supply to drop (good for reselling properties!), as people are willing to buy and rent any available space. The competition by buyers causes prices to rise, and pushes market values higher.

On the other hand, when population rates are trending down, supply outpaces demand for housing, and consequently housing supply will increase, and it will be harder and harder to resell real estate. As property sales decrease in this buyer's market, the value of the properties themselves drop, and market values will fall.

To get an idea of where population trends are heading for your area, look at the website for the U.S. Census Bureau (www.census.gov) and the Bureau of Labor Statistics (www.bls.gov).

EMPLOYMENT TRENDS

Employment growth or contraction is important because it's a key indicator of what is likely going to happen with population growth. For example, when a big company moves into a city, it has a big impact on population. Not only does it bring employees with it and hire local talent, but it also provides a stable population of consumers who need services such as restaurants, auto repair shops, and hairdressers. Therefore, while a company may move into town with 1,000 employees, the service industries to support those 1,000 employees may bring another 1,000 or 2,000 people to the area. Employment growth can quickly drive population growth.

Of course, when companies leave town or lay off employees, it tends to have a negative effect on population trends, and also on the real estate market. Again, not only might the employees leave town, but there will now be less demand for the accompanying service industries, and those service workers will likely leave town searching for greener pastures elsewhere.

As a real estate investor, you should always try to stay on top of what is happening with the major employers in your farm area, and whether new employers or new industry will be moving in.

OVERBUILDING

When populations are increasing, builders go crazy trying to keep up with the demand for housing. New housing builders are so focused on getting as much housing inventory on the market as quickly as possible that they don't notice when supply starts to overtake demand. This leads to overbuilding, where there are too many new houses and rental units on the market than are being demanded. With too much inventory, sales start to drop, which leads to falling housing prices, and falling market values. Eventually, builders will stop building, but by then it's often too late, as the market is more than saturated.

If there is still a strong underlying economy in the local area, population should continue to grow, and eventually the oversupply of housing units will be absorbed. If the underlying economy is not strong, it may take many years for the excess housing units to get absorbed, and the local real estate market may stagnate for long periods of time.

SOCIO-ECONOMIC TRENDS

Trends in number of households and household income play a key role in the vacancy and income rates experienced in the surrounding markets. For example, in locations where there is a high divorce rate, families will tend to be smaller, and the demand for housing will tend to be higher. Changes in household income also play an interesting role in investment real estate; for example, when household incomes drop, many people start to rent houses as opposed to buying, thereby hurting investors who prefer to resell their properties.

6. Getting a "Feel" for the Location

Last but not least is the purely qualitative information you're going to get by spending hours driving around your potential farm area, getting an idea of the types of houses, types of neighborhoods, and types of people in the area.

While there is nothing scientific or quantitative about this approach, here are some things you should be cognizant of while driving around:

- Many times, the best areas to flip houses are those that have strong middle class and blue-collar neighborhoods. You want areas where there is pride of ownership (nice, well-kept lawns, few eyesores, and neighbors who know and interact with one another) and where families who are considering settling down would feel welcome and comfortable.
- Typically, older established neighborhoods that are 20–30 years old tend to make the best candidates, because those are the areas where homeowners have equity and prices are reasonable. That said, in a down market, like what we saw after the 2008 recession, you shouldn't rule out newer houses or newer neighborhoods as well. Not only do foreclosures and short sales bring down the prices of newer houses in a bad market, but builders are often willing to dump unsold inventory at rock-bottom prices.
- You're going to want areas where the majority of houses are lived in by the owners as opposed to being rented out. Owners tend to take

better care of their houses than tenants do, and neighborhoods with lots of owner occupants tend to be closer knit than neighborhoods comprised mostly of renters.

- Areas where many owners have lived for long periods of time are generally better than areas with lots of turnover. These areas have solid roots, tend to have less crime, and, because the owners have a good bit of equity in their properties, there is less chance that the houses in the area will fall into foreclosure. The one exception is neighborhoods where there is a lot of newly rehabbed houses and new construction; these neighborhoods often see more turnover but are attractive to buyers looking for up-and-coming areas.

- Any areas that have convenient consumer amenities and shopping are good; any areas that mix commercial businesses (auto shops, warehouses, etc.) with residential tend to be less desirable for rehabbing and reselling houses, as many families don't want the noise and activity associated with these types of businesses.

While I often tell people, "The place you rehab houses doesn't necessarily have to be a place where *you* would choose to live," I do prefer areas where I could feel safe and would be comfortable raising my children. If the gut feeling you get from a particular area isn't good, it shouldn't matter what the quantitative data tells you—you're going to be much happier, and therefore more successful, in an area where both the data and the "feel" is right.

My Farm Area

Just to give you an idea of the size and scope of the farm area you might want to target, let me tell you about the farm area I had for the first several years of my investing career. Remember, your path doesn't need to follow mine, and there's no reason your farm area can't be much bigger or smaller, but this may give you some perspective on what worked well for me in my early years.

When I started, I decided to invest close to home. In fact, because work/life balance is so important to me and I hate sitting in traffic, this was one of my primary goals. At the time, I lived in Cobb County, a suburban county just northwest of Atlanta, Georgia:

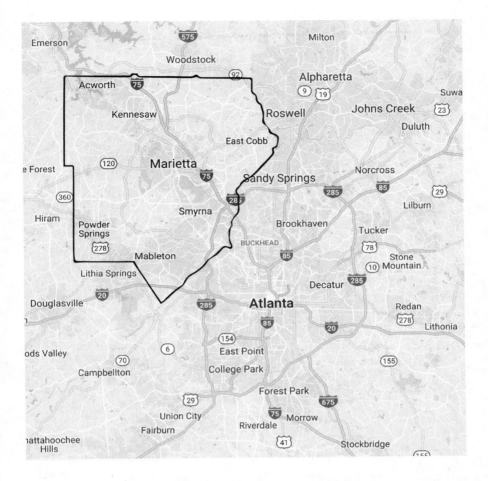

Cobb County is actually pretty large; it encompasses about 345 square miles and, when I started investing, had a population of around 700,000. At first, I decided to focus on a single city within Cobb County—Austell, Georgia:

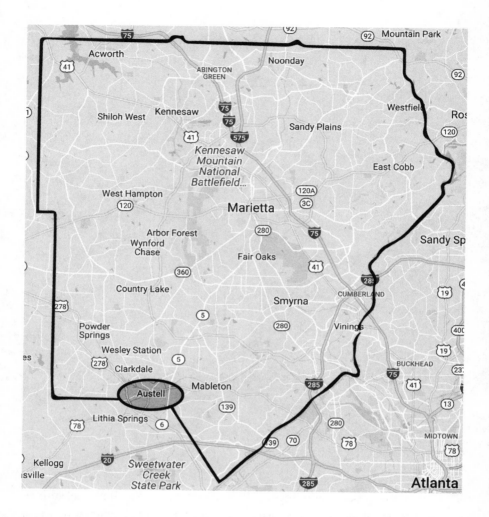

Austell has two zip codes, an area of about six square miles, and, back in 2008 when I was getting started, it had a population of about 8,000. After doing some MLS research on Austell property sales, I noticed that about half of Austell seemed ripe for investing (one of the two zip codes) while the other half seemed not so ripe (the other zip code). The bad half had large amounts of inventory and few retail sales, and the ratio between distressed and retail property sales was small.

So, I decided to focus on half of Austell, Georgia:

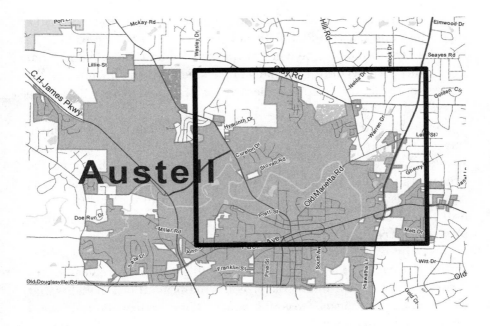

This farm area—this one zip code—encompassed about three square miles and a population of about 4,000 people. Having such a small farm area meant it might take a long time to find a deal, but it also meant that I could learn the area inside and out in just a couple weeks.

I spent the next two weeks driving every street and through every neighborhood in that zip code of Austell. I started to see patterns; the same half-dozen builders had come in between 1995–2000 and put up a massive number of houses in this city. In fact, the neighborhoods were all very similar, with houses selling at almost identical price points.

Within a couple of weeks, my wife and I knew every street and every subdivision in that half of Austell. When our agent brought us a deal, all we needed to know was the address before we had a good idea of what the house looked like and what the neighborhood was like. That small farm area paid off for us; during the 2008–2012 period, my wife and I bought and sold more properties in that zip code than any other investor and nearly any other real estate agent.

In fact, focusing on that small farm area led to our name becoming synonymous with investing in that area, and we often had other investors calling us to sell their rehabbed houses. Additionally, it led to us being able to build solid relationships with all the buyer's agents in the area, which helped us move our rehabbed properties. When an agent had a buyer in Austell, it wasn't uncommon for us to be the very first phone call the agent made to see what properties we had for sale and what properties we had coming available. Likewise, it wasn't uncommon for agents selling distressed properties in Austell to call us to see if we were interested in buying.

Within a year of starting our business, we had built an automated buying and selling pipeline in our farm area. Within a couple of years, we were focused on several cities within that same county, but our farm area was still relatively small. By 2011, our total farm area was about 35 square miles and encompassed a population of about 100,000. Even several years into our business, there were still no houses in our purchase area that we couldn't drive to in 30 minutes or less.

My point is, don't be afraid to start small. While many investors feel the need to cast a wide net—thinking it will get them more deals—becoming an expert in a small area provides many additional benefits that can be more advantageous to your business. If you realize that your small farm area doesn't provide enough potential deal flow, you can always expand to a larger area; incremental expansion is always easier than starting big in the first place.

CHAPTER 5

WHAT YOU SHOULD BUY

One of the hallmarks of a successful investor is good time management, and when it comes to investing, one key to time management is knowing what kinds of properties you should be focusing your energy on and what kinds of properties are just a waste of your time. While any property can be a potential deal if you're persistent enough (and skillful enough), new investors should be focusing their time and energy on the types of properties that are most likely to result in successful acquisitions and great deals.

Distressed Properties

The key to being a successful real estate investor is being able to target and find distressed properties. You'll often hear that term in this business, and you'll hear it used in many different contexts. But generally speaking, a distressed property is one where either the owners of the property or the property itself are in a position where it is likely that the property will sell below market value.

Conditions Leading to Property Distress

There are typically three situations that will cause a property to be distressed, and will in turn lead to a property being sold below market value:

1. **Financial Distress of Owners**
    - By far the most common situation that results in property distress is the adverse financial situation of the owners. There are

two common financial situations that lead to the bulk of distressed properties:

- ◆ Homes are "underwater" on their mortgages. In other words, owners owe more on their mortgage than their house is worth. This means that the homeowner either needs to sell for less than what they owe, or they need to find a creative solution where they can sell the property (or transfer control of the property) without having to pay off their loan at the time of the sale.
- ◆ Homeowners are having trouble making their mortgage payments. Even in situations where a home isn't underwater, if the homeowner is having trouble making their mortgage payments—due to loss of their job, underemployment, etc.—they will find themselves at risk of foreclosure if they can't sell their property quickly. This often leads to discounts on the sale of the property, especially if the buyer can close quickly without requiring much from the owner in terms of financial help.
- Whether a homeowner faces one or both of the above financial situations, there is an opportunity for the smart investor to help solve the homeowner's problems, and in return get a great deal on a house.

2. **Personal Distress of Owners**

- Owner distress isn't always caused by financial situations. In many cases, the distress of the homeowner can be caused purely by life circumstances out of their control. Sometimes common life situations will require a homeowner to want or need to sell their house quickly, and when owners are put in a position where they are forced to sell quickly, they will generally be willing to sell at a discount to make that happen.
- The four most common situations you'll run into where a homeowner wants or needs to sell their house quickly are as follows:
  - ◆ Divorce of the owners.
  - ◆ Death of one or more owner.
  - ◆ Job change requiring a quick relocation.
  - ◆ Tired and overworked landlord.
- These circumstances often translate into a situation where the seller is extra motivated to get rid of the property quickly, creating a great opportunity for a savvy investor.

3. **Poor Property Condition**
   - In many cases, the distress is more related to the condition of the property than to the circumstances of the owner. When a property is in poor condition, the potential set of buyers for the property is reduced. Typical homeowners don't want to buy a house where they will need to do a lot of work and spend a lot of money, even if it means the house can be purchased at a discount. They'd rather spend more money for a house where they can just move in and not have to deal with property issues.
   - In fact, even if a typical homeowner were willing to buy a property in poor condition, their lender probably wouldn't allow it. Most traditional mortgage lenders will not lend money to buyers for properties that aren't in move-in-ready condition, meaning all the major systems in the house work. Even little stuff like a non-functioning water heater or missing stove can be enough for a lender to refuse to provide a mortgage.
   - Properties in distressed condition may just need basic updating or they may need a huge overhaul, but what they have in common is less competition from retail buyers. In some cases, where the houses need a lot of work, there is even less competition from other investors who are scared of big renovations. These situations provide great opportunities for investors who are unafraid to jump in and get their feet wet.

As an investor, you should think of yourself as a problem solver; one of your biggest keys to success will be finding problems and then figuring out creative solutions. If you can find homeowners who are facing the situations we discussed above, and if you can position yourself to help solve their problems in a way that is a win-win for both sides, you'll find that great deals are constantly falling into your lap.

Retail Properties

I want to quickly touch on the opposite of distressed properties—retail properties. I know of many new investors who, even after being told time and again that they should focus on distressed properties, instead spend their days looking at and making offers on retail properties. They get discouraged as offer after offer is ignored or rejected. As an investor, it's important that you know the difference between a retail and a distressed property, and also that you understand why you should be focusing your time and energy on distressed properties and not retail properties.

"Retail" simply means that the sellers and the property are not distressed, and that the property is in good enough shape that it would likely sell to a homeowner who will move into the house. Retail properties are the most common type of property that you'll encounter as a real estate investor; they are everywhere, which is why they are such an allure for so many new investors.

However, you don't want to get caught up in the trap of thinking, "If there are so many retail properties out there, it shouldn't be too hard for me to find a few bargains to buy and resell." There are several reasons why retail properties are nearly impossible for investors to buy at a discount and why investors generally shouldn't bother focusing on them:

- Retail properties are by definition in good condition, and there is going to be a lot more competition for these houses than for other houses in worse condition. The reason for this is simple: Houses in good condition require less work from their buyers and are much easier to get mortgages for.
- Retail properties have a large buyer pool, and because the sellers aren't desperate to sell, it is often very difficult to buy these properties for less than market value, which means there's almost never much financial room to buy a retail property, add value to it by fixing it up, and resell it. For this reason, fewer investors will spend much time looking at or considering purchasing retail properties.
- Retail properties are generally marketed very widely. Often, they are listed on the MLS and other real estate websites for everyone to see, which means that you will have no competitive advantage over other buyers looking for a property.

So, now that I've hopefully convinced you that distressed property is the key to successful investing, it should also be obvious that the more distressed the property or the more distressed the homeowner situation, the better the opportunity for a great deal.

With that in mind, I want to talk a bit about the foreclosure process. In many markets and at many times, foreclosed properties are an excellent way to acquire good deals; in fact, many investors build their entire real estate business around buying foreclosures.

Keep in mind that there are several phases of the foreclosure process, and the further along in the foreclosure process a property is, the more distressed the homeowner, or the bank, is likely to be.

The Foreclosure Process

First, let's define—in very simple terms—what foreclosure is:

Foreclosure is the legal process whereby the lender on a property can gain ownership of the property should the borrower default (stop paying) on the loan. When a homeowner cannot pay the monthly mortgage on his property, the lender (generally a bank) can gain control and ownership of the property. The lender will usually attempt to sell the property at auction in attempt to recoup the loan amount, and if that fails, will often sell the property using a real estate agent and the MLS.

Depending on which state you live in, you will see one of two sets of processes around foreclosures:

- **Non-judicial foreclosure:** This is a foreclosure process that doesn't involve the courts or the judicial system and where the rules for foreclosure are defined by state statutes.
- **Judicial foreclosure:** This is a foreclosure process that is processed through the court system, much like any other type of lawsuit.

Many states support both types of foreclosure process, though one or the other will typically be the standard.

Non-Judicial Foreclosure Process

In most non-judicial foreclosure states, in order for a property to be foreclosed upon, the lender must go through a several-month process to regain control of the property and then sell it. While every state has their own particular set of rules to be followed, the timeline below indicates the most common high-level process of non-judicial foreclosure:

NOTICE OF DEFAULT

The first step in the foreclosure process is the filing of a "notice of default" (NOD) with the county recording office in the county where the property is located. This happens after the borrower misses several months of payments. This puts the homeowner on notice that the foreclosure process has begun and that the house will be scheduled for auction or sale.

NOTICE OF TRUSTEES SALE

If the borrower doesn't bring the loan current within a set period of time after the NOD is filed, the lender will post a notice of sale on the property. This notice will also be recorded with the county recording office and will typically be published in a local newspaper or publication over the next several weeks.

TRUSTEES SALE

At the time and location specified on the notice of sale (usually on the county courthouse steps or at the property itself), the property is auctioned off to the highest bidder, who must pay the high bid price in cash. The winner of the auction receives ownership of the property.

The opening auction bid on the property is made by the foreclosing lender, and this opening bid is usually equal to whatever amount was owed on the property by the borrower, plus any accrued fees. But most properties aren't deemed by most investors to be worth the amount owed, so the majority of properties don't receive a bid at or above the opening bid price. And, if there are no bids higher than the opening bid price, the property will be purchased by the lender.

REAL ESTATE OWNED (REO)

Properties that don't sell at auction and are purchased by the lender are called "real estate owned," or REO, properties. These properties are then sold by the lender almost exactly the same way as any other property sold on the open market. At some point after the trustee's sale, the lender will put the REO property up for sale by listing it with a real estate agent on the MLS. The amount of time that a lender will wait before listing the property for sale on the MLS varies based on the whim of the lender. A lender may put an REO property up for sale within a couple weeks or may hold onto the property for months or even years before listing it for sale. This is why so many houses that look foreclosed may sit vacant for months or years before you notice a "for sale" sign in the yard.

In some states, this entire process can be as short as just three to five weeks, and in other states could be as long as one to two years. Additionally, some jurisdictions will auction off property as little as once per month, while other jurisdictions may hold auctions every day of the week. You'll want to get familiar with your state's laws if you're buying in a non-judicial foreclosure state.

Judicial Foreclosure Process

Because the judicial foreclosure process is complicated and will be controlled by lawyers and the court system, these types of foreclosures are beyond the scope of this book. But, you should note that once the process is complete, the lender will typically resell the foreclosed property—the REO—much the same as in non-judicial foreclosures. Specifically, the lender will list the property with a real estate agent who will use the MLS to market it and find a buyer.

Property Criteria

When I started in this business, people would often ask me, "What are your criteria for buying houses?" And my answer was very specific:

> I look for traditional style, single-family houses that were built after 1990, with at least three bedrooms, at least two bathrooms, and a level and usable backyard, and that will resell after renovations for between $100,000–$150,000.

If you asked me why I focused on those types of houses, my answer was simple: Those are the types of houses that were selling in my area! It didn't matter if I personally liked or disliked these types of houses; all that mattered was that buyers in my area tended to like them. If buyers in my area preferred 5-bedroom ranch houses built in the 1950s, then that would have been my buying criteria.

The point is, when targeting properties, personal preference is important to a degree—if you like it, others will also—but much more important than what you prefer is what the buyers in your market tend to prefer. They are your customers, and your job as a business owner is to provide the product that your customers want.

It's also important to realize that just because a certain type of property may be selling very, very inexpensively, that doesn't make it a good deal. Here's an example of that from personal experience.

In my original farm area back in 2008 through 2011, you could find some amazingly cheap single-family homes that had just 1.5 bathrooms. Banks and homeowners were practically giving these houses away, in some cases literally. Some investors in the area got very excited by the low prices on these properties, without considering that it was nearly impossible to resell those types of houses at that time.

Here was the relevant data that I pulled up when trying to decide if I should be buying some of those houses:

In 2010, in the zip code where I focused most of my investing, there were 318 retail sales. Of those 318 sales, exactly six of those had fewer than two full bathrooms. In other words, at that time, only 2 percent of sales in my market were of properties with fewer than two bathrooms! I'd have been crazy to try to rehab and resell homes with fewer than two full bathrooms, regardless of how cheaply I might have been able to buy them.

(And in case you're wondering, it's not easy to turn a half-bath in a small house into a full bath. The 1.5-bath floorplan is typically too small or cramped to convert a half-bath into a full bathroom within the existing square footage, and it's often too expensive to add the necessary square footage to make an enlarged bathroom.)

Any investor who didn't do the research and assumed that buying cheap houses with 1.5 bathrooms was a brilliant move probably ended up with a lot of unsold houses that year. Luckily, I did the research, and I knew what types of houses I'd be able to resell. You should do the same.

What Characteristics Should You Consider?

Based on the above anecdote, it should be obvious that I can't tell you specifically what types of houses you should be investing in, and what property characteristics you should be looking for. However, I can give you a general overview of the property characteristics you should be thinking about and then you can do some research to determine what specifically is selling, and not selling, in your market.

Here are the most important property characteristics you should be investigating when determining what your specific property criteria is:

- **Property age:** In most areas, there were housing booms at several points over the past 100 years. In my experience, houses built during the most recent boom—ignoring any current new construction spikes—will be the most desirable to potential buyers, while the boom previous to that makes for the best rentals. For example, in Atlanta, prior to the current wave of new construction, there was a housing boom in the 1970s and then again in the mid-1990s. As a rehabber starting in 2008, I focused on houses built in the 1990s; many of the landlords I know focus on properties built in the 1970s. Again, this is a general rule, and your data will tell you for certain.

- **Property style:** In most areas, there are going to be certain styles of houses that predominate the landscape. In general, these are the types of houses buyers prefer in that area. However, that's not always the case. For example, historically, there have always been many single-story ranch style houses in my farm area, and you'll still see many of these houses around. However, buyers now prefer more traditional style houses to the ranches, which tend to be more popular as rentals. So again, make sure you have the data.

- **Construction type:** You'll want to know if your buyers prefer framed houses, brick, stucco, etc. While most construction types will get the job done, there will be some preferred styles in your area, and these will be the houses that the buyers are naturally attracted to.

  Remember, don't assume that others want the same thing you want, especially if you come from a different area. A great example here is that I dislike basements, both as a homeowner and as an investor. To an investor, they are money pits. However, most of the buyers in my area love basements, so I'd be a fool to pass up a great house with a basement just because of my personal preferences.

- **Number of bedrooms and bathrooms:** In all areas, there will be a minimum number of bedrooms and bathrooms that are needed to sell a property quickly. In my area, it used to be three bedrooms and two bathrooms was the minimum; over the past few years, it's transitioned to the point where buyers are demanding at least four bedrooms and two baths. So, this is our new criteria.

- **Lot size:** Depending on your area and your buyer demographic, you may see trends in the types and sizes of lots that tend to sell quickly. For example, in more rural and suburban areas, buyers are going to be accustomed to larger lots, with flat lots preferable to hilly lots; in cities, any private exterior space may tend to help the property sell quickly and at a premium. It's important to know what types of lots are expected by the typical buyer and ensure that your property has it.
- **Subdivision or stand-alone:** You will often hear that you shouldn't buy investment property on busy roads, but I'll take that one step further: In many areas, buyers are going to expect not just non-busy roads, but also a well-defined subdivision. Subdivisions may have amenities that buyers want, aesthetic standards that buyers find attractive, or may just provide the privacy that your buyers expect. When considering a property, make sure to consider whether your potential buyers will expect it to fall within a subdivision or not, and how that will affect your future sale.

You may find several other property characteristics that tend to be common or uncommon in your particular market, and you'll be wise to take note of how those characteristics will impact your ability to buy and sell properties in that area. This doesn't mean that different is always bad, but consider that if most buyers are looking for a certain type of house, it will be easier to sell that type of house than another type.

All that said, here are some general rules that I've come to learn over the years. Keep in mind that some of these may be difficult to glean by just looking at historical sales data:

- When buying in a subdivision, the nicer the subdivision, the farther back from the main road you'd like the house to be; the more run-down the subdivision, the closer to the front of the neighborhood you'd like the house to be. In other words, the more unkempt houses potential buyers see before they arrive at yours, the less likely they are to be impressed with yours.
- Houses where the neighbors have barking dogs or other animals in their yards can be very difficult to sell.
- Houses with no attached garage are harder to sell.
- Houses with fewer than three bedrooms and two baths are very

difficult to sell.

- Houses without usable yard space are difficult to sell in areas where the bulk of the buyers are families.
- Houses on busy streets are difficult to sell in areas where the bulk of the buyers are families.
- Houses near schools are difficult to sell in areas where the bulk of the buyers have no kids.
- Houses with outdated floor plans are very difficult to sell.
- Houses with pools can be tricky. Make sure you have a good understanding of who your target buyer is before buying a house with a pool. In my experience, a house with a pool may sell for a premium, but your target group of potential buyers will be much smaller.

Level of Renovation

Especially early in your rehabbing career, you're going to want to be selective about the types of renovation projects you jump into. I've seen a lot of new investors get in over their heads on their first or second project by trying to tackle a renovation that was either risky or required a great deal of construction knowledge, scheduling ability, or custom design work.

While you don't necessarily have to stick to "paint and carpet" rehabs when you start out, you should have an idea of what your skill set is, what your level of risk tolerance is, and how much stress you're willing to incur on the early projects. When I look at a house, I will often characterize the level of renovation by placing the project into one of four levels, as follows:

COSMETIC	ADVANCED COSMETIC	MECHANICALS	ADVANCED
PAINT	CABINETS	HVAC	FOUNDATION
CARPET	COUNTERTOPS	RE-PIPING	MOLD
APPLIANCES	DOORS	RE-WIRING	STRUCTURAL
LIGHTS/FANS	WINDOWS		ADDITIONS
SINKS/FAUCETS	ROOF		
DOOR HARDWARE	SIDING/GUTTERS/TRIM		
OUTLETS/SWITCHES	MAJOR TRIM/DESIGN		

Level 1: Cosmetic

The most basic type of renovation is what is referred to as a cosmetic renovation. It involves making changes and repairs to only the most basic finishes in the property—painting, replacing carpet, putting in new appliances, replacing lighting and plumbing fixtures. This is the type of renovation many new rehabbers will look to start with, and even the most inexperienced investor should be able to tackle a basic cosmetic renovation. In the industry, these types of renovations are often called "paint and carpet" renovations, as painting and replacing carpet constitute the bulk of the renovation effort.

Level 2: Advanced Cosmetic

The next level up from a cosmetic rehab is what I call an "advanced cosmetic" renovation. These types of renovations will include everything in a basic cosmetic rehab plus some more complicated cosmetic repairs, including replacement of cabinets and countertops, some doors and windows, some basic exterior work (roof, gutters, siding) and some upgraded trim work on the interior. This is the type of renovation I recommend that most new investors start with; it's difficult enough that you'll have less competition from other investors and easy enough that you shouldn't get yourself into any major trouble during the actual rehab.

Level 3: Mechanicals

The next level of rehab includes everything from the advanced cosmetic category plus the mechanicals. In general, mechanicals refer to the electrical, plumbing and heating/air conditioning (HVAC) systems of the house. This level of rehab might entail things like rewiring the electrical system, re-piping the house with new plumbing, or replacing pieces or even all of the HVAC system. While some mechanical work isn't overly complicated, I call out this group of tasks separately, as these are the first level of renovation tasks you'll encounter that will require permits from your county or local jurisdiction.

Level 4: Advanced

This type of renovation presents risks over and above typical rehab projects. Advanced projects include renovation work such as foundation repairs, mold remediation, structural repairs, or additions. These tasks all present certain risks, both during the renovation itself and once the renovation is complete, as future buyers will need to deal with issues that weren't properly addressed. These types of renovations shouldn't be taken lightly, as they can present potential lawsuit risks should any of the work be done improperly. Once you have some rehabbing experience, these types of projects will present some unique opportunities, as most other investors won't want to get involved, so you can potentially pick up these projects at prices that offer large potential profits.

CHAPTER 6
WHO TO BUY FROM

In the previous chapter, we discussed the differences between retail properties and distressed properties; and hopefully, by now, you're convinced that you should be buying distressed properties. And we discussed what specific characteristics you should be looking for in your investments.

In this chapter, I'll discuss the most common acquisition strategies being used today by active investors, and hopefully get you thinking about which of these strategies will be best for you and your investing business.

In general, there are five types of sellers and situations you should be focused on as an investor:
1. Owners with equity (typically distressed homeowners)
2. Absentee owners with equity (typically landlords)
3. Owners without equity (typically short sale sellers)
4. Bank owned foreclosures (REOs)
5. Foreclosure properties at auction (trustee sales)

Purchasing from Owners with Equity

In the last chapter, we talked about the various personal circumstances that many homeowners encounter that motivate them to sell their property at a discount. If you recall, the big ones were divorce, death, and relocation. In some cases, these hardships result in financial distress as well, and in those situations, it may be difficult to buy from these sellers if they owe more on their mortgage than their property is worth.

But, in other cases, the homeowners are desperate to sell, *and* they owe little enough on their mortgage that they can sell at a substantial market discount and still get their mortgage paid off. They have equity in their property. When a distressed homeowner has equity in their property, there is often a great opportunity for an investor to swoop in, help the homeowner with their tough situation, and create a great deal for the investor. It's a win-win all around.

Here's an example:

My closing attorney and good friend of mine called me on a Sunday morning to tell me about a yard sale in his neighborhood. Apparently, the woman who owned the house had recently died and her daughter was selling off the bulk of the stuff in the house. She indicated that she might be interested in selling the house at some point.

My wife and I were in the area, so we stopped by and my wife struck up a conversation with the daughter. The daughter was still pretty upset about her mom's death, but indicated that once everything settled down, she would be looking to sell the house; she wasn't looking forward to the sale, as the house was in pretty rough shape and she knew it wouldn't sell quickly or easily in that condition. She also indicated to my wife that the house was nearly paid off, and only had a small mortgage remaining.

My wife gave the woman her business card, collected the woman's name and address, and told her to call us if and when she was ready to sell. A couple months went by, and my wife sent the woman a Christmas card and a nice note offering some kind words. She never mentioned the house. About two weeks later, my wife got a call from the woman saying, "I've been meaning to call you. We'd love to sell the house, but we just don't have the energy to clean it out or fix it up for sale. We can't even bear to visit the house anymore."

We told the woman that if she wanted to sell to us, we'd take the house as-is, we'd clean it out ourselves and we'd do all the necessary repairs. She never needed to set foot in the house again if she didn't want to. We negotiated a fair price and closed on the house a week later. She made a great profit and we got a great deal.

After an extensive rehab, we made over $40,000 on the deal. Years later, we still exchange Christmas cards with this woman.

Why did this situation work out as well as it did? Because we understood what the seller's main problem was—she just wanted to be rid of the house quickly and painlessly. Had we told her she'd have to clean the house out or if we had asked her about needed repairs or if we had dragged out the closing, we wouldn't have been solving her core problem, and we likely wouldn't have gotten the deal. However, by closing quickly and easily, and not asking her to do any work or investigation, she was happy to walk away with a little less money than she probably could have gotten had she cleaned the house, gotten an inspection, and done some minor repairs.

The lesson here is that sometimes there are more important things to a seller than money. If you can figure out what those important things are and provide them to the seller, oftentimes they are willing to give up some money in return, allowing you a great deal and a win-win situation all around.

For distressed homeowners, some of those non-monetary things they may be looking for include:
- Quick closing so they can get cash for an upcoming expense.
- Not having to deal with packing and moving.
- Not having to clean and repair the house.
- Not having to remove stuff from the house, especially things that bring back memories.

Remember, just because money may be your biggest motivator when it comes to buying a house doesn't mean that money is the seller's biggest motivator!

Why Buy from Owners with Equity

To summarize, here are two of the biggest reasons why you might want to be targeting distressed homeowners with equity in their properties:
- **Great deals.** Assuming the homeowner has enough equity, it's possible to buy the property at a price where you can make a lot of money. Again, the key is being able to solve the homeowner's non-monetary problems.
- **Quick closings.** Oftentimes the problem the homeowner is trying to solve is getting a quick sale, which means you could go from a first discussion with a homeowner this week to owning the property next week. Working with distressed homeowners with equity is by far the fastest way to a quick deal.
- **No real estate agents involved.** This makes our lists of both benefits

and drawbacks. The benefit to not having any real estate agents involved is that you don't need to worry about another party influencing the seller based on the sales price. Real estate agents will often try to get their clients the most money possible, even if it means ignoring their other problems. Unfortunately, you are going to be looking for a discount in return for helping with those other problems, and an agent can often get in the way.

The Drawbacks to Buying from Owners with Equity

Despite the possibility of getting a great deal very quickly, there are a few big downsides to working with distressed homeowners:

- **Difficult situations.** Because buying from distressed homeowners often means dealing with people who are going through difficult life situations, you need to be prepared to have difficult conversations with people who may be in a vulnerable state of mind. Those sellers who are not receptive to your pitch may get angry or even violent; and even those who are receptive may not be in the best position to cope with whatever situation brought you to them.

- **Potential ownership and title complexities.** These types of deals are often prone to ownership complexities. Especially when you are dealing with a divorce or a death, it may not be clear who has the authority to sell the property. Or you may find yourself in a situation where you require the approval of several people, some of whom may be less agreeable than the others.

- **May require cash and quick closing.** The benefit of these types of deals is a quick closing—that is, unless you *don't* want a quick closing. If you're going to need time to get your finances in order and get the deal funded, this might be frustrating to the seller and you may find that you can't really solve their problems. Be aware that many sellers are going to want a quick close in return for providing you a great deal.

- **No real estate agents involved.** On the negative side of not having agents involved, you're going to need to hold the seller's hand throughout the entire process. They may know nothing about selling a house and will be looking to you to facilitate the deal and ensure that everything gets done quickly and smoothly. If you don't have a lot of experience buying and selling houses, this can put you in a tough spot. Likewise, if you happen to be a licensed real estate agent yourself, you'll want to insist that the sellers be represented by their own agent in order to avoid any appearance that you are using your professional status to take advantage of the seller. If you're licensed, make sure you talk to your broker before engaging with distressed homeowners with you as the buyer.

Purchasing from Absentee Owners with Equity

You often hear reference to buying properties from absentee owners. This simply refers to property owners who don't live in the property, and in most cases an absentee owner is a landlord for the property. In some cases, the landlord will be an investor who purposefully bought property as an investment; in other cases, the landlord will be a homeowner who has become a "reluctant landlord," meaning they moved out of their home, couldn't sell it, and put a renter in there as a short-term solution.

While both of these situations—investors and reluctant landlords—can be profitable to you, you'll want to approach the two very differently. Investors (at least the smart ones) will usually have equity in their properties, while the reluctant landlords usually won't; if they did, they wouldn't have had difficulty selling. Therefore, while you may be able to purchase an investor's property outright, when dealing with a reluctant landlord you'll have to approach the situation as a potential short sale, which we'll discuss in the next section.

With that said, I'm going to focus the rest of this section on targeting investor-landlords who have properties with equity.

You may be asking, "Why would someone who is an investor and who purposefully bought a property to hold as a rental be interested in selling to me at a below-market price?" The answer is that many landlords underestimate the amount of time and effort it takes to manage a rental property. This is especially true for landlords who own properties out of state; they may have difficulty finding good property managers they can trust and may be tired of dealing with the headaches that come from having tenants.

In fact, the best situation (for you) is to find an out-of-state landlord who is between tenants. They're likely facing some rehab from the last tenant, dealing with the prospect of having to get the place rented again, and not looking forward to the tediousness of getting a new renter into the property. Moreover, they're trying to do all of this from afar! You can bet that these landlords are often very motivated to sell, and if you catch them on the right day, they may be willing to practically give their property away.

Why Buy Absentee Owner Properties

As alluded to above, there are plenty of great reasons to focus on properties owned by absentee landlords:

- **Tend to have equity.** Many landlords purchase their properties for cash, and even those who get financing will put 20–30 percent down. Therefore, it's common to find professional landlords who have properties with equity.
- **Are often motivated.** Again, if you catch an absentee landlord at the right time, there can be a tremendous amount of motivation, and you can sometimes walk away with a fantastic deal. One strategy to leverage this opportunity is to call the number on "for rent" signs and ask the owner if they've considered selling. You may find that selling is *exactly* what they're looking to do, as opposed to receiving all those annoying calls from prospective tenants. In fact, some of the best real estate deals I've ever heard about have come from landlords who are getting ready to retire and are interested in selling their entire portfolio of houses. In some cases, they're willing to provide substantial discounts to someone willing to buy them all at once.
- **Are easy to find.** There are many services that can provide lists of absentee owners, where the list can be filtered by data such as location, amount of equity the owner has, and amount of time the owner has held the property. In other words, finding these leads can be easy if you're willing to do the legwork to follow up on them.

The Drawbacks of Absentee Owner Properties

While absentee owner deals can be tremendously profitable, there are also some downsides to focusing on this type of seller:

- **Owners tend to be savvier.** The big downside to dealing with absentee owners is that many of them are professional investors and tend to be savvier than your typical homeowner when it comes to real estate transactions. They often have access to the MLS and they know how to use it. Thus, they may be familiar with what their property is worth and may not be willing to part with it for less than market value. This is especially true if they haven't gotten to the point where they're tired, frustrated, and sick of dealing with tenants.

- **You may inherit a tenant.** Because absentee owners usually rent out their properties, there's a good possibility that there will be a tenant in the property when you purchase it. And it's also quite possible that that tenant will have an enforceable rental agreement that you can't legally break. You may have to be willing to hold onto the property until their lease expires, or you may have to figure out a way to incentivize the tenant to leave.
- **Properties may not make good flips.** I've found that in some areas, the type of property that makes a good rental won't make a good flip, and vice versa. If you're buying a property from a landlord, it runs the risk of being a property that is more suited to being rented out than to being someone's primary residence. It may relate to the style, the floor plan, or the lot—there are many aspects of a property that can make it more suitable to be a rental than a primary residence. These factors can sometimes stand in the way of the deal being profitable to a rehabber.

Purchasing from Owners Without Equity

In many cases, you'll be dealing with homeowners or investors who are underwater on their property and may consider doing a short sale. A short sale is a special kind of purchase directly from an owner who owes more on the loan than his property is worth. In a short sale, the homeowner asks permission from their mortgage lender to sell the property for less than what they owe on the mortgage, generally because they are having trouble making the payments on the loan due to some financial hardship.

For example, let's say John Smith owes $200,000 on his house, but recently lost his job and can't afford to make his monthly payments. John knows that his house is now worth less than $200,000, and he asks his lender for permission to sell at a lower amount. The lender, who doesn't want to deal with a foreclosure, which I'll discuss below, gives permission. John lists his house with a real estate agent.

You—the investor—come along and offer to buy John's house for a price that works for you; let's say $150,000. Assuming John is okay with selling you the property, he accepts the offer and sends it to the lender for approval. The lender will do a basic appraisal to find out what the property is worth and may take into consideration the condition of the property as part of that appraisal. If the lender determines that your offer of $150,000 is reasonable (we'll discuss what that means below), the lender may approve the sale, allowing you to purchase the property for that amount—substantially less than what John owes.

Now, you may be asking yourself, "Why would the bank allow John to sell the property for $150,000 when he owes $200,000—isn't the bank losing money?"

First, yes, the bank is losing money. However, the bank may determine that they will lose *less* money by allowing John to sell the property for less than what is owed than they would if they had to foreclose on the property. Not only is a foreclosure expensive (the bank needs to pay attorneys, real estate agents, and others), but it's quite possible that after all is said and done, the bank may end up reselling the foreclosed property for less than what the short sale generated. In the end, a short sale can be a win-win for everyone involved.

There are some potential downsides for the homeowner by selling their property as a short sale. You should be aware of these, as they may come up in discussions between you and the seller, or you and the seller's real estate agent:

- **Deficiency judgment.** First and foremost, the bank has a right to ask the homeowner to promise to repay the difference between the sale price and what's owed (in our example, $50,000) or to file a deficiency judgment against the homeowner in an attempt to recoup that difference later.
- **Owe taxes to the IRS.** In addition to potentially owing money to the lender, the difference between what a short sale is sold for and what the owner owes on the loan is going to be subject to capital gains taxes by the IRS. In our example above, the $50,000 would be considered a gain by the homeowner and would be subject to taxes.
- **Credit impact.** Lastly, the homeowner will take a hit to his credit when completing a short sale. This credit hit will typically not be as bad as a foreclosure or bankruptcy, but can impact FICO scores by 150-250 points. The actual impact will be based on the specific borrower and will be impacted by whether the seller missed payments prior to the short sale or whether they were current on their mortgage the entire time.

Why Buy Short Sale Properties

In normally appreciating housing markets, you won't find a lot of great short sale deals, simply because most houses are worth more than what the homeowner paid for them. But in struggling real estate markets, short sales can be a great opportunity for investors. There are several reasons for this:

- **Easy to find.** In struggling markets, you'll find that short sales are everywhere. You can find them on the MLS, you can find them while searching through foreclosure listings, and just talking to people on a daily basis will often reveal situations where a distressed homeowner needs to sell their property quickly.
- **Less competition.** There is typically less competition from both owner-occupants and other investors when buying short sales. This is because the short sale process can take a long time, and most buyers don't like waiting around.
- **Substantial discounts.** While banks will do an appraisal on the property, they will often accept as little as 80 percent of that appraised value at the sale. If you can prove that there are serious defects with the property (by providing pictures, contractors estimates, etc.), you can often get even larger discounts.
- **Fewer hidden defects.** Because the owners often still live in the property they are short selling, you can be fairly certain that most of the major renovation items—HVAC, plumbing, electrical—are in basic working order. And because you can often talk directly with the seller (and sometimes even get a full disclosure document), you can often find out everything that's wrong with the house before you buy.

The Drawbacks of Short Sale Properties

There are a few drawbacks to short sale purchases as well. While these tend to be of little concern to seasoned investors who buy and sell a lot of properties, to a new investor who only plans to buy one at a time, these can be showstopper issues:

- **Long timeframe.** The biggest downside to buying short sales is that they can take a very long time. I've worked on short sales where I've waited six months to get a response from the bank. There's always the possibility that the response will be a rejection, or even that the lender will move forward with a foreclosure before you get a response to your offer.
- **Resale restrictions.** Many short sales have resale restrictions imposed by the lender. In most cases, the lender will make you sign an agreement that says you won't resell the property for at least 90 (and sometimes as long as 120) days.

Purchasing Bank Owned Foreclosures (REO)

An REO property is a property that has gone through the foreclosure process, didn't sell at auction, and is being sold by the lender—usually a bank—through the typical real estate sales process.

When I say a "typical real estate sales process," I mean that the property is listed on the MLS through a licensed real estate agent, and all potential buyers can submit offers exactly as if it were a retail property. Offers are reviewed by bank asset managers assigned to oversee the sale of the bank's REO properties. Asset managers have the authority to initially accept or reject offers on the property, and if an asset manager accepts an offer, it goes to a more senior decision-maker at the bank for final approval.

Once a sale is approved, the contracts are signed—including a bank-specific addendum to the typical contract—and the property goes through a standard closing process, sometimes taking between three and six weeks to complete.

Why Buy REO Properties

REO properties have been the bread and butter for many real estate investors since the 2008 real estate bubble burst. While the number of great REO deals drops in hot real estate markets, in many areas investors can find profitable REOs.

There are many good reasons why thousands of real estate professionals focus on the purchase of REO properties, either exclusively or as part of a larger acquisition strategy:

- **Low prices.** While the opening bid at the trustee's sale will likely be whatever is owed on the house, once the house gets listed on the MLS as an REO, the price is often much lower. You're probably thinking, "Doesn't that mean the bank is now losing money on the sale?" Yup, and that's why REOs often provide great bargains. Banks don't like holding REO inventory, so they are often willing to lose money to get the property off their books.
- **Easy to find.** As I mentioned, REOs are often listed right on the MLS or publicly searchable websites, so anyone who has access to the MLS or the Internet has access to REO properties. And anyone who has access to a real estate agent has access to the MLS.
- **Opportunity to inspect.** We discussed the foreclosure process above. Investors can actually purchase properties at any stage of the foreclosure process, including during pre-foreclosure (the 115 or so days after

the NOD is filed but before the trustee's sale) and at auction. During pre-foreclosure, you only have access to the property as much as the homeowner will grant it, and during the auction process, investors often can't get into the houses to inspect them. However, once a property becomes a REO, potential buyers are free to enter and inspect the property—and have their contractors inspect the property—as much as they'd like before, during, and after submitting an offer.

- **Less negotiation.** While many real estate investors enjoy the negotiation process, there are many who would prefer not to have to stand toe-to-toe with a homeowner and try to negotiate a ridiculously low offer for their house. With REO offers, you will never actually speak with the seller (the asset manager); you will simply submit an offer on a contract, and any further negotiations will come through either your real estate agent or the seller's real estate agent.

- **Standard process.** With REO purchases, the process takes a little bit of time to fully understand, but once you understand it, it's never going to change. While each bank might have its own set of quirks to deal with during the transaction, for the most part every REO purchase will require the same set of steps to get from beginning to end. And the best part is, your real estate agent will take care of 95 percent of the work related to the transaction.

- **Excess inventory.** While this won't be true in hot markets, when the economy turns down or your local market softens, there is generally a good bit of REO inventory. In these markets, where it may be difficult to find motivated sellers or sellers with equity in their homes, finding motivated banks looking to liquidate their REO inventory is oftentimes very easy.

The Drawbacks of REO Properties

Despite all the good aspects of buying REOs, there are some downsides as well:

- **Higher earnest money deposit.** First and foremost, there is going to be a higher upfront cost for purchasing REOs. When you put a property under contract, you will generally need to provide the seller with a deposit, called earnest money, that proves you are a serious buyer. This earnest money is refundable under certain conditions if you don't buy the property, but under other conditions (for example, if you don't make good on your contract), the earnest money can be kept by the seller. Once the house is purchased, the earnest money is generally credited towards the purchase as part of your down payment. When dealing with a homeowner, you can sometimes negotiate the earnest money amount as low as $10 or $100. But with REO purchases, the bank will require that your earnest money deposit be a minimum of $500 or $1,000. Of course, you will need to come up with more than that for your down payment (we'll talk about financing in the next chapter), so hopefully coming up with $500 or $1,000 isn't a showstopper.

- **Buyer unfriendly contracts.** Because REO purchases can often provide great deals to investors, some banks will make a point to ensure their contracts are as one-sided as possible—in the bank's favor. For example, I've seen contracts that say that if the bank can't close the transaction on schedule, the buyer needs to wait around for as long as it takes to get the deal closed, with no recourse on the part of the buyer. When you sign these contracts, you are agreeing to these terms, so make sure you understand everything you sign, and make sure you are okay with any unintended ramifications that might arise.

- **Little opportunity for negotiation.** I mentioned in the section above that one of the benefits of buying REO properties is that there is less need for negotiation with the seller. On the other hand, for those of us who really enjoy—and are good at—negotiating, buying REOs takes away some of that advantage. When negotiating with homeowners, buyers have the opportunity to get creative and to use their negotiating tactics to cut deals that focus on things other than purchase price or closing date. With REO properties, there is no room for creativity; banks tend to care only about the amount being offered, the amount of earnest money being submitted, the way the buyer is paying (cash or financing), and when the buyer can close. Negotiations beyond those terms will usually not be considered by the bank.

- **Missed deadlines.** If you're in a hurry to buy a property, REOs are probably not for you. Most banks operate inefficiently, and the chances of a quick transaction are slim. In general, expect the bank to need anywhere from three to eight weeks from the time the contract is signed to the time you ultimately own the house. Of course, if you need time to get your financing lined up, this might actually be a good thing.

- **Deed restrictions.** Some banks will require that buyers agree to a selling restriction when they purchase one of their REO properties. For example, if you purchase an REO from Fannie Mae (a quasi-government lender that ends up with many of the foreclosed properties purchased with FHA loans), expect that you will be required to sign an agreement that says you will not resell the property within 90 days of purchase for more than 20 percent above the purchase price. In other words, if you buy a Fannie Mae REO for $100,000, expect that you will not be able to resell that property for more than $120,000 (20 percent above the purchase price) for at least three months. While this might not be a big deal if you expect the rehab and resale to take several months, for some house flippers, waiting three months to sell might as well be an eternity.

Purchasing Foreclosures at Auction (Trustee Sales)

As we discussed in the previous chapter, the foreclosure process in most states will culminate in a public auction, where the property will be sold to the highest bidder if the bid is above the opening price set by the foreclosing lender.

While I would definitely not recommend that most new investors purchase properties from trustee sales, I do want to include them here for completeness sake. Trustee sales can often provide opportunities for seasoned investors to find great deals, but there is a lot of due diligence that goes into the process, and if you make even a minor misstep, you can face great financial risk.

Unlike properties purchased from a retail owner, an absentee owner, through a short sale, or as an REO, purchasing at trustee sale is one of the few situations where the seller won't guarantee clear title to the property at purchase. In other words, when you purchase a property at trustee sale, you inherit any claims, liens, or other title clouds that were part of the property prior to purchase.

While you may think you're getting a steal of a deal at auction, you'd hate to find out later that there were $50,000 worth of liens and other debts that are now yours, and that now makes the deal far less than a steal. Of course, there are ways to avoid these types of risks and still get fantastic deals at auction, but if you plan to go that route, I highly recommend doing some additional research outside of this book.

In addition to not getting a guarantee of clear title when purchasing at a trustee sale, there are several other downsides you should be aware of:

- **All cash purchase.** You will be required to pay all cash for the property at the time of the sale. If you don't have the cash or ready access to the cash, you can't buy at county auction.

- **Few actual deals.** While there are some great deals at auction, they tend to be few and far between. Because many lenders will start the opening bids at what was owed on the property (plus any legal fees, etc.), most auction properties aren't worth the cost and won't be sold—they'll go back to the lender to be disposed of in an alternate manner. You could spend months looking for a deal at county auctions and never find one.

- **Redemption periods.** In some states, the foreclosed homeowner has the right to try to "cure" the foreclosure by paying off the owed amount plus any fees or penalties. They may even have the right to stay in the house for some period of time after the foreclosure, while attempting to repurchase the property. As an investor, you may be forced—or decide it's in your best interest—to hold off on doing any work on the property until after the redemption period is up, which can be up to a year.

Finding the Seller Who's Right for You

When deciding which types of sellers and situations you should be focusing on, there are several things I would encourage you to consider:

- **Your personality.** Do you enjoy dealing with people face-to-face? Do you have the empathy to tactfully involve yourself in a seller's difficult personal situation? If so, working with homeowners may be right for you. If not, you may want to consider focusing on REO and trustee sale properties, where the seller is a large, faceless corporation. More than anything else, your personality should factor into the types of sellers you deal with. I'm not suggesting that you always stay in your comfort zone, but it's a great place to start.

- **Your timelines.** Are you determined to get a project started right away? Or are you willing to spend a couple of months hammering out a deal? If you need that quick fix, you may be able to go down to the courthouse steps and buy a foreclosure at auction tomorrow or next week. If you're more patient, the several weeks that it may take to get an REO under contract might be for you. And if you're in no hurry to get moving on a deal, spending several months working on buying a short sale property may result in a great opportunity. Your patience, or lack thereof, will certainly be a factor in deciding which types of sellers you should be targeting.

- **Your location.** Are there are a lot of owners in your area with equity? If so, targeting absentee landlords or distressed homeowners may produce great leads. If not, you could spend months searching for that elusive seller with enough equity and distress to make for a good deal. Is your MLS overflowing with REO and short sale deals? If so, there may be some great low-hanging fruit for you to take advantage of. If not, you could make dozens of offers on listed properties and never even get a response. Your location—and the current real estate market there—will factor prominently in the types of sellers you'll be targeting.
- **Your marketing skills.** Regardless of from whom you plan to buy your deals, you're going to need to make the effort to find those deals. This is where your marketing, advertising, and scoping out of deals comes into play. That's the focus of our next chapter...

CHAPTER 7
HOW YOU'LL FIND DEALS

There are lots of ways to find real estate deals, and everyone has their favorite. In fact, many real estate investors will spend years getting great at one single strategy for acquiring deals and will use that method exclusively to build and grow their business. Unfortunately, this idea of putting all your marketing eggs into a single basket can have a massive impact on your business if and when that sole method of finding deals slows down or goes away.

For example, early in our investing career, we focused exclusively on finding REO deals right off the MLS. If a potential deal came to us through another means, we ignored it, as we felt the MLS was the most efficient route and the one we knew best. Then, in late 2011, we started to find that deals on the MLS were drying up, and competition for the small number of deals that did remain was fierce. With the market picking back up, lots of investors were jumping back into the fray, and they all seemed to be looking for deals in the same place I was!

That's when we finally decided to expand our marketing focus to include other methods of deal flow. It turned out to be the best decision we ever made in this business! With multiple streams of marketing effort, we started to find more deals in a market that was becoming tougher and tougher with every passing month. We quickly realized that if two sources of deals were better than one, three or four were even better; we made a concerted effort to try lots of different methods of acquiring deals, and we got pretty good at several of them.

Below I discuss several of the most common methods of acquiring deals, with some involving heavy marketing and some not; some involving a heavy time commitment and some not; some involving large cash expenditure and some not. Just like everything else in business and marketing, there are a lot of ways to be successful; it's up to each business owner to evaluate the various methods of potential success and focus on those. I would recommend that you think about which of these methods of deal flow best suits your personality, skill set, cash position, and time availability, and then focus on two or three that are the best match.

The Acquisition/Marketing Grid

The first thing to realize when you start marketing is that not every marketing avenue will work to attract every type of deal. In Chapter 6 we discussed the various sources of deal flow, and now it's time to determine what marketing approach to take in order to attract the types of deals you'll be pursuing.

The following chart provides a general overview of which acquisition and marketing strategies can successfully be used to attract which types of deals. This chart should help guide you to the type(s) of acquisition and marketing mechanisms that you should be considering and using to generate your deals.

	MLS	ONLINE/ AUCTION	DIRECT MARKETING	ADVERTISING	WHOLESALERS	ON-SITE
ABSENTEE OWNER	NO	MAYBE	YES	MAYBE	YES	NO
DISTRESSED HOMEOWNER W/ EQUITY	MAYBE	MAYBE	YES	MAYBE	YES	NO
DISTRESSED HOMEOWNER W/O EQUITY (SHORT SALE)	MAYBE	MAYBE	YES	MAYBE	YES	NO
TRUSTEE SALE	NO	NO	NO	NO	YES	YES
REO	YES	YES	NO	NO	YES	NO

We'll spend the rest of this chapter detailing each of the acquisition and marketing strategies, hopefully giving you a better idea of which you'll want to try. We'll talk about the pros and cons of each strategy, provide an introduction on how to get started with the strategy, and provide tips based on our real-life experiences with each.

Remember, to be a successful, well-rounded investor, you'll want to get familiar with—and become an expert in—at least one or two of these strategies.

The MLS

The Multiple Listing Service is the vast online marketplace where listing agents (real estate agents who represent sellers) market (list) the properties they have for sale; and where selling agents (real estate agents who represent buyers, sometimes called buyer's agents), search for properties for their buyers.

Despite what many people believe, there is no national MLS; each major city will have an MLS, and some cities have multiple listing services. Pretty much any property for sale through a real estate agent will get put on the MLS, including retail sales, REOs, and most short sales.

As I mentioned above, for the first several years of our investing career, we focused exclusively on buying deals right off the MLS. And not just any deals; we only bought bank-owned REOs. In fact, of the first 30 deals we ever did, 29 of them were bank-owned properties that we purchased right off the MLS.

I'm a big proponent of leveraging the MLS, but I also believe that all investors need several channels by which they can acquire property. Markets change quickly, and if you don't have multiple strategies for acquiring property, you could quickly find yourself without income and without much hope of finding more property. If you plan to rely on the MLS for some deals (and I believe you should), just make sure you don't put all your eggs in that basket.

Benefits of Using the MLS for Deal Flow

There are lots of benefits of focusing on the MLS for your deals. First and foremost, using the MLS requires very little—if any—marketing effort. A decent percentage of distressed property sales are listed right on the MLS, meaning the deals come to you as opposed to you having to market for them. This can potentially save you a lot of money on marketing costs and save a lot of time on other marketing efforts.

Second, if you rely on real estate agents to bring you MLS deals, there is no cost to using the MLS. During the first four years of our investing career, we never spent a dime on marketing costs, as all our deals came right off the MLS.

Third, if you're going to be investing in distressed properties, there is no single resource for finding available properties better than the MLS. Nearly all the REOs sold by major banks are going to be listed by local real estate agents on the MLS, short sales are listed on the MLS, and many retail and absentee owners in distressed situations will market their properties directly through the MLS.

Drawbacks of Using the MLS for Deal Flow

The biggest drawback to using the MLS to find deals is that lots of other investors are doing the same thing. Because the MLS is so easy to use and is free to search, competition for deals on the MLS is often fierce, with some properties attracting dozens of offers from investors and home-owners alike. And because you're going to be more conservative (i.e., more successful) than many of your fellow investors, you're not going to be offering as much as they are for the same properties. This means that you're going to make a lot of offers but end up with very few deals.

In fact, many deals that hit the MLS are already sold before they ever got listed! Listing agents will sometimes pass the best deals to their favorite investors, who lock the deal up before it ever officially gets listed for sale, and then put it on the MLS just to make it look like the agent was doing the right thing. Likewise, with short sales; most lenders require that short sales be listed on the MLS before they will consider taking a reduced payoff, but oftentimes, listing agents are only listing the properties on the MLS to satisfy this condition. In many cases, the property was already under contract well before the agent actually put it on the MLS for sale.

The biggest downside to relying on the MLS for deals is that getting direct access to the MLS can be difficult. In most states, in order to gain direct access to all the MLS data, you need to be a licensed real estate agent. If you're not licensed, there are websites that will provide you with much of the same data as the MLS (www.realtor.com is a great example), but these sites won't provide some of the most important information, such as the confidential agent remarks and lockbox codes to get you into the property. Likewise, when you find a real estate agent to work with, she will have the ability to automatically email you listings that match your buying criteria as they become available on the MLS, but again, you won't be getting all the important data this way.

If you decide that you want to focus on the MLS for deal flow, I highly recommend that you consider getting your real estate license just for this purpose.

Deciphering MLS Listings

If you're going to be using the MLS as a source of deals, you'll need to get good at deciphering which MLS listings are distressed properties, and which are retail properties. Sometimes the listing agent will make it very easy to tell—for example, they may put "BANK OWNED FORE-CLOSURE!" in big bold letters right in the comments.

But other times, it's a lot more difficult to determine a property's status. And even if you can tell which properties are distressed by looking through the listings, that still requires you to look through every new listing to see which are potential deals and which are not.

Experienced investors have learned that there are a number of ways you can filter distressed listings on the MLS without having to look through each listing one by one. To give some examples of how I filter for the potentially good deals, I use an advanced search across all listings, looking for the following words and phrases:

To indicate that the property is likely an REO:
- "Sold as-is"
- "Foreclosure"
- "No disclosure from seller"
- "Lender owned"
- "Call agent for lockbox code"
- "Must pre-qual w/ preferred lender"
- "Pre-qual or proof of funds required with all offers"
- "Corporate owner"

To indicate that the property is a short sale:
- "Potential short sale"
- "Lender approval required"
- "Pending lender approval"

To indicate that the property is distressed:
- "Handyman special"
- "Fixer upper"

- "Cash only"
- "Will not qualify for FHA financing"
- "Needs some TLC"

Online and Auctions

Over the past several years, marketing and selling online have become huge outlets for distressed property sales. You can find house sales on websites run by everyone from the U.S. government to large auction houses to mom-and-pop wholesalers looking to move a property every now and again. While it would be impossible to cover all the different online property sale websites, I'm going to give an overview of some of the most popular and discuss the types of properties they sell and why you might—or might not—want to consider looking for houses on each.

HUD Properties (HudHomeStore.com)

The biggest operation for selling houses online is run by the U.S. government's Department of Housing and Urban Development (HUD). To give some background, if a homeowner buys a house using an FHA loan and later gets foreclosed upon, the foreclosed home reverts to ownership by HUD, which then sells the foreclosed house online to any buyer. Because HUD has so many homes in their inventory these days, many investors will build their entire strategy around buying HUD foreclosures.

The HUD website is www.hudhomestore.com, and anyone can browse the site to see what properties are listed in a given area. To bid on a HUD house, you must work with a real estate agent who is registered with HUD to place bids, and most buyer's agents have the ability to do this. When first listed for public bidding, HUD properties are targeted at owner-occupants—investors cannot bid on them. But if a property doesn't sell to an owner-occupant within a specified period of time (either five or 30 days, depending on property condition), it is then opened up to investors for bidding.

Houses in good condition often sell to owner-occupants without investors ever getting a chance to bid, but those houses in more distressed condition, or in areas where HUD has more inventory than there are buyers, will often become available to investors. The way the bidding works is that each day HUD will take all the offers submitted during the prior day and review them. They will rank the offers based on how much money HUD will net on the sale, and if the offer that nets them the highest amount meets their minimum acceptable amount, that offer will be accepted.

Unlike other foreclosure/REO sales, the seller (in this case HUD) doesn't care about any terms, conditions, or stipulations other than the net amount of money they receive on the sale. Therefore, there is no preference for owner-occupants vs. investors or for cash buyers vs. financed buyers. It's a level playing field, and the highest offer wins. If none of the offers provides a net amount to HUD that meets their minimum requirement, the house stays listed, and HUD will repeat the offer review process every day until they get an acceptable offer. As a buyer, you can submit a new offer as often as you like (either a different offer or the same one), and you may find that HUD will eventually accept your offer.

While it's not publicized anywhere, it's accepted that HUD is willing to accept a net amount that is about 15 percent below list price. Therefore, if a HUD property is listed for $100,000, your best chance to get HUD to accept your bid is to ensure that the net amount they will receive on the offer is at least $85,000. Below that amount, they will likely reject the bid and leave the property listed. That said, if a HUD property has been listed for a long time, HUD will often reduce the listing price and start considering bids lower—and sometimes much lower—than 15 percent off the list price.

With HUD properties, investor buyers do not have an inspection period. Once you submit your signed contract and earnest money (after your offer is accepted), you're committed to buying the property or losing your earnest money deposit. There are no exceptions. That said, you typically have two days from the time your offer is accepted until the contract and the earnest money is due. If the HUD office is local, your agent can drop the package off in person at the office. However, if the office is not local, you'll have to overnight it the day before it's due.

With that said, here's a little trick: While you technically don't have an inspection period with HUD purchases, you can use the day or two between the time the offer is accepted and the completed package is due to do some quick inspections. If you decide not to go through with the purchase, you just don't send in the contract or earnest money and HUD will just relist the property, with no penalty to you.

Home Path and Home Steps

Two of the most common types of REO property are those being sold by Fannie Mae and Freddie Mac, two quasi-government agencies that underwrite and insure much of the conventional lending in the United States. When a conventional loan gets foreclosed upon, the property will often revert back to Fannie Mae or Freddie Mac to be sold off, often as an REO.

Both of these agencies sell their REO inventory through real estate agents (on the MLS), but they also list their inventory on their websites: www.homepath.com and www.homesteps.com. And, they typically require agents to make offers directly through the websites.

One downside to Fannie and Freddie REOs is that they give preferential treatment to owner-occupants; most inventory isn't made available to investors until 15 days after homeowners get the first opportunity to buy. However, if the 15 days goes by without an accepted offer to a homeowner, the property is opened up for investor bidding, and it's often possible at this point to get some good deals. Because owner-occupants will generally buy the nice houses in the first 15-day period, the houses that open up to investors tend to be in more need of renovation, but again, these are often the houses that provide the most profit potential as well.

Auction.com and Other REO Auction Sites

The second major classification of online property website consist of the auction sites. Some of the most popular sites in this category are Auction.com (www.auction.com), Williams & Williams Auctions (www.williamsauction.com) and Hubzu (www.hubzu.com). These sites typically auction off REO properties that didn't sell through the standard REO channels (meaning they didn't sell when they were publicly listed on the MLS).

The auction takes place over several days, or even weeks. If the bid reaches a certain amount, it may be accepted immediately, or the seller may choose to let the auction run its entire duration before determining the high bid. While some of these sites are true auction sites, many of them are just lead generation systems for the sellers.

Let me explain...

With a true auction, the highest bidder will win. Sometimes the high bid may have to be above some minimum threshold (the reserve), but assuming it's above the reserve and the buyer has the ability to pay, the sale is final once the bidding is complete.

Unfortunately, with many of the so-called online auction sites, this isn't the case. Instead, the highest bidder hasn't actually won anything; the auction house will just take the highest bid and submit it to the seller just like any other offer and wait for the seller to decide if they want to take the offer, reject it, or make a counter-offer. Sometimes, bidders need to wait weeks to find out if their high bid was accepted or not.

In addition, some of the sites will hold auctions both online and in-person; Auction.com is known for going city to city and auctioning off large inventories of REO properties, some of which were previously available for purchase online and some of which are only available in person. In some cases, properties that don't sell the first time around (either in person or online), or where the seller doesn't accept the high bid, are re-auctioned multiple times until sold.

While there is no rhyme or reason to whether a seller will accept the high bid or not, sellers are looking for at least 65 percent of the value of the property as it's listed. (The auction house always lists what they believe is the market value.) However, it often takes at least 80 percent to ensure the seller will seriously consider the offer.

While I've known many investors to find good deals using these auction sites, the process can certainly be frustrating; if you're expecting a traditional auction experience, you're likely to be disappointed.

Classified Websites

There are a few large nationally recognized websites where private sellers can list and sell stuff that they own—eBay (www.ebay.com) and Craigslist (www.craigslist.org) are two of the largest. And many cities, especially the larger ones, will have their own sites specifically geared to local trade.

These sites are typically referred to as "classifieds" sites, as they are extensions of what used to happen in the classified sections of newspapers. While eBay isn't a traditional classifieds site, it does have some similarities, which is why it's lumped into this category.

On these sites, private sellers (both homeowners and investors) will often list real estate for sale. These are usually privately-owned properties that are being sold as part of a traditional sale; in many cases, the owners may not be overly motivated, and the properties may not be distressed, so not every listing will be a potential deal. But there are enough distressed sellers and investors who sell on these sites that it's worthwhile to spend some time there looking for bargains.

Personally, when I look to resell a property to another investor, my first course of action is to email all the investors I know, and my second course of action is to list the property on Craigslist. While much of the response I get from the listings is spam and tire-kickers, I have found some serious investor buyers on Craigslist, meaning they are constantly keeping their eyes open for deals on the website, and you should too.

Wholesaling Websites

The last major category of online property sites consists of websites that are geared towards allowing investors to sell to other investors. This is typically called wholesaling, where one investor will purchase or take control of a piece of property, and instead of improving the property himself and making a hefty profit, he would rather sell it to another investor to do the work and take a smaller profit instead.

While the idea is great in theory, in reality, most wholesalers aren't very good at finding deals, so by the time they find a property and mark up the price to account for their profit, the property isn't much of a deal. On top of that, wholesalers are notoriously bad at estimating resale value and rehab costs, so any information they give you about a property should be considered highly suspect.

Personally, I don't like the wholesaling websites, as I've never found a deal at any of them. Nevertheless, if you have a keen eye, there is no harm in looking, as most of these sites are free for buyers.

Direct Marketing

Direct marketing involves communicating directly with your potential customers (sellers, in this case) and can be done through many different means including through the internet, through the mail, over the phone, and in person. For the purposes of this discussion, I'm going to define direct marketing as a *one-on-one direct contact* with your customer, as opposed to blanket marketing and having customers contact you via your advertising.

I'll discuss the blanket advertising mechanism later in the chapter.

The two most common types of direct marketing used to attract real estate deals are *direct mail marketing* and *cold calling* (which can be done over the phone or in person). I'll discuss each in more detail below.

Direct Mail

Direct mail (DM) is still one of the most reliable forms of marketing for real estate deals. Because DM will allow you to target the widest range of potential sellers quickly and at a reasonable cost, many real estate investors spend the bulk of their marketing time and money focused on DM leads.

Direct mail consists of creating postcards or letters that indicate your interest in buying property, sending them to a target audience of potential sellers, and then waiting for those sellers to contact you, either by phone, email, or through your website. Your target audience of sellers could consist of distressed or retail owners, and your method of purchasing from different sellers may vary.

Distressed Direct Mail Targets

When targeting distressed sellers through DM, you are more than likely going to be targeting homeowners who are underwater on their house; this means that the homeowner owes more than the house is worth, and the most common scenario for you to purchase that property would be through a short sale transaction.

When focusing a DM campaign on distressed owners, here are some of the most common groups of sellers to go after:

- Owners who are 30, 60, or 90 days late on their mortgages.
- Owners who have been notified of a pending foreclosure.
- Owners who have listed their house for sale on the MLS, but the listings have expired.
- Owners facing distressed situations, such as divorce or death.

Retail Direct Mail Targets

In strong markets where homeowners tend to have equity in their homes, it's possible to find great retail deals through well-created DM campaigns. The nice thing about buying retail—meaning the homeowner is above water on their property and can sell without doing a short sale—is that you won't need approval from the owner's lender, making the deal much faster and hassle-free.

While retail DM campaigns can be targeted at homeowners, they are oftentimes targeted at other investors as well, such as landlords. This is because these other smart investors may have bought their properties long ago or for all-cash and may have a lot of equity. Also, many landlords own property out of state, and managing those properties can get tiresome; many landlords don't want to be landlords anymore and are willing to sell their properties at deep discounts if the right buyer comes along.

Here are the most common groups of retail sellers the direct marketers tend to go after:

- Absentee owners (generally landlords) who have owned their property for at least seven to ten years (meaning they likely have equity) or who purchased their property for cash.
- Homeowners who have owned their properties for at least seven to ten years.
- Blanket mailings to all houses within a subdivision, community, or geographic location.

Creating Your Direct Mail Campaign

Putting together a direct mail campaign isn't rocket science, but it will take a good bit of time and effort. Here are the basic steps that go into creating a DM campaign:

1. **Set up your phone line or website for your DM leads.**
   You're going to need at least one way for your potential leads to contact you, and the two most common and effective ways are via phone or website. Most contact will be done via phone, and while you most certainly won't want to be giving out your personal cell phone number, there are plenty of options for getting a free or inexpensive phone number that you can use instead. Personally, I use Google Voice. I can set up a free phone number (or several), have the number forwarded to my cell phone and customize a voicemail message for when I don't answer. If I miss a call and receive a voicemail, Google Voice will transcribe the message and text it to me, along with the calling number.

   I also have a website set up to capture leads, as some people would much prefer to check out a website prior to placing a phone call, and some never want to initiate a phone call. My website has all the basic information about who we are, what we do, and what the sales and purchase processes are when dealing with us. It then allows the potential lead to contact me directly via a web form that goes to my email.

2. **Find or generate your target mailing lists.**
   Once you have your method(s) of contact set up to receive communi-

cation from potential leads, you're going to want to put together (or purchase) your list of contacts. There are many options for direct mail targets—a few pages back, we discussed the most common distressed and retail targets. While you can certainly build your list by hand by sorting through public records and driving around town trying to find run-down properties, my recommendation is to work with a list provider who can give you names for a reasonable price.

There are many national companies that can provide lists of absentee owners or 30/60/90-day mortgage lates, and in most markets, there are local companies who can provide pre- and pending-foreclosure lists. For lists of expired MLS listings, you shouldn't have too much difficulty finding a local real estate agent who will work with you, especially if you're willing to pay a small fee or bring the agent in on the deal by allowing him or her to represent the seller in some way.

3. **Create your marketing letter or card.**

The most important step in the process is to create the mailer that you will be sending to prospects. Letters and postcards are the two most common types of mailers, and there can be plenty of variety of mailings within those two groups. For example, some direct marketers prefer very short, very vague handwritten notes on yellow paper ("yellow letters"), while other marketers prefer page-long letters that go into great detail on what the investor is looking for and proposing. There is no one right answer, but below I will discuss some of the things you should consider when creating—and tweaking—your direct mail campaigns.

To give you an idea of the wide range of direct mailers you should be considering and trying, here are a few letter and card samples (these are taken from www.YellowLetters.com and www.YellowLettersComplete.com, two popular turnkey direct mail services):

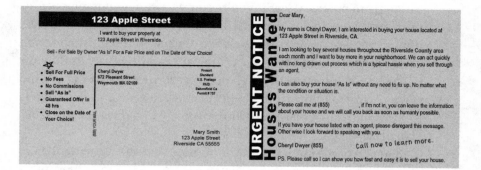

Dear Crystal,

Hi,

My name is Kevin Ross
and I would like to

$ BUY $

your house at 123 Main St.

Please call me at 555-123-4567

Thanks,

Kevin

Dear Crystal,

I am interested in purchasing your house at 123 Main St.

I can buy your house "As Is," so you won't have to fix anything up, and I have cash so I can close quickly. To discuss your options, please call me at 555-123-4567.

Please call!

Thanks,

Kevin Ross

4. **Address, stuff, stamp, and mail your direct mail pieces.**
Once you have your mailing list in hand and your mailer created, it's time to put the package together. For non-postcard mailings, you're going to need the following:

- *Copies of your mailer.* If you'll be handwriting, it's time to get to work. Other options are to print your mailer or to handwrite one and make color copies of the handwritten letter.
- *Envelopes.* Remember, one of the big keys to a successful direct mail campaign is to get as many prospects to open that envelope as possible. To achieve this, think about the types of envelopes you're more likely to open:
  - Envelopes that are handwritten.
  - Envelopes that aren't standard 4" × 9".
  - Envelopes that are non-white (especially pastel colors).
  - Envelopes that appear to contain an invitation.
- *Stamps.* There are many options for stamping and sending your mailers. While bulk mail options are cheaper than first class, they will cause your mailer to be opened at a lower rate. I prefer first-class stamps, despite the high price tag ($.49 per envelope at the time of this writing). You'll need to determine what works best for you based on your budget and goals. One trick here is to go to the post office and ask for decorative stamps as opposed to the standard first-class flag stamps; while they won't cost anything additional, it's just another way to get your mailer to appear to be personal, increasing the chances it will be opened.
- *Return address labels.* You'll want return address labels, as a high percentage of your mailers may get returned, especially if you're targeting homeowners who are near foreclosure and have already moved out of their homes. By getting the returned mail, you can remove these names from your list and save money on your follow-up mailings. I would recommend not using your home address on the label, but also not using a P.O. box address. Many UPS Stores will provide mailboxes at a low cost that can be received using an attractive street and suite address. This is what we use.

The Keys to Great Direct Mail Marketing Campaigns

Creating successful direct mail marketing campaigns will take a lot of time and practice. The first set of letters or postcards you send won't receive the response you were anticipating; this is why good direct marketers will spend lots of time honing and testing every aspect of their campaigns in order to get the highest response rate.

If you want to be a great direct marketer and have effective direct mail campaigns, you will need to be willing to test many, many different approaches and not give up in the face of adversity or low response rates. Here are just a few things that good direct marketers do in the course of creating and optimizing a DM campaign:

- Test different sized letters or postcards.
- Test different sized envelopes.
- Test handwritten vs. typed letters and envelopes.
- Test different color papers and inks.
- Test different kinds of postage (first class vs. bulk).
- Test different marketing messages.
- Test different calls to action (phone number vs. website, etc.).
- Test different target groups (distressed vs. retail, homeowner vs. investor, etc.).

There are thousands of different permutations for how you can put together your marketing campaign, and there is no one right way to be successful with direct mail. You need to figure out what works for your target sellers in your area and in your market. Remember, what works for one group of potential sellers at one particular time and in one particular market may not work for another group of potential sellers at another time or in another market.

As an example from personal experience, we used a handwritten yellow letter in our first absentee owner mail campaign that said:

Dear [First Name],
Hi,
My name is J
I would like to BUY your house at
[Address]
Please call me at
[Phone]
Thanks, J

This campaign got a 13 percent response! Unfortunately, it didn't generate any quality leads and we quickly determined that we'd rather focus on distressed sellers instead. We tried the same letter for our first pre-foreclosure and 30/60/90-day-late mailings and got 0 percent response. That's right—13 percent response from one group and zero responses from another group using the exact same letter and marketing techniques.

All that said, there are four main keys to be a successful direct marketer:

1. **Getting your audience to open your letter.** If you're sending letters, this means getting the receiver of that letter to open the envelope and read what's inside. We've found that the best way to do this is to personalize the envelope in a way that makes it look more like an invitation than a formal business letter. Use a greeting card-sized envelope, handwrite the address, don't include your name (and definitely not a business name) on the return address label, and use pastel colored envelopes.

2. **Getting your audience to read your message.** Getting your message read and creating an emotional attachment with the prospect will lead him or her to pick up the phone and call you (or hop on your website for more information). To accomplish this, your message should be personalized and either handwritten or appear handwritten. Using a handwritten font and using mail merge to personalize the message with the prospect's name and address, you not only have a great likelihood of getting your message read, but you have a greater likelihood of generating an emotional response that leads the prospect to act. More importantly, you've created something that looks and feels personalized, but is still completely automated.

3. **Getting your audience to act on your call to action.** This means getting the receiver to pick up the phone, visit your website, send you an email, or whatever it is you want them to do. The best way to do this is to craft your message in a way that tells the receiver that you can and will solve their problem; people will respond when they believe that responding will help solve their problem.

4. **Converting that potential lead into a sale.** The most important step is taking that phone call, email, or website hit and actually convincing the person on the other side to sell their property to you. This won't be done in the course of a single communication—it may take days or weeks—but it's your job to convince the seller that you have the ability to solve their problem and give them the

confidence that you will. This is by far the hardest of the steps to be a successful marketer; if you don't have the ability to communicate with your potential leads or don't want to communicate with your potential leads, you'll need to find someone who can do that for you. It doesn't matter if you can get 100 percent of your target audience to contact you if you don't have the ability to convert the lead into a profitable transaction.

The Secret to Direct Mail Marketing Success

There is one HUGE secret that successful direct marketers do that other, less successful, direct marketers don't do. And that's REPETITION.

Too many new marketers assume that if they don't get a response from a prospect on the first mailing, they're never going to get a response. Nothing could be further from the truth. In fact, you're more likely to get a response (even if it's just a "TAKE ME OFF YOUR LIST!!!") on the second, third, fourth, or fifth mailing than you are on the first. Even if the prospect is only calling to ask to be removed from the list, that's still an opportunity to try to convert a lead.

If you want to be successful with direct mail marketing, be consistent in your communication. Send a second mailing two to three weeks after the first, a third mailing four to six weeks after that, and then follow up with additional mailings every six to eight weeks for the next several months.

Cold Calling and Door Knocking

The other side of direct marketing for real estate deals involves a much more personalized approach. Cold calling involves directly contacting prospects either via phone or in person by knocking on their door and hopefully getting an answer.

While I don't advocate phone calls to try to generate leads or deals— they don't have a very high success rate in this industry—I know several investors who have been very successful at door knocking to generate leads and close deals. Door knocking works best in this market when targeting distressed sellers. Many investors will use pre-foreclosure and mortgage late lists to generate their leads, and then spend their days knocking on doors trying to get motivated prospects to speak with them and potentially put together a deal.

Here are the biggest benefits and drawbacks to using this technique:

Benefits of Door Knocking for Deal Flow

While I'm personally not a fan of door knocking (I don't have the personality for it and don't like personal rejection), there are many investors who believe this is by far the best form of marketing and generating leads and deals. Door knocking has some great benefits:

- **Low cost.** Other than gas money, it doesn't cost anything to knock on doors of potentially distressed sellers and talk to them about their problems and how you might be able to help solve those problems.
- **Personalized.** Unlike direct mail and other marketing techniques, knocking on doors and talking to homeowners face to face is about as personal as it gets. If you're good at building rapport and are comfortable talking to people one on one about their situations, the likelihood of finding deals may be higher with door knocking than with any other marketing avenue.
- **Guaranteed to get message across.** With other types of direct marketing, there is no guarantee the prospect will get, open, or read your message. However, with door knocking, you know whether your message was delivered, and you have immediate feedback to help improve or change your message to future prospects.

Drawbacks of Door Knocking for Deal Flow

While door knocking for deals can generate some amazing deals, it's not for everyone. Here are just some of the drawbacks associated with using door knocking as your preferred method of generating deals:

- **Not easily scalable.** While you may be able to target thousands of people per day with direct mail, you may only be able to knock on a couple dozen doors per day, so your success rate will need to be much higher in order to generate the same results from door knocking as you get from other direct mail strategies.
- **Safety risk.** There is an inherent risk to knocking on doors of people who are likely in a difficult place, both financially and emotionally. The risk of verbal abuse is very real, and there is even the risk of violence in some situations. If you're not comfortable with this risk, door knocking is not for you.
- **Requires skill and a specific personality.** Not everyone has the personality to be able to build rapport quickly and easily enough to put together a deal at the owner's doorstep. Additionally, those who are more introverted and can't deal with rejection will find door knocking

to be frustrating and demoralizing.
- **Solicitation rules (could be illegal).** Lastly, there are legal risks with door knocking in communities or subdivisions where solicitation is not allowed. You may need to get a permit to knock on doors.

Some Tips When Knocking on Doors

There are many different tactics and strategies that door knockers use to build rapport and gain the trust of potential sellers. Here are just a few tips that will help you be successful if you decide to go this route:

- Don't start the discussion focused on the homeowner. A good opening line might be, "Hi, I was looking at the foreclosure right next door and was hoping you could give me some information about it?" After that discussion ends, continue with, "Great, thanks. I really want to buy something in this neighborhood. Do you know of anyone else around here who might be looking to sell?"
- If you want to reach people when they're home, focus on knocking in the late afternoon (4–6 p.m.) and later evenings during the summer. This is when prospects are more likely to be physically present at the house.
- Dress business casual and don't wear perfume, sunglasses, or a hat. You want to put the homeowner at ease and looking as average and non-threatening as possible will help achieve that goal.
- Don't pull up in a fancy car; again, average is to your benefit.
- If you're going to knock in pairs, I would recommend either a man/woman or two women together, never two guys. Two guys will seem threatening, even to a male homeowner.
- Be discreet—you never know when the homeowner may not want others (even those he lives with) to know he's facing a distressed situation with his house.

A Twist on Traditional Door Knocking

If you're concerned about the safety of knocking on the doors of potentially distressed and emotional sellers, there is another alternative that some investors use to drum up leads—leaving either a personalized note or even an actual offer on the property attached to the door. This will guarantee that you get your message in front of the owner (assuming they still live there), and while it's not as personal as a face-to-face conversation, it has some benefits over direct mail marketing and cold calling over the phone.

While door knocking certainly isn't for everyone, it can be very successful for those who are good with people, don't mind rejection, and are willing to get doors slammed in their face every once in a while.

Advertising

I use the term "advertising" in this chapter to mean marketing strategies that are targeted towards large groups of people, as opposed to one-on-one or targeted marketing, like direct mail and door knocking. The most common forms of advertising for real estate leads are internet marketing and bandit signs. Both attempts to get your message in front of large volumes of potential targets in the hopes that some of them will contact you and you'll have an opportunity to close a deal.

Internet Marketing

The concept of internet marketing is simple: You create a website that is used to capture information, and then you create online marketing campaigns to drive potential sellers to your site and provide that information. However, while the concept of internet marketing is simple, the real-life implementation can be anything but. There are many different ways to drive traffic to your website; some are "organic" (meaning visitors get to your site via search engines or other cost-free mechanisms), and some are paid (meaning you pay to get leads sent to you).

Organic Internet Traffic

The best way to drive organic traffic to your lead-capture site is to create a content-rich website that ranks high in the search engines for the types of internet searches your potential sellers are doing. For example, let's say you want to buy distressed houses in Baltimore, Maryland. People who are interested in selling their distressed house in Baltimore may type the following into Google or another search engine:

"How can I sell my Baltimore home very quickly?"

When they type that or a similar phrase in a search engine, you'll want your website to show up at or near the top of the page of results. If the potential seller clicks on the link to your website, you have an opportunity to capture their information and generate a lead. Again, while it's easy in principle, if you live in a larger or more popular geographic area, there are likely already many other investors with websites competing for these leads. You'll need to work hard to get your site ranked higher than theirs for the potential search traffic you're trying to get.

To get an idea of the competition you'll face for leads from organic search traffic, try this:

Go to one of the popular search engines, such as Google.

1. Do a search that is similar to what your potential targets might search for when looking to off-load their properties (for example, "sell my house quickly in Baltimore").
2. Look at how many results were returned for that search. (The actual example above netted 123 million results.)

In order to be successful using this marketing route, you'll want your website to show up on or very near the first page, meaning in the top ten results. With 123 million competing results, that will take time and some seriously dedicated effort!

Paid Internet Traffic

The alternative to trying to get free traffic to your website is to pay for it. This is done by placing ads in various places on the internet where potential sellers might see them. The most common form of paid advertising on the web these days is Google AdWords.

Google will allow you to pay to place ads around the internet to drive traffic to your website. The cost of getting your ad to appear varies, based on other advertisers looking to advertise in the same spot at the same time. For example, if you want your advertisement to appear on a webpage that talks about how to do short sales in Baltimore (remember above where you were trying to get distressed seller leads in Baltimore?), you will be competing with others who are interested in advertising space on the same page. These are either other investors like you who are trying to attract seller leads or real estate agents who are looking for clients. If you are willing to pay more than they are for the advertising space, Google will give it to you; if your competitors are willing to pay more, they will likely get it. It's an auction system: The more you're willing to pay, the higher ranking your ad gets.

In addition to Google AdWords, smart internet marketers will try to convince owners of worthwhile websites to dedicate advertising space for a fee. Using the example above, you might approach the owner of the Baltimore short sale webpage with an offer to pay a monthly fee to provide your advertisement a permanent spot on their site. In general, using this type of paid advertising, you'll pay the site owner every time a page is displayed with your ad on it, regardless of whether your ad is clicked or not.

There are lots of intricacies of internet marketing that I won't go into here—that would be a separate book!—but if you have an aptitude for working online and you have the time and energy to become an expert internet marketer, this is another great way to develop investment leads from your target sellers.

Bandit Signs

Another popular mass marketing technique used to generate real estate leads is using yard signs, known as bandit signs, to advertise your services as a real estate buyer. You will create and place these signs in public areas where your target sellers are likely to drive by and see them. For example, if you're looking to buy in a particular neighborhood, you may place signs at the entrance to the neighborhood, across the street, or at busy intersections near the neighborhood.

Signs can be pre-printed, and there are plenty of companies on the internet who will print standard 12" × 18" or 18" × 24" color signs for between $1 and $2 each. Alternately, blank signs can be purchased at the big box stores and handwritten.

A typical bandit sign might read something like the following:

STOP FORECLOSURE!
WE WILL BUY YOUR HOUSE
WE PAY CASH, CLOSE QUICKLY
CALL 999-123-4567 NOW!

Once you have your signs, you can purchase wire stakes to plant the signs in the ground or you can use a sign stapler to staple signs to trees or telephone poles.

Dealing with Local Laws Regulating Bandit Signs

Many cities have laws prohibiting marketing using bandit signs, and you should check with your city before installing signs. The "nicer" the city, the more likely city code enforcement will restrict bandit sign use and will physically remove your bandit signs. Even in cities where bandit signs are legal, many code enforcement agencies and agents are intolerant of the signs and will take them down.

Many investors will put up signs on Friday evening after 5:00 p.m.—after city enforcement agents are done for the week—and then collect their signs on Sunday evening or Monday morning before code enforcement is back to work. This can help keep the signs from being removed and destroyed by the city, saving money in having to replace them. The worst-case scenario is that the city may call you and threaten you with a fine if they find any more of your signs placed in public locations. If this happens, it's best to find another locale for the signs or try another marketing technique.

One way to determine how lenient code enforcement might be is to track the signs of other marketers. Do they routinely get pulled down shortly after being put up? Or do they linger in public areas for weeks at a time?

Hopefully it goes without saying, but never put bandit signs on private property, unless you have the permission of the property owner.

Some Tips When Using Bandit Signs

If you try marketing with bandit signs, here are some tips and tricks that will help get you started:

- Many investors who use bandit signs prefer stapling to poles vs. the wire stakes. The stakes are almost as expensive as the signs and increase shipping costs, making the marketing campaign much more expensive.
- When placing signs, be cognizant of where they are most likely to be seen. When putting signs on poles, put them at the height of the typical driver. When putting your signs at major intersections, place them on the right-hand side of the road where traffic stops so drivers can see your sign while they are waiting for the light to change. And you don't want to place signs in the median between traffic lights, as speeding drivers are unlikely to notice them or have time to write down your phone number.
- If you're targeting drivers, you don't want to put a website on the sign. Advertising is impulse-based, and you want people to have the option to act on your marketing message immediately. While they can do that by calling you on their cell phone, they won't have the option to visit your website while on the road.
- If you want to save your time, you can pay someone to put signs out for

you. This way, you can spend your time doing the high-value activities like talking to potential sellers who call you. In general, expect to pay about $1 per sign to hire someone to install for you.

Wholesalers

I talked a bit about wholesaling in the section about wholesaling websites. While I'm not a huge fan of finding houses on these sites, working directly with local wholesalers—people who find deals specifically for the purpose of reselling them to investors—may provide a great opportunity to acquire some deals.

My first word of warning is that most wholesalers are very bad at what they do. Many wannabe investors become wholesalers because they have no money and no knowledge of investing but believe that wholesaling will allow them to make some quick cash without much work. Unfortunately, there is nothing further from the truth. Wholesaling is very difficult and requires nearly all the skills that rehabbing requires, plus the ability to get deals at such a great discount that there is room for two people to make money on the deal!

Most wholesalers don't have this skill. They don't know what a good deal looks like, they can't determine a resale value accurately, and they don't know how to estimate rehab costs. That means that many wholesalers will do little more than waste your time bringing you deals that aren't really deals.

All that said, there are a few professional wholesalers who happen to be good at their jobs, have the ability to consistently find good deals, can help you evaluate those deals, and then leave enough room in their markup to allow both of you to make a decent profit. If you can find one or two successful wholesalers, it may be worth your time and effort to build a solid relationship, as they will have the ability to bring you a steady flow of deals. While your rehab profits won't be quite as large— wholesalers have to mark up their prices, so they can get paid—the fact that you won't have to spend a lot of time and money marketing for deals is a huge benefit.

Throughout the years, I've found several wholesalers who have been able to bring me one or two deals per year. While not enough to keep my pipeline of deals filled, it's certainly been a great way to supplement my deal flow. And had I focused more time and energy on building relationships with a few great wholesalers, there's a good chance that they might have accounted for a lot more of my deals.

On-Site (Trustee Sales)

The last acquisition strategy I want to touch on is attending trustee (foreclosure) sales at your local courthouse. I mentioned in the last chapter a number of downsides and risks associated with buying properties at trustee sales; for these reasons, I don't recommend relying on trustee sales as a means to acquiring properties when you're first starting out.

That said, I would recommend attending the sales, networking with other investors who are present, and starting to get familiar with the process and the intricacies of buying on the courthouse steps. However, until you feel like you have a handle on all other aspects of the rehabbing process, relying on these auctions for your deals is likely going to be too much work to take on.

Other Marketing Techniques

While I've covered many of the techniques popular among investors to generate leads and deals, this certainly isn't meant to be an exhaustive list. There are dozens, if not hundreds, of ways to market for potential deals. These are just some of them.

To name just a few of the other potential ways to find deals:
- Newspaper/magazine classified ads
- Display ads in restaurants/bars
- Radio spots
- Television spots
- Billboards
- Social networking
- Partnering with professionals who deal with distressed sellers (agents, attorneys, etc.)

The most successful investors are constantly figuring out new ideas and techniques for marketing and advertising their business. Get creative, and you'll find that you have more leads than you know what to do with!

CHAPTER 8
THE FLIP FORMULA

This chapter may be the most important in this book. While the formulas and the math behind the formulas are not very complex, understanding the formulas and applying them correctly will make the difference between your first investments being profitable or unprofitable.

If you have any questions while you're reading this chapter, go back and reread. If you still have questions, send me an email at flippingbook@biggerpockets.com, and I'll do everything I can to help clarify.

I've had countless newbie investors ask me how I decide whether to take on a flip project. What they're asking is, "How do you know if the numbers work out in your favor?"

Most investors have some quantitative analysis technique for determining whether to pursue a project. Some use analysis techniques that require spreadsheets or complex formulas; others don't use any formulas, but just go off a gut feeling they may have for the property or the location.

While I'm certainly not a fan of the gut feeling method, I'm also not a huge fan of the complex analysis method either. This may surprise some people—especially those who know my tendency to sit in front of large spreadsheets for hours on end—but one of the main goals of my financial analysis is to be able to do it in my head in less than ten seconds while standing on the property I'm considering.

Certainly, the whole analysis can't be done in ten seconds, but most of it can be. The goal of this analysis is simply to determine the highest price I can pay for a property while still making my desired profit. If I can purchase the property for that amount (or less!), I'll take the deal. If not, I'll pass.

The Flip Formula

My formula for the maximum purchase price (MPP) of a flip property is this:

MPP = Sales Price - Fixed Costs - Profit - Rehab Costs

where

Sales Price equals the conservative estimate of what I can sell the property for (not the list price!) after rehabbing.

Fixed Costs equal all the costs, fees, and commissions that I can expect to pay during the project, excluding rehab costs.

Profit is the minimum amount of money I want to make off the project when it's complete.

Rehab Costs are the material and labor costs required to rehab the property into resale condition.

As an example, let's say that I have a property that I'm considering purchasing. I believe I can easily resell the property in rehabbed condition for $95,000. Additionally, I know my fixed costs throughout the project to be $17,000 (we'll discuss how to calculate this later in the chapter). I've decided that my desired minimum profit is $15,000, and I've estimated the rehab costs to be $13,000 (we discuss estimating rehab costs later in the book and in our companion book, *The Book on Estimating Rehab Costs*).

In this case, my maximum purchase price can be calculated as follows:

MPP = Sales Price - Fixed Costs - Profit - Rehab Costs

MPP = $95,000 - $17,000 - $15,000 - $13,000

MPP = $50,000

In this example, if I can purchase the property for $50,000 or less, I'll jump on the deal.

Using our Flip Formula, we can accurately determine how much we're willing to pay for a given piece of real estate (our MPP). But to arrive at our MPP, we need to understand how to determine our sales price, our fixed costs, our desired profit, and our rehab costs. Let's discuss each of those now.

Determining Sales Price

Determining a property's selling price after renovations is as much an art as it is a science. Appraisers can spend years honing their skills at property valuation, and even many seasoned real estate agents can have a difficult time assessing the resale value of a property before it is rehabbed. As a successful real estate investor, you will need to be able to determine what your properties will sell for, and you'll need to be able to do it reliably and consistently.

Doing a Comparable Market Analysis (CMA)

While the least time-consuming way to do it is to hire an appraiser or to allow your real estate agent to do it for you, I firmly believe that understanding how value is determined and being able to determine it yourself will go a long way towards making you a more successful—and more independent—investor.

So, while you might end up consulting someone else to determine resale value—and you should certainly validate your assumptions with others who are knowledgeable in this area—I want to spend some time discussing the process for doing it yourself.

It boils down to three steps:

STEP #1: PULLING COMPS

This first step is one that you're going to need some help with. You will need information about comparable properties ("comps") that have sold in your area, and that information isn't always readily available. While websites like Zillow.com and Trulia.com are useful, the best and most up-to-date information is found on the MLS, which you'll need a licensed real estate agent to access for you. If you already have an agent you're working with to help you find properties, he or she should be happy to help you get this data; if you don't currently have an agent, this is your incentive to start building those relationships now.

Once you have an agent or someone else with access to the MLS who is willing to pull some data for you, you want to ask them to provide you a list of comps. These are other properties that are very similar to what your property will be *after* the rehab. The real estate market is relatively efficient, so if you can get a good idea of what similar properties have sold for, you should get a good idea of what your property will sell for. It's a simple concept, even if it's not always simple to do.

Before I go any further, let me explain what I mean by "similar" property. This is actually the biggest point of confusion for many new investors learning this process. They assume that because two houses have a roof, a front door, and a kitchen, that they are "similar." For the purpose of determining resale value, nothing could be further from the truth. When looking for comparable properties, here are the top five things you want to see:

- **Time of sale.** Most importantly, you are looking for properties that have sold within the previous six months (three months is even better). Notice I say "SOLD" properties, and not properties that are currently listed for sale. Many investors assume that if there are ten other properties listed for sale at $150,000 in the same neighborhood, this must be an accurate representation of what the properties are worth. Wrong! If the properties were actually worth $150,000, they wouldn't all be for sale, would they? Most likely, the properties will sell for less than the asking price, and maybe for a *lot* less. In fact, in a down market, many of these properties will not sell at all. Perhaps all the neighbors bought at the height of the market, they all owe $150,000 or more on their properties, and they can't afford to sell for any less. Does that mean they'll get $150,000? Of course not. Some of these houses may soon be foreclosed on, and instead of being your comps, they could end up being your competition. So, when looking for comps, remember to *only* use *sold* properties, and stick to the previous six months.

- **Location and proximity.** You want to find properties that are close to yours. How close? It depends. If you're in a large city where real estate values can double from one street to the next, you're going to want to find other properties on the same street. If you're in a sprawling suburban area with large homogenous neighborhoods (planned developments or communities), then you're going to want to find properties in or around the same subdivision. And if you're in a rural area where there are many acres or even miles between houses, you'll probably be looking within several miles. In general, for most properties in typical suburban areas or small cities, you'll be looking for properties that are within a half-mile of the subject property.

- **Age and style.** You want to find properties that are similar in age and style. A 1967 brick ranch is unlikely to sell for the same price as a brand-new two-story McMansion with a finished basement (in my area, the ranch would sell for more!). The best-case scenario when looking for comps is that your property is in a planned community, where most or all of the houses were built by the same builder within a year or two of each other. However, even if you're not this lucky, you should still be able to find other properties that were built in the same time period and of similar style.
- **Size.** When it comes to comps, size very much matters. If your property is more appropriately sized for a single couple than for a family of six, that's going to affect how much it's worth. And when I say size, I'm not just talking about square footage. I'm also talking about the number of bedrooms and bathrooms, as well as finished basement areas. Best case, you should be looking for comps that have within 10 percent of the same finished square footage, the same number of bedrooms, and the same number of bathrooms. Of course, the more bedrooms and bathrooms your property has, the more room you have for variance. In other words, while the difference between a 2-bedroom/1-bath house and a 3-bedroom/2-bath house is huge, the difference between a 6-bedroom/5-bath house and a 7-bedroom/4-bath house is minor. However, even these small differences will play into your sales estimate.
- **Condition.** The last very important criterion for assessing a comp is the condition. A fully renovated property in move-in-ready condition will most certainly sell for more than a run-down, ready-to-be-foreclosed on house that hasn't been updated since the 1970s. Unless you're looking in an area that has lots of other investors, you may be hard pressed to find comparable properties that have been fully remodeled; so you at least want to find properties that are in good shape, are move-in-ready, and have the same level of finishes that yours does. Along with the condition of the property, you also want to ensure that the comparable was not a distressed sale. If the house sold as a short sale or a foreclosure—even if it was in good condition—it's not a comparable for your property. This last point is very important... don't forget it!

Now, your job is to find at least three other properties that meet all the requirements above. In many areas, and especially in a down housing market where there aren't many houses selling, it may be difficult to find three other properties that are good comps for your property.

If you absolutely can't find three properties that meet the criteria, it's okay to expand your search a bit—we'll account for that in the next step. Start by going back nine months instead of six; if necessary, go out a mile from the subject property instead of a half-mile. Perhaps find a house that's a few years older, has a few hundred more square feet, or isn't in quite as good of condition.

STEP #2: ADJUSTING YOUR COMPS

Ideally, you should have at least three good comps to use for your analysis. For this next step, there is a little bit of math involved, but it's pretty straightforward, and if you can add, subtract, multiply, and divide, you should have all the tools you need.

The purpose of this step is to adjust the value of the comps to ensure that they resemble the subject property as closely as possible. Remember, the goal of a valuation or appraisal is to have an apples-to-apples comparison of your subject property with the comp properties. If the properties are different, you'll need to adjust their values to make them apples-to-apples.

For example, let's say your subject property and one of the comp properties are nearly identical, with the exception that the subject property has three bedrooms and the comp property has four bedrooms. Clearly, if this is the only difference, then the comp property is going to be considered more valuable than the subject property, as it has an extra bedroom. Therefore, if the comp property had recently sold for $150,000, then it's likely that your subject property is worth a little bit less than $150,000. In other words, the 3-bedroom property is worth less than the 4-bedroom property.

In order to do your adjustments, you must compare each of the comp properties—one at a time—to the subject property and perform an adjustment on each of the comps to determine an apples-to-apples value. Note that I said to "adjust the comps." What this means is that we need to determine what the comp property would have sold for had it been equivalent to the subject property. In the example above, where the comp sold for $150,000, but had an additional bedroom than the subject property, we'd have to adjust the $150,000 sale price *downwards* to achieve an apples-to-apples comparison.

In my area, an extra bedroom may be worth about 3 percent more in sales price, so for this adjustment, we'd subtract about 3 percent from the comp sale price to get an apples-to-apples comparison. Subtracting 3 percent from the $150,000 sales price would put the comp value at about $145,500. There are no hard-and-fast rules about how much various property features are worth—this is going to be highly dependent on the level of house, the area, and what is typical for local properties.

It's sometimes confusing to figure out which direction to adjust the comp values, but remember, the goal is always to try to figure out what the comp *would have* sold for had it been *exactly equivalent in features* to the subject property. Here is a list of features you should consider when doing your adjustments, and also how the differences should be adjusted for:

- **Date of sale.** If the comparable sale was more than six months old, the value may need to be adjusted depending on how the market has changed since the sale. If the market has improved, the comp value may be adjusted upwards; if the market has declined, the comp value should be adjusted downwards.
- **Age.** If the comp is older than the subject property, the comp value may be adjusted upwards; if the comp property is newer than the subject property, the comp value may be adjusted downwards.
- **Condition.** If the comp is in worse condition than the subject property, the comp value should be adjusted upwards; if the comp is in better condition than the subject property, the comp value should be adjusted downwards.
- **Living area square footage:** If the comp has *less* square footage of living area than the subject property, the comp value should be adjusted *upwards*; if the comp has *more* square footage than the subject property, the comp value should be adjusted *downwards*. Also, note that living area above grade (above ground level) is worth more than living area below grade. Therefore, an extra room on the second floor of the house would be worth more than a similar sized extra room in the basement. Lastly, note that unfinished area may be worth a little extra, but not nearly as much as finished living area.
- **Bedrooms and bathrooms.** If the comp has fewer bedrooms or bathrooms than the subject property, the comp value should be adjusted upwards; if the comp has more bedrooms or bathrooms than the subject property, the comp value should be adjusted downwards. Note that extra bedrooms and bathrooms are not worth as much as extra square

footage, but certainly add value. Also note that the fewer bedrooms and bathrooms the subject property has, the more the comp adjustment should be (in other words, going from two to three bathrooms is going to be much more valuable than going from five to six bathrooms).

- **Garage/carport/driveway.** If the comp has less garage space, carport space, or general parking area than the subject property, the comp value should be adjusted upwards; if the comp has more garage space, carport space, or general parking area than the subject property, the comp value should be adjusted downwards. Again, the value difference is going to depend on the relative differences, not just the absolute difference; for example, going from a carport to a 2-car garage is going to be more valuable than going from a 3-car garage to a 5-car garage.
- **Porches/patios/decks.** If the comp has less desirable outdoor spaces than the subject property, the comp value should be adjusted upwards; if the comp has more desirable outdoor spaces than the subject property, the comp value should be adjusted downwards.
- **Fireplaces.** If the comp has fewer fireplaces than the subject property, the comp value should be adjusted upwards; if the comp has more fireplaces than the subject property, the comp value should be adjusted downwards.

Let's look at an example of an actual property that I recently did a valuation on.

We are trying to determine the value of our subject property that has the following features:

Age	12 years
Condition	Excellent
Square footage	1,940 SF
Beds	3
Baths	2.5
Parking	2-car attached garage
Porches/decks	Front porch/back patio
Fireplaces	1

We have found three properties within one mile of the subject property that we believe are good comparables and should give us a decent idea of what our property should resell for.

The three comparables have the following features:

	COMP 1	COMP 2	COMP 3
AGE	12 YEARS	12 YEARS	5 YEARS
CONDITION	EXCELLENT	EXCELLENT	GOOD
SQUARE FOOTAGE	1854 SF	1875 SF	2650 SF
BEDS	3	3	4
BATHS	2.5	2.5	3
PARKING	2-CAR ATTACHED	2-CAR ATTACHED	2-CAR ATTACHED
PORCHES/DECKS	FRONT PORCH/ PATIO	FRONT STOOP/ PATIO	FRONT STOOP/ PATIO
FIREPLACES	1	1	1

Now it's time to do our adjustments of the comps to give an apples-to-apples comparison of each of them to the subject property. Remember, this was the actual analysis I recently did for one of my properties, and the values below are the values I assigned based on my experience:

	SUBJECT	COMP 1	COMP 2	COMP 3
AGE	12 YEARS	SAME	SAME	- $3,000
CONDITION	EXCELLENT	SAME	SAME	+ $5,000
SQUARE FOOTAGE	1940 SF	+ $1,000	+ $1,000	- $8,000
BEDS	3	SAME	SAME	- $1,500
BATHS	2.5	SAME	SAME	- $1,500
PARKING	2-CAR GARAGE	SAME	SAME	SAME
PORCHES/DECKS	PORCH/PATIO	SAME	+ $1,000	+ $1,000
FIREPLACES	1	SAME	SAME	SAME
TOTAL ADJUSTMENTS:		+ $1,000	+ $2,000	- $8,000

What this chart is telling us is that our Comp #1 is very close to our subject property in terms of features, and if we added $1,000 to the price it sold for, that should give us a good idea of the value of our subject property. Likewise, with Comp #2, if we added $2,000 to its sales price, we'd get a good idea of the value of our subject property. Lastly, with Comp #3, if we subtracted $8,000 from its sales price, we should get a good idea of the subject property value.

STEP #3: DETERMINING THE VALUE OF THE SUBJECT PROPERTY

Now that we have our comps, and we've adjusted them against our subject property, it's time to use this information to determine a reasonable valuation for our subject property. Remember, we determined above that if we take the actual sales prices of the comparables and adjusted them using our adjustment values, we should get a good idea of the valuation of our subject property.

Here are the actual sales prices of the comparables, along with the adjustments and the final adjusted value:

	COMP 1	COMP 2	COMP 3
SALE PRICE	$105,000	$105,000	$120,000
ADJUSTMENTS	+ $1,000	+ $2,000	- $8,000
ADJUSTED VALUE:	$106,000	$107,000	$112,000

Therefore, based on this analysis, it's likely that our subject property is worth somewhere between $106,000 and $112,000. From here, depending on how conservative you want to be, I would suggest that you either assume your subject property is worth the lower of the three values ($106,000 in this case) or the average of the values (about $108,333 in this case).

Like I said, this was an exercise I did recently on an actual property with these characteristics and the actual comps I used for my analysis. In the end, the property sold for $110,000, and when the buyer's appraiser did his appraisal, he used the same three comps I did as his main comps.

Below is a copy of the adjustments page from the actual appraisal (with personal information blacked out). As you can see, the appraiser used several additional property features to do his adjustments and was a lot more scientific about how he determined the adjustment values, but in the end, the appraiser came up with values that weren't too different than the quick and dirty analysis I provided above.

Uniform Residential Appraisal Report

File #

There are 19 comparable properties currently offered for sale in the subject neighborhood ranging in price from $ 95,000 to $ 150,000
There are 31 comparable sales in the subject neighborhood within the past twelve months ranging in sale price from $ 105,000 to $ 135,000

FEATURE	SUBJECT	COMPARABLE SALE # 1	+(-) $ Adjustment	COMPARABLE SALE # 2	+(-) $ Adjustment	COMPARABLE SALE # 3	+(-) $ Adjustment
Address							
Proximity to Subject		0.11 miles SE		0.04 miles E		0.93 miles SE	
Sale Price	$ 110,000	$ 105,000		$ 105,000		$ 120,000	
Sale Price/Gross Liv. Area	$ 56.70 sq.ft.	$ 56.63 sq.ft.		$ 56.00 sq.ft.		$ 45.28 sq.ft.	
Data Source(s)		FMLS#4182148;DOM 10		FMLS#4221355;DOM 29		FMLS#4166186;DOM 177	
Verification Source(s)		Market Data Center		Market Data Center		Appraisal/Field	
VALUE ADJUSTMENTS	DESCRIPTION	DESCRIPTION	+(-) $ Adjustment	DESCRIPTION	+(-) $ Adjustment	DESCRIPTION	+(-) $ Adjustment
Sales or Financing Concessions		ArmLth FHA;5395		ArmLth Conv;4600		Short FHA;1500	
Date of Sale/Time		s03/11;c02/11		s07/11;c06/11		s08/11;c07/11	
Location	N;Res;	N;Res;		N;Res;		N;Res;	
Leasehold/Fee Simple	Fee Simple	Fee Simple		Fee Simple		Fee Simple	
Site	11326 sf	9583 sf	0	10454 sf	0	10890 sf	0
View	N;Res;	N;Res;		N;Res;		N;Res;	
Design (Style)	Traditional	Traditional		Traditional		Traditional	
Quality of Construction	Q4	Q4		Q4		Q4	
Actual Age	12	12		12		5	0
Condition	C3	C3		C3		C4	+3,500
Above Grade	Total / Bdrms. / Baths	Total / Bdrms. / Baths		Total / Bdrms. / Baths		Total / Bdrms. / Baths	
Room Count	7 / 3 / 2.1	7 / 3 / 2.1		6 / 3 / 2.1	0	8 / 4 / 3.0	-1,500
Gross Living Area	1,940 sq.ft.	1,854 sq.ft.	+1,300	1,875 sq.ft.	+1,000	2,650 sq.ft.	-10,700
Basement & Finished Rooms Below Grade	0sf	0sf		0sf		0sf	
Functional Utility	Average/Good	Average/Good		Average/Good		Average/Good	
Heating/Cooling	FWA/CA	FWA/CA		FWA/CA		FWA/CA	
Energy Efficient Items	Standard	Standard		Standard		Standard	
Garage/Carport	2 Car Attached	2 Car Attached		2 Car Attached		2 Car Attached	
Porch/Patio/Deck	FPch/Patio	FPch/Patio		Stoop/Patio	+2,500	Stoop/Patio	+2,500
Fireplaces	1	1		1		1	
List/Sales Price Adjust(98.33%)							
Net Adjustment (Total)		☒ + ☐ - $	1,300	☒ + ☐ - $	3,500	☐ + ☒ - $	-6,200
Adjusted Sale Price of Comparables		Net Adj. 1.2% Gross Adj. 1.2% $	106,300	Net Adj. 3.3% Gross Adj. 3.3% $	108,500	Net Adj. 5.2% Gross Adj. 15.2% $	113,800

Using Tax Assessments for Comps

Before I move on, I wanted to address a mistake that I see a lot of new investors make and have even seen some very seasoned real estate professionals make as well. Many newer investors will see the tax assessment for a property and will assume that the assessed value of the property is in some way indicative of the value of the property. This is flat-out *not the case*.

While the assessed value of a property *could* end up being close to the actual value of the property, it is more likely to be coincidence than anything else.

There are a few reasons for this:

- Local assessments are done infrequently. It's possible that the last time an assessment was done, the housing market was very different, and values were far from where they are now (in either direction).
- The city or county often doesn't have the best data on the property characteristics. For example, a property may have originally been intended to be a 3-bedroom/2-bath property, but due to changes in the planning or work done by previous owners, it could now be a 4-bedroom/3-bath property. If the proper permits weren't pulled (or even if they were, but not recorded correctly), the local government wouldn't know about the change, and no new assessment would be triggered.
- Local assessors don't enter the property, so they have no idea what the inside looks like. From the outside, two condos may look identical, but inside, one might have granite, hardwood, upgraded fixtures, a Jacuzzi tub, and $15,000 worth of upgraded appliances, while the other might use all builder-grade materials.

In my experience, local assessments can be off by 30 percent or more (in either direction). So be careful, and don't ever rely on the tax assessment to help you determine a property's value.

Calculating Fixed Costs

In my Flip Formula above, I refer to "fixed costs" and I mentioned that my fixed costs for a recent project were about $17,000. In this section, I'll discuss how I arrived at my fixed costs number and how you can determine what your fixed costs will be for your projects.

Fixed costs are composed of the various fees, commissions, and costs associated with all parts the investment project (outside of the actual rehab costs). While each investor (and each project) likely has his own specific fixed costs, for me they can be broken down into the following three categories:

1. Purchase costs
2. Holding costs
3. Selling costs

Each of these categories can be broken down in more detailed expense line items.

Purchase Costs

Purchase costs refer to those fixed expenses that contribute to the purchase of a property. For my projects, purchase costs can specifically be broken down as follows:

- **Inspection costs.** When I first started, I would have an inspection for each of my properties prior to purchase. I used the same inspector for every inspection, and he charged about $400 for a full inspection of a typical property.
- **Closing costs.** Each purchase comes with a fixed set of closing costs paid by the buyer. In Georgia, this includes a title search, attorney fees, courier fees, recording fees, state taxes, and document review fees. All those ridiculously inflated costs are charged by the closing attorney to ensure clear title and recording of the new deed. Across all my purchases, these costs usually come in around $1,000. Note that some states also have transfer taxes, which can amount to 1–2 percent of the total price, both on the buy and sell side. Do your research on your state's fees so that you aren't surprised at closing!
- **Lender fees.** For the most part, I use the same lender to finance each property purchase. The lender charges a set of up-front fees to fund the loan, including a loan origination fee, appraisal, underwriting fee, flood certification, document preparation fee, processing fee, and credit report fee—again, all those ridiculous and inflated fees that contribute to the lender's bottom line. While every investor and every lender will have a specific set of fees—and while these fees are somewhat tied to the purchase price of the property—for a typical acquisition I do, these lender fees total around $2,000 per property.

Holding Costs

Holding costs refer to those expenses that add up between the time I acquire the property and the time I sell the property. For my projects, holding costs can specifically be broken down as follows:

- **Mortgage payments.** On a typical project, my monthly mortgage payment will be about $500. In addition, a typical project—from purchase to sale—will typically run between four to six months. Therefore, during that time, I'll generally make about $2,500 worth of mortgage payments to my lender to keep the property.
- **Property taxes.** On the properties I purchase, the typical yearly property taxes are on the order of $1,400. Again, if I hold the property for

four to six months, this will average out to about $600 in property taxes per project.

- **Utilities.** While performing rehabs, I like to ensure that all utilities (electricity, water, and gas) are turned on. This is both for the convenience of my contractors as well as to help diagnose any issues with the property. Because the seasons in Georgia tend towards extreme temperatures, I've found that my utilities in my properties run about $200 per month for the duration of the project. Again, over four to six months, this averages about $1,000 per project in utility costs.
- **Insurance.** Typical insurance costs for my properties are about $350–$400 per year. On average, I pay about $200 in insurance costs for each project.

Selling Costs

Selling costs refer to those fees and commissions that must be paid for me to sell a property. Again, different investors will use different marketing mechanisms to sell their houses, so selling costs for each investor may be quite different. For my projects, selling costs can be broken down as follows:

- **Commissions.** Because my wife is our real estate agent, we save about half of the commissions we would otherwise incur when selling a property. That said, if our buyer has their own agent—they generally do—we must pay about 3 percent of the purchase price to that agent at the sale. A typical property of ours sells at about $120,000, so that 3 percent comes out to about $3,600 paid to the buyer's agent at the sale of our property. Add to that the fees my wife pays to her broker, and the total commissions average about $3,900 per property sale.
- **Closing costs.** In this market, most buyers ask the seller to pay some or all of their closing costs. On our sales, we've been asked to pay anywhere from $2,000 to $6,000 in closing costs for the buyer. On average, we're asked to pay about $4,000 in buyer closing costs, and because it is a buyer's market, we usually agree to it.
- **Home warranty.** Most first-time home buyers (the type we cater to) request that the seller purchase a home warranty as a condition of the sale. We always expect to do this and almost always have, and this adds about $500 to the cost of the sale for us.
- **Termite letter.** In addition to the home warranty, many buyers and their lenders require us to provide a proof of termite inspection at the

sale. This runs somewhere just below $100.

- **MLS fees.** Because my wife is our agent, she is required to pay a fee to the local MLS for listing the property. This runs about $100.

As you can see, buying, holding, and selling a property can cost a lot of money in fixed fees. Let's see how these add up on a typical project of mine (see next page).

On average, it costs me about $16,500 in commissions and fees to just buy, hold, and sell a property in this particular area (I like to round up to be conservative, which is why I use $17,000). Many investors ignore these costs when calculating their potential profit on a deal; but consider that if you plan to earn about $15,000 to $20,000 on a typical project, these costs can actually mean the difference between earning your desired profit and losing money!

So, before you start using the Flip Formula to analyze your deals, sit down with a pen and paper and write down all the costs you can think of that you will incur throughout your project. Start with the ones I've listed; you may find that you have greater or fewer costs, and you may find that your specific costs will vary, but it's important that you calculate your fixed costs sooner rather than later.

PURCHASE COSTS	
INSPECTION COSTS	$400
CLOSING COSTS	$1,000
LENDER FEES	$2,000
HOLDING COSTS	
MORTGAGE PAYMENTS	$2,500
PROPERTY TAXES	$600
UTILITIES	$1,200
INSURANCE	$200
SELLING COSTS	
COMMISSIONS	$3,900
CLOSING COSTS	$4,000
HOME WARRANTY	$500
TERMITE LETTER	$100
MLS FEES	$100
TOTAL:	**$16,500**

Your Profit

At some point, you are going to have to determine what the minimum amount of profit is that you are willing to work for on a particular rehab. This is often determined by a number of factors:

- **Price point.** Most investors understand that rehabbing and reselling a $100,000 house is unlikely to generate as much profit as rehabbing and reselling a $500,000 house. Because the amount of cash required to make bigger deals and the risks involved are greater, the profits tend to be greater as well. While many investors might be happy with a $15,000 profit on a $100,000 resale, these same investors might require a $50,000 profit on a $500,000 resale.
- **Experience.** New investors are likely to settle for smaller profits than more experienced investors. For investors doing their first deal, a $5,000 profit might sound like a huge accomplishment. But once these investors realize the amount of time and energy involved in flipping a house, they won't want to settle for such small gains.

- **Amount of risk.** Obviously, projects that incur greater risk should also have opportunity for greater reward. While an investor may be happy with a small profit on a condo that only required new paint and carpet, that same investor is going to want to see the possibility for much greater profits if there is risky foundation or waterproofing work that needs to be done. Because these major repairs run the risk of budget and schedule overruns, extra profit should be built in to compensate for those risks.
- **Amount of time.** Most investors will demand higher returns for projects that take several months than they will for projects that only take a couple weeks. Not only does the extra time decrease the overall rate of return, but the investor likely will have to invest a much larger number of hours, so the higher profits will be needed to maintain an hourly wage.

All that said, how much profit should you expect to earn on your first few deals? As a general rule of thumb, for rehabs that resell for under $300,000, I like to assume that profits will be at least 10 percent of the sale price, with a minimum return of at least $15,000.

For example, if I plan to sell a rehab for $250,000, I would be looking for a minimum profit of $25,000. If I plan to sell a rehab for $90,000, my profit target would be closer to $15,000.

By ensuring that my minimum profit target is $15,000, this also builds in an extra $15,000 cushion. In other words, even if I go over budget by $15,000 (or sell for $15,000 less than expected), in the worst case I will still break even.

For larger projects—over $300,000 sales price or new construction—I may take other factors into consideration when determining my minimum profit targets, such as the length of the project timeline or any added risk the project might incur.

There's no right or wrong answer to how much profit you should be trying to earn on each deal. You need to decide what makes a project worthwhile for you to undertake, and your profit targets may be much higher or much lower than mine.

Estimating Rehab Costs

The most common question I get from new investors is, "How do I accurately estimate rehab costs for a flip project?" Unfortunately, the answer to this question isn't simple, and for more investors, is the single biggest road-block standing in the way of them feeling like they are ready to invest. While there is no magic bullet to estimating rehab costs, there are several options at your disposal, and the one thing I can promise you is that the more rehabs you do, the easier it will get.

One thing to keep in mind is that before you can determine renovation costs, you're going to need to do an inspection and put together a *scope of work* (SOW) document, which is a list of renovation items you plan to complete during the rehab. The scope of work is your detailed renovation plan and will serve as your roadmap to the renovation project. We discuss SOWs in great detail in Chapter 12.

The other important point to keep in mind is that at this point in the process, where you don't yet have the property under contract and aren't committed to buying it, the goal isn't necessarily to get a precise estimate, but instead get a ballpark figure. If you can get within 10–20 percent of your actual renovation estimate, that should be good enough for this stage of the process. When you get a property under contract, you will have some time to complete your due diligence checklist, and one of the major checklist items will be to get an *accurate* renovation estimate for the project. We discuss how to create that level of detailed budget in Chapter 13.

Rehab Cost Estimation Options
In the meantime, here are some options for generating a ballpark rehab estimate that will allow you to complete your initial analysis:

Do It Yourself
While I wouldn't recommend relying on your own inspection and rehab estimate right out of the gate, it's important to have at least a cursory understanding of the process so that you can determine whether the inspections and rehab bids you're getting from others are reasonable. I would highly recommend picking up a good book that details the ins and outs of doing a property inspection, such as *Inspecting a House: A Guide for Buyers, Owners, and Renovators,* by Carson Dunlop & Associates, LTD.

Once you feel comfortable with basic inspection techniques, Chapter 12 of this book provides a detailed introduction into the topics of creating a SOW and then using that SOW to generate a renovation budget (Chapter 13).

Again, if this is your first serious undertaking of a major renovation project, I would recommend that you supplement your own inspection and rehab estimate with one of the methods below; but hopefully, after a couple of projects, you'll start to gain the knowledge and confidence to do these things yourself.

General Contractor Inspection and Bid

This is the estimation process I would recommend a new rehabber use to get a rehab estimate prior to actually getting a property under contract. While this method won't generate highly precise and accurate estimates, it also won't cost you a whole lot. The idea is to find a good general contractor (GC) who is accustomed to doing investment renovations and working with investors. The GC will visit your property with you to do a walk-through and basic inspection, discuss options for renovation work, and then provide a ballpark estimate for that renovation. We discuss finding a great GC later in this chapter.

In my experience, a good GC would charge about $50-$100 per hour for this service, and a typical walk-through and inspection could be completed in an hour to an hour and a half. So, you'll wind up spending between $40-$80 to generate an estimate this way. That said, a good GC may agree to do this service for a fixed fee of perhaps $75, especially if he knows that you are serious about entering the business and may eventually use him for your renovations.

Here are a bunch of other thoughts regarding this method for estimating your rehab that you'll want to keep in mind:

- Not all GCs are alike (see Chapter 15 for more on this), and some are more accustomed to doing high-end renovations while others are used to working with investors. On my first project, I got bids ranging from $30,000 to $80,000 for work that I could probably get done now for $20,000, simply because I was talking to the wrong kind of contractors. These were contractors who mostly did high-end remodels for homeowners; they were not "investor friendly" contractors. Try asking other investors for GC recommendations in your area, or at the very least, ask the GC if he is accustomed to working on investment rehabs. Once you get your bid, take it to an experienced investor you know and see if he believes it looks reasonable.
- The estimate the GC will give you will include the overhead associated with having him manage the entire project for you. This overhead cost

could range anywhere from 10–25 percent of the total renovation costs, depending on the GC. If you plan to manage the project yourself and hire your own subcontractors, the total rehab cost could be considerably less than what the GC estimates. Don't be afraid to ask the GC specifically to tell you his overhead for the project.

- While the GC will walk the property with you, point out concerns and issues, test some of the major mechanical systems, and provide you a list of items that may need to be repaired, he won't be nearly as thorough as someone doing a full property inspection. In addition, he probably won't inspect obvious things like doors and windows opening and closing correctly, or appliances working or not working. A GC shouldn't replace a full property inspection at the appropriate time (see Chapter 11). That said, a good GC will very likely be able to catch some issues that a typical property inspector wouldn't, as most GCs are more familiar with building codes, building practices, and engineering issues than a typical property inspector. So, even if you plan to eventually have a full property inspection done (and you should), having a GC walk the property with you is still a great idea.

- While the GC can tell you what works and what doesn't, the GC may not be able to tell you exactly what you should and shouldn't do for your rehab. For example, he might be able to tell you that the countertops can't be salvaged and need to be replaced, but that doesn't mean you should trust his judgment about whether to replace the countertops with laminate, granite, or tile (though we'll discuss those topics in Chapter 12). Likewise, the GC can tell you how much it will cost to reconfigure a floor plan or move walls, but he's not necessarily going to have the experience to recommend if and when you should be considering these types of changes.

Remember, the goal at this point in the process is to determine a ballpark renovation estimate in order to complete your analysis of the deal without spending too much money. Once you have the property under contract you can start to consider more expensive options that will allow you to create very detailed rehab plans and budgets.

Direct Sub-Contractor Inspections and Bids

Now, let's say you have a little bit of experience with construction, you know how to create a SOW and you've worked with sub-contractors ("subs") in the past. You have a good idea which contractor to call to do each portion of the project, and you may have a list of these subs or know another investor who can recommend subs to you. If that's the case, you may be able to bypass paying a GC to give you a pre-purchase estimate and bring in the subs directly to give you bids. This, of course, may or may not be done in conjunction with a prior home inspection.

For this method of estimation, you will need to break down the rehab into parts that will be sub-contracted out to individual contractors (this will often be part of your SOW). Then you bring in those individual contractors for estimates on those parts of the project, add the estimates together, and you have your total renovation budget.

For example, you'll get a plumber to give you an estimate on things like replacing toilets, faucets, and hot water heaters. You'll get a flooring professional to give you estimates on replacing carpet, wood, or vinyl flooring. Because you will be hiring these contractors to do the work if you get the project, you shouldn't expect to have to pay for these estimates.

If you don't have much construction experience, the next question you're probably asking yourself is, "What contractors will I need to give me an overall estimate on my project?"

Depending on the scope of the project, you'll want some or all of the following contractors to give you bids and help you complete your project:

- Plumber
- Electrician
- HVAC (heating & air conditioning)
- Painter/sheetrock/siding
- Carpenter
- Flooring supplier/installer
- Roofer
- Landscaper
- Cabinet supplier/installer
- Handyman

Bringing in subs for bids also makes the most sense when you plan to manage the rehab yourself, and going this route provides two big benefits over the other estimation techniques I mentioned above:

- You will get a more accurate estimate of what the costs will be. Because you will need a detailed SOW when bringing in subs directly, the subs will be able to provide very detailed cost estimates for each line item on the SOW.

- It will generally be free, as subs are more willing to look at a project and provide free bids on a detailed list of tasks than a GC would be. Of course, the subs may or may not be willing to help you with inspections (or may want to get paid for that effort), so again, this method may only be free if you are able to complete the inspections yourself or were to get a property inspection prior to bringing in the subs.

When you're first starting out, if you don't have any construction experience, it may be highly confusing on how to find all these contractors and determine who is responsible for which portions of the work; if you're not sure where to start with all these subs, stick with finding a GC for your estimates. But once you've gone through the renovation process a time or two, you'll get a lot more comfortable talking to and working with subs directly and will be better prepared to start getting estimates directly from them on future projects.

I started using this method on my fourth project, and never looked back. I haven't paid for a property inspection or for a bid on the repairs in many years.

Square Footage Estimations

While I don't recommend this—especially for new investors—there is another way to generate ballpark estimates on cosmetic rehabs. By using rules of thumb for costs in your area, it's sometimes possible to estimate the cost of a cosmetic rehab based on the high-level scope of work and the square footage of the property.

For example, after doing many dozens of renovations on properties in my area, I know that I can do a semi-complete interior cosmetic overhaul (replacing all the paint, flooring, cabinets, light fixtures, plumbing fixtures, door knobs and electrical outlets and switches, including demo and hauling away of the trash) for about $10 per square foot.

I know that I can do a full cosmetic overhaul (everything above, plus new HVAC system, water heater, roof and gutters, doors, and windows) for about $22 per square foot.

I can do a gut rehab (everything above, plus all new siding, sheetrock, decks, new plumbing, and new wiring) for about $35 per square foot.

These estimates are based not only on where I live and the types of houses I renovate, but also on the *specific* contractors I use and their prices. This is why I don't recommend this method of estimation to new investors and would only ever use this method myself to generate a quick-and-dirty ballpark estimate on a property for which I'll later do a more detailed estimate.

Finding a GC for Pre-Purchase Inspections and Bids

I mentioned above that using a GC to inspect properties and estimate rehab costs was my preferred method of doing pre-purchase estimates. But not all GCs are created equal, and it's important that you find a GC who has experience working with investors and will understand that as an investor, your needs are much different than a typical homeowner.

With that said, here are a few thoughts on where you might find a good GC:

- Ask other investors in your area for recommendations. For the same reasons I mentioned when looking for a buyer's agent, this should be the first place you go whenever you're looking for a new team member.
- If you've found or know any other great subs, ask them which GCs they've worked with in the past they would recommend. Good subs like to work with good GCs, so they often have strong opinions on who's good and who's not.
- Hang out at your local Home Depot or Lowe's, especially early in the morning. Good contractors are buying materials at 6 a.m. so they can be on the job by 7 a.m. Start handing out cards and making friends at your local hardware store.
- If necessary, look for (or post) ads on Craigslist or other websites where you can find local talent. While this is the most hit-or-miss method (you'll certainly get a lot of response, but not all of it will be quality), it's a way to start if you have no other good options.

Once you find a bunch of potential GCs, it's important to do some screening.

Here is the list of questions I recommend you ask the GC before trusting him to help you:

1. **Are you licensed?** While not absolutely necessary for the buying part of the process, a licensed GC is likely more professional and experienced than an unlicensed contractor. When looking for a GC to actually do your rehab work—that's another team!—being

licensed is an absolute requirement.

2. **Where are you located?** If I need someone on short notice, I don't want someone who has to drive an hour to the job site.

3. **How much notice would you need to schedule a walk-through of a property I'm considering purchasing to give a rehab estimate?** A short response time is better.

4. **Have you had experience doing rehabs for investors?** The GC needs to understand my business needs and what investor pricing looks like.

5. **How much would you charge to provide a pre-purchase inspection and estimate on rehab costs?** I'm happy to pay, but I want to see what they think they're worth.

6. **What types of projects would you be qualified to evaluate, and which are outside your areas of expertise? Purely cosmetic? Basic remodeling? Major rehab? Structural?** You want the right person for the right job, and when analyzing properties, you want a GC who is comfortable with at least basic remodeling and hopefully a lot more.

7. **What contracting areas would you be able to estimate material and labor costs for houses I'm considering purchasing? Plumbing? Electrical? Roofing? Carpentry? Exterior? Landscaping? Other?** I don't want to have to bring more than one person out to get an estimate.

8. **Would you be able to provide references upon request?** I will check them before giving them a job.

There may be several GCs who fit your criteria, but at this stage of the game, you'll want to pick one with whom you feel you'd be comfortable working, whom you trust, and who has a good grasp of all aspects of home renovation. More importantly, he should be comfortable and excited about working with you.

Your First GC Consult

Once you find a GC you think you'll be comfortable working with, I highly recommend setting up a walk-through of a house. It doesn't have to be any particular house, just a house that is representative of the type of house you're likely to buy as your first project. Perhaps it's old and dirty, the cosmetic components (floors, paint, appliances, light fixtures) all look worn out, and the place needs a good overhaul, but you don't notice any major issues—for example, no mold and nothing that would indicate foundation issues. This is the type of house you might consider for your first deal: It's a job, but nothing you can't handle.

This is going to be the house where you get a basic education on how to estimate rehab costs. I want you to call your GC (the one you found using the criteria above), offer him $100–$150 to come to the property, spend an hour or two walking through and helping you learn how to do some very basic inspection techniques, and then provide you a very rough estimate of how much it will cost to rehab the major components.

The purpose of this exercise isn't to determine precisely what needs to be fixed or how much the renovation will cost—this will be determined after you have an accepted offer on a property—but for the next step of this process, you will want to have a rough idea in order to know whether you should even be putting in an offer. Is it in the $10,000 range? The $20,000 range? The $50,000 range? Or the $100,000 range?

The Myth of No-Rehab Rehabs

There's one last thing I want to discuss before I close out this chapter, as I see many rehabbers fall into the same trap. In the course of a typical week, I see and hear about a lot of properties for sale. Inevitably among them are properties advertised by sellers or wholesalers as "No rehab needed!" or "Move-in ready condition!"

Every time I read an email from a wholesaler that says a property needs no rehab (or even "very little" rehab) and has a bunch of built-in equity, I laugh a little bit. While I imagine there are houses out there that could be purchased and resold for a profit without putting in any time, effort, or money, if they existed they'd be major exceptions to the rule.

There are two reasons for this:

First, if a property needs absolutely no rehab (or even pretty much no rehab) and can be bought and resold for a profit, then why isn't the seller just selling it to a retail buyer at a higher price? For example, if a wholesaler tells me that he has a property for sale at $50,000 that is worth $75,000 with no rehab, then why isn't that wholesaler selling the property to a retail buyer for $75,000 and leaving me out of the deal?

Of course, if you ask them about this, most wholesalers will tell you that "I don't have the cash to buy the property myself," or "I'm not in the flipping business." Sorry, those reasons don't make a whole lot of sense to me. If a wholesaler has the opportunity to either make $5,000 by whole-saling to me or to make $25,000 by flipping himself without having to do any rehab, he'll figure out a way to borrow the money and become a flipper for this one deal.

The very fact that a wholesaler is trying to sell to me for a lower price instead of immediately reselling to a retail buyer for what he says it's worth is all the information I need to know that the deal isn't as lucrative as he'd like others to believe.

Secondly, I'll occasionally have a wholesaler or seller tell me that a house only needs a few thousand dollars in repairs. They'll often call these "paint and carpet" rehabs, as that's all the rehab that's needed— new paint and new carpet.

Again, as far as I'm concerned, rehabs that cost under $5,000 are just a myth.

In all the houses I've bought and rehabbed, the minimum amount of work I would ever consider doing before reselling to an owner occupant is as follows:

- **Interior paint**. I would never consider trying to sell a retail rehab without fresh interior paint.
- **Updated flooring**. As a very minimum, carpet in the shared living areas and bedrooms, vinyl flooring in the kitchen and bathrooms.
- **New appliances**. Without appliances, a house probably won't be able to sell with an FHA loan (at minimum, a range/oven). Adding a fridge, dishwasher, microwave and washer/dryer isn't that much more expensive and will make your house stand out.
- **Updated electrical fixtures**. New light fixtures and fans make an old house look updated.
- **Updated plumbing fixtures.** Likewise, new plumbing fixtures bring a touch of renovation to an older house.
- **HVAC maintenance.** A dirty furnace will be a red flag to inspectors, so get them cleaned and maintained.
- **New light switches, outlets, covers, registers, smoke alarms.** Want to make a house look brand new? Replace the little things like out-lets, switches, and HVAC registers.
- **Cleaning**. Most importantly, I'll never try to sell a house without getting a house cleaner to scrub it from floor to ceiling.

This is the very minimum that I'd do in any house. I'll occasionally come across a house that doesn't need one or more of these things, but that's *very* rare, and I'd probably do it anyway.

Even a bare bones rehab with only these things would cost $10,000-$15,000 with decent and insured contractors. Even using uninsured day laborers and builder-grade materials would cost at least $5,000-$7,000 to do this type of rehab. And only painting the interior and installing new carpet is likely to cost at least $5,000 for a typical 3-bedroom house.

So, if a wholesaler tells me that a house "only needs a few thousand dollars' worth of rehab," a big red flag is going to go up in my head.

CHAPTER 9
LOOKING AT PROPERTIES

Are you ready to start looking at properties? It's time!

In this step, you're going to be doing several things simultaneously:

- You will start looking at lots of houses to get familiar with the relationship between the condition of properties and their value;
- You will start your house search and your marketing campaign;
- You will start evaluating potential candidates to be your first—or next—project.

The 100 House Rule

This is the point where we start putting all your hard work into action. I normally recommend that new investors look at 100 houses before they start making offers. This is my "100 house rule." But, if you've done all your homework, are comfortable you know what you're looking for, and are confident you have a grasp of The Flip Formula for analyzing potential deals, you may be able to cut some corners on the 100-house rule.

That said, at a minimum, I would recommend visiting at least 25–50 houses over the first few weeks. The houses should be in all different conditions, neighborhoods, and price points. The goal here isn't to necessarily find a deal, but to get familiar with what houses in your area look like.

This is where having a strong relationship with your real estate agent is very important. You're going to be asking your agent to do a decent amount of legwork over the first several weeks including getting you lists of properties and getting you into houses, and they likely won't be getting compensated for their efforts. Make sure you recognize the time and effort your agent is putting in, and make it clear how appreciative you are. While I don't want to belabor the point, this is also where having your own license would come in very handy. How nice would it be if you could view any property you wanted at any time without needing an agent to hold your hand?

Regardless, let's assume that you're ready to start looking at houses. Where do you begin? Here is the process I recommend when starting to look at properties:

1. First, look at some houses that are very distressed (you might be surprised at how bad a house can look!), and then look at some houses that have been rehabbed and are listed for sale. This will give you an idea of what your before-and-afters are going to be like.

2. Then take a look at some retail houses for sale (sales by owner occupants). These will tend to be in better condition than the distressed properties, but not nearly in as good condition as the rehabbed houses. These will make up the bulk of your competition and will define the very minimum standard for your rehabs. What finishes do these houses have? Your rehabbed house should have at minimum the same finishes, and some upgrades. Are you taking notes?

3. Next, you'll want to take a look at properties that are under contract, but not yet closed. It might be tricky to get into these houses (the agents won't really understand your motivation) but try being creative. Looking at properties under contract will give you an idea of what a house needs to look like to *sell* in your area. How much nicer are these houses than the houses for sale that haven't been put under contract? How do the prices compare between the houses that are currently for sale and currently under contract?

At this point, you should be getting an idea of what it takes to sell a property in your area and at what prices they tend to sell. This is tremendously important; while doing a comp analysis to determine resale value can all be done on paper, having a gut feeling for what a house will be worth after rehab will make finding houses much easier. It might take a while, but eventually you'll find that you can drive past a neighborhood, peek at the exterior of a few houses, and instinctively know for how much they would sell once renovated.

Start Looking for Deals

Now is also the time to start your marketing and acquisition strategy. Whether you'll be actively marketing or advertising for properties, or whether you'll be buying right off the MLS and just need to start reviewing properties, now's the time to get moving and start looking for houses.

Generating Seller Leads

If you're not going to be buying off the MLS, or if you have a dual strategy that involves marketing and advertising for properties, it's time to put those marketing and advertising plans into action.

Will you be using direct mail? If so, it's time to get your list, put together your marketing pieces, and start mailing envelopes. Will you be using the internet for your marketing? If so, it's time to create your website and start building your keywords. Will you be putting out bandit signs? If so, it's time to get those ordered and start deciding where you will put them. (See Chapter 7 for more information about marketing and advertising for leads.)

Regardless of the type of marketing and advertising you're doing, the goal at this point is to get your phone ringing. Investing is a numbers game—most of the leads you get (whether off the MLS or through your marketing) will not turn into deals. Unfortunately, that's just the reality of the business. You may look at 50 properties or talk to 100 sellers before you find a serious lead. And you may have to go through many serious leads before you land your first deal.

If you'll be marketing and advertising for leads, expect the process to take several weeks, or even a month or two, before the calls roll in. Maybe you'll be lucky and that first motivated seller will call you on day one; but if that doesn't happen, don't get discouraged. Remember, every day that you take action, you're one step closer to closing that first deal.

Okay, you've been patient, you've ramped up your marketing, and now the calls are starting to come in. What do you say when the person on the other end of the phone says, "I saw your marketing and I'm considering selling my house"?

Talking to Sellers

When you get a phone call from a potential seller, it's important to know which of your marketing channels it came from.

This is important for two reasons:

1. Knowing where your leads are coming from will allow you to optimize future campaigns. If you know one channel is working well, you can double-down your efforts on that channel; if you know another channel isn't working well, you can focus on revamping or terminating that part of your marketing strategy.
2. It's important to understand as much as you can about the situation of the person on the other side of the phone *before* you answer. This will allow you to tailor and personalize your discussion to the situation of the caller from the very moment you pick up the phone. For example, are you about to be speaking with an investor or homeowner? Does the person have equity in their property or are they underwater? Is the person simply late on their mortgage or is foreclosure right around the corner? The best way to identify the type of caller prior to answering the phone is to have set up different phone numbers for different groups of targets or different marketing campaigns. So, if you receive a call on 555-1234, you'll know instantly that it's from someone who saw a bandit sign, because that's the number you put on the sign.

While every phone call will need to be personalized to the specific caller and every situation will be unique, in general you'll have one of two types of discussions: Either you will be speaking to a seller with equity in their house or you'll be speaking to a seller who is underwater and will need to get agreement from their lender to sell below the current mortgage amount (a short sale). There are other options when speaking to a seller who is underwater, but those types of creative deal structures are beyond the scope of this book.

Owners with Equity

When speaking with a seller who has equity in their house, you want to get to the two most important questions:
1. "Why are you selling?"
2. "What's the best price you could give me if I were to pay cash and close this week?"

That information will give you an idea of how to approach the purchase. Remember, understanding the seller's motivation will give you an idea of how to negotiate, and will give you an idea of their motivation level.

The more motivated they are, the lower their initial offer to sell will be.

Here is a script I like to use when speaking with sellers who have equity:

Date: _____

Address: _____

Seller Name: _____

Seller Phone: _____

Points to Note Somewhere in Conversation:
- We always buy properties "as-is," so you won't need to do any repairs
- We pay cash and actually purchase the property—we're not looking to wholesale
- We can close quickly—generally 1-2 weeks if there are no title issues
- We are licensed real estate agents, and we will use all state-approved contracts

Initial Questions (to Determine if You Should Continue):
- Are you ready to sell your house in the next couple weeks? — *Must be "Yes"*
- Is the house currently listed with a real estate broker? — *Must be "No"*
- What do you think the house will be worth in today's market? $_____
- What are you hoping to sell the house for? $_____

If the answer to #4 is MORE than the answer to #3, don't bother continuing...

Follow-up Questions:
- Confirm owner's name (and that the person on the other end of the line is the owner): _____
- Is this the best number to reach you? If "No": _____

- Confirm address of house: _____
- Out of curiosity, why are you selling?_____
- When do you want the house sold?_____
- On a scale of 1 to 10, to being highly motivated, how would you rank your motivation to sell? _____
- Is the home vacant or occupied?   *Vacant   Occupied*
- If occupied, when is the lease up?_____
- Do you have a mortgage? About how much do you owe? $_____
- Are you current or behind on your mortgage?   *Current   Behind*
- If "Behind," has the bank started the foreclosure process?   *Yes   No*
- I always buy "as-is," but can you tell me a little about the condition of the property?_____
- Without needing to do any repairs, with closing next week, and for a cash offer, how much would you be willing to sell the house for? $_____
- How did you come up with that price?_____
- Would it be okay if we came by in the next day or two to see the property for ourselves and present an offer?   *Yes   No*
- If "No," dig a bit more into why not and how the issue can be resolved…

Notes: _____

Thank you! I'm going to sit down, do a little research, and we'll give you a call back in just a bit to schedule a time to see the property. Is that okay?

Potential Short Sale Leads

When dealing with sellers who are underwater on their property and would consider a short sale, it is important to gather the information necessary for your real estate agent to begin the short sale process.

Here is a script I like to use when speaking with sellers who might consider pursuing a short sale:

Date: _____

Address: _____

Seller Name: _____

Seller Phone: _____

Seller Email: _____

- Do you currently live in the house?   *Yes   No*
- Is your house currently listed with a real estate agent: *Yes   No*
- Are you the owner of the home: *Yes   No*
     If not, who is? _____
- Whose name is on the mortgage loan? _____
- What type of loan is it?   *FHA   VA   Conventional*
- About how much is owed on the loan? $ _____
- How many mortgages do you have on the home?   *1   2   3*
- About how much do you think the home is worth $ _____
- 1st Mortgage info:
     About how much is owed? $ _____ Lender Name: _____
     Monthly Payment Amount: $ _____ Interest Rate: _____
- 2nd Mortgage info:
     About how much is owed? $ _____ Lender Name: _____
     Monthly Payment Amount: $ _____ Interest Rate: _____
- Current?   *Yes   No*
     If "NO," how many months are you behind? _____
- Is your home in foreclosure?   *Yes   No*
     If "Yes," what is the auction date? _____
- Property Details:
     Condition of home: *Very Good   Good   Average   Poor*
     Year Built: _____ Square Footage: _____
     # Bedrooms: _____# Bathrooms: _____
- What is your hardship? Why are you having trouble making your mortgage payments? _____
- We are going to have one of our licensed agents/short sale specialists contact you to set up a face-to-face meeting—is that okay?   *Yes   No*

Buying Off the MLS

If you will be buying short sales or REOs right off the MLS, now is the time to have your agent automate a daily feed that will send you emails with any properties that meet your criteria. You'll want to review the newly available properties (or those with a price reduction) each morning and determine if any might meet your criteria.

This is where having visited 25, 50, or 100 houses will pay off. If you had started to notice location, price, and condition trends while looking at these houses, you can now use this information to help determine if there are any "diamonds in the rough" in the list of properties you're receiving from your agent.

Hopefully your agent is also reviewing the list of properties that might meet your criteria and is helping you sort through the listings as well. Not only should your agent be looking at new properties to determine if they'll meet your criteria, but they should also be looking at properties that have been sitting on the market for more than 60 or 90 days to determine if there are any potential opportunities to pick up a house for well below list price. Sellers are often willing to discount prices significantly if a property has been on the market for a long time without any offers.

If you find a property that intrigues you and strikes you as a potentially good deal, take a drive past it. Look at the exterior, take note of the houses on either side and observe the rest of the houses in the neighborhood. You can often get an idea of what the interior of a property looks like just by looking at the exterior. If the exterior was neglected and in rough shape, there is a chance the interior is as well; if the exterior was kept up for the most part, the interior likely was as well.

For reference, the picture below is what a typical MLS listing looks like in my area (this will vary for each MLS and each location, so don't necessarily expect your MLS listings to look the same):

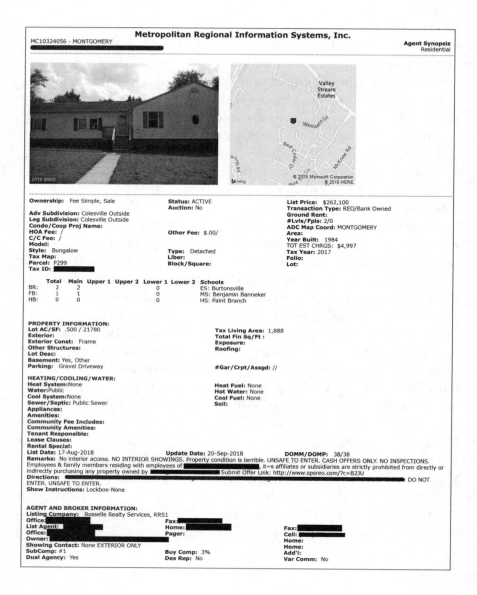

Ownership: Fee Simple, Sale

Adv Subdivision: Colesville Outside
Leg Subdivision: Colesville Outside
Condo/Coop Proj Name:
HOA Fee: /
C/C Fee: /
Model:
Style: Bungalow
Tax Map:
Parcel: P299
Tax ID:

Status: ACTIVE
Auction: No

Other Fee: $.00/

Type: Detached
Liber:
Block/Square:

List Price: $262,100
Transaction Type: REO/Bank Owned
Ground Rent:
#Lvls/Fpls: 2/0
ADC Map Coord: MONTGOMERY
Area:
Year Built: 1984
TOT EST CHRGS: $4,997
Tax Year: 2017
Folio:
Lot:

	Total	Main	Upper 1	Upper 2	Lower 1	Lower 2	Schools
BR:	2	2			0		ES: Burtonsville
FB:	1	1			0		MS: Benjamin Banneker
HB:	0	0			0		HS: Paint Branch

PROPERTY INFORMATION:
Lot AC/SF: .500 / 21780
Exterior:
Exterior Const: Frame
Other Structures:
Lot Desc:
Basement: Yes, Other
Parking: Gravel Driveway

Tax Living Area: 1,888
Total Fin Sq/Ft :
Exposure:
Roofing:

#Gar/Crpt/Assgd: //

HEATING/COOLING/WATER:
Heat System: None
Water: Public
Cool System: None
Sewer/Septic: Public Sewer
Appliances:
Amenities:
Community Fee Includes:
Community Amenities:
Tenant Responsible:
Lease Clauses:
Rental Special:
List Date: 17-Aug-2018

Heat Fuel: None
Hot Water: None
Cool Fuel: None
Soil:

Update Date: 20-Sep-2018   **DOMM/DOMP:** 38/38
Remarks: No interior access. NO INTERIOR SHOWINGS. Property condition is terrible. UNSAFE TO ENTER. CASH OFFERS ONLY. NO INSPECTIONS. Employees & family members residing with employees of ▮▮▮▮▮, it~s affiliates or subsidiaries are strictly prohibited from directly or indirectly purchasing any property owned by ▮▮▮▮▮ Submit Offer Link: http://www.spsreo.com/?c=B2JU ▮▮▮▮. DO NOT ENTER. UNSAFE TO ENTER.
Show Instructions: Lockbox-None

AGENT AND BROKER INFORMATION:
Listing Company: Rosselle Realty Services, RRS1
Office:
List Agent:
Office:
Owner:
Showing Contact: None EXTERIOR ONLY
SubComp: #1
Dual Agency: Yes

Fax:
Home:
Pager:

Buy Comp: 3%
Des Rep: No

Fax:
Cell:
Home:
Home:
Add'l:
Var Comm: No

If the MLS listing indicates the house is empty (likely if the house is an REO and less likely if the house is a short sale), then feel free to discreetly peek in the windows and see if you can get an idea of what the inside of the house looks like. The goal is to get as much information as you can prior to calling your real estate agent to look at the house. The agent will be spending time, effort, and gas money each time you want to look at a property, so you should be fairly confident that the house might be a deal before getting your agent involved.

Once you determine that a property is worth looking at more closely, immediately call your agent and arrange a time to meet at the house. Your agent will call the listing agent (the agent representing the seller) to get some important information. Not only will the listing agent be able to give showing instructions, but the listing agent can also tell your agent whether there are any other offers, how flexible the seller may be in price, and other information that could give you some insight into the status of the property.

When you meet your agent at the property, your goal is to get a general idea of the condition and a rough estimate of the repair costs. This is when that first GC consult (from the last chapter) comes into play. Based on what you learned during that session, you should have a very rough idea (to the nearest $10,000 or so) what this rehab might cost. If you're not sure, take your best guess and add 50 percent, or even double it.

If you can't even guess how much it might cost to renovate the property (it's not uncommon to be overwhelmed at this point), get your GC on the phone, have him come over to the property and start working on a more precise rehab estimate *for this particular property*. At the same time, have your agent put together a detailed comp analysis to determine more precisely for how much the property would resell after rehab. You'll be using both this rehab estimate and this resale estimate in the next section when deciding whether to submit an offer.

Deciding to Make an Offer

You've now looked at lots of houses and you think you might have one or two that could potentially make a good project. How do you determine if you should submit an offer?

It's time to go back to The Flip Formula that we learned about in Chapter 8:

MPP = Sales Price - Fixed Costs - Profit - Rehab Costs

As you recall,

Sales price equals the conservative estimate of what I can sell the property for (not the list price!).

Fixed costs equal all the costs, fees, and commissions that I can expect to pay during the project.

Profit is the minimum amount of money I want to make off the project when it's complete.

Rehab costs are the material and labor costs required to rehab the property into resale condition.

At this point, for every property you see, you should start running numbers through this formula. Plug in the estimated sales price (based on information from your real estate agent and based on sales pending houses you've seen), plug in your estimated fixed costs (go back to Chapter 8 to see how to estimate those), plug in your desired profit (use 15 percent of the estimated sales price if you don't have a price in mind) and plug in the rough rehab cost estimate you've determined (based on your discussions with your GC).

Where is the resulting maximum purchase price (MPP) in relation to the list price of the property? If the MPP is anywhere close to the list price (within 20 percent), you should consider submitting an offer. For example, if the list price of a particular property is $80,000, and the MPP you've computed for that property is $70,000, it's a candidate to make an offer.

At this point you may be thinking, "How can I make an offer with only a very rough estimate of all the costs? What if I miscalculated or missed something?" Don't worry about this right now. You will figure out all the actual numbers and costs if and when your offer is accepted (during your "due diligence period") to provide a way for you to back out of the deal should you later determine that your estimates were way off.

If after all the extra work you determine that your maximum purchase price is significantly below the list price, you're still free to make an offer, but you shouldn't get your hopes up about getting the property under contract. But don't be discouraged! I looked at many, many properties before I made my first offer, and I made lots of offers before I got my first property under contract. The time I spent looking at properties and the money I spent on my GC during that time wasn't wasted one bit, because every time I looked at a property and ran the numbers, I learned more about assessing value, estimating costs, and analyzing deals, making the next properties that much easier to evaluate.

Remember, it's a learning process, and as long as you're gaining knowledge and confidence every step of the way, you're making progress.

CHAPTER 10
MAKING OFFERS

You've found a property that you think might be "the one," and you're ready to make an offer. Whether the property is right off the MLS or being made to a seller with whom you've been talking for days, once you've determined that you're ready to make an offer on a property, you're going to want to do so *in writing*, at least until you gain some experience.

There are several reasons for this:

- If the property is listed on the MLS, the seller will likely require that the offer be in writing and will not even consider a verbal offer. This is typically true for any property listed by a real estate agent.
- Even if a written offer isn't required (for example, if you're verbally negotiating with a private seller), the formality of putting the offer in writing will discourage the seller from backing out of the deal if they agree to an offer and later change their mind before the offer can be written up.
- Negotiating in person can be very difficult for someone who doesn't have experience. Sellers may react emotionally to your offer, and if you're not prepared to respond to the emotional reaction, you may find yourself in a difficult situation that you don't know how to handle.

If you submit an offer on an MLS listed property and are represented by a buyer's agent, he or she will most likely be handling the writing of the contract. If you submit an offer to a private seller without an agent involved, you should obtain a copy of your standard state contract and fill it in yourself.

In either case, you're going to want to be familiar with the basic components of a real estate contract, and there are some important decisions you need to make before submitting your offer.

State Contract vs. Custom Contract

The first question you're going to need to answer is what contract you'll be using. The two choices boil down to using either a *standard state contract* or a *custom contract* that suits your particular needs.

If you'll be making offers through an agent on properties listed on the MLS, you won't have a choice—your agent will require you to use the standard state contract. The state contract is just a fill-in-the-blank document that all licensed agents/brokers in your state use. By using the same contract, agents can essentially "speak the same language" and there's less concern about an agent putting something in the contract that doesn't hold up to legal review.

While the agent will not want to make any major changes to the contract, they can add small components (called "stipulations") that add to or change the contract in small ways. For example, the agent could add a stipulation that says you get to keep the dining room table when you purchase the house; if both sides agree and sign the contract, it's now legally binding.

If you make an offer without an agent, it still may be possible to use the state contract. While technically this may not be allowed—many states copyright their contracts—it's often not too difficult to get your hands on a blank copy that you can fill in yourself. The advantage to this is that you can be assured that your contract is fully legal for your state, has most of the legal components you'll need, and is most likely skewed towards protecting the buyer over the seller, which most state contracts are.

If you don't have access to the state contract or for some reason you don't want to use the state contract, you can go with a custom contract. Some people will download contracts off the internet, some will pay an attorney to create one, and some will share contracts with other investors they know. The big reason why some investors choose to use their own contract is that the state contracts are often long and complicated. By using a custom contract, an investor can create something that is much shorter—sometimes a single page—that is more easily readable than the state version.

There are some risks to using a custom contract, especially if not written or reviewed by a qualified attorney.

First, much of contract law is state specific; it's possible that a custom contract will have components that may not be legal in your state. In the worst-case scenario, a custom contract may not even contain the minimum components that make up a real estate contract, meaning that either party could just back out at any time without legal ramification.

The other big risk is that your "simple" contract won't contain all the important provisions that will come into play if something about the deal goes awry. Remember, when everything goes smoothly, contracts are nothing more than a formality. It's when things go wrong that a contract is important, and if your contract doesn't cover the specific situation when something goes wrong, it may not be worth the paper it's written on.

I'll leave it at this: If you plan on using a custom contract, make sure that you spend the couple of hundred dollars it will take to have it reviewed by a qualified real estate or contracts attorney. While we all hope that our deals will go smoothly and there will never by any contentious legal battles, it's always better to be prepared for a worst-case situation.

The 5 Major Contract Components

Regardless of whether you plan to use the state contract or your own custom contract, there are several key components to your offer that will need to be addressed in the contract. If you're working through an agent, you'll want to provide this information to them; if you're writing the contract yourself, you'll want to ensure each component is adequately covered.

Specifically, here are five big decisions you'll need to make in order to prepare your offer:
1. Form of payment: cash or financing
2. Purchase price
3. Earnest money
4. Closing costs
5. Contingencies

Let's discuss each of these in more detail...

1. Form of Payment: Cash or Financing

The first thing you'll need to determine is whether you'll be offering to purchase the property in cash or with financing. This decision will impact several other parts of your offer, and if your offer is accepted, will dictate how the seller views the deal throughout the closing process. Generally speaking, a cash offer is one where you intend to purchase the property using cash you currently have available in your name (you will be asked to prove it when you submit your offer), and a financed offer is one where the funds are intended to be borrowed or otherwise obtained before the closing.

Sellers tend to be very biased towards cash offers and being able to offer 100 percent cash will increase your odds of getting your offer accepted, or at least seriously considered. But many sellers (especially banks, if you'll be offering on REOs) are very strict with their definitions, and if you can't provide a statement from a bank or brokerage account with your name on it and showing the full amount of the funds available, the seller may not consider you an all-cash buyer. Even if you fully intend to have access to the cash by the closing date (perhaps you're borrowing the money from a family member or are in the process of selling another property), if you can't prove that the cash is in *your* account at the time of the offer, you run the risk of not being considered a cash buyer, and in the eyes of the seller your stretching of the truth may cost you the deal.

While this may not be what you want to hear, if you can't include a bank statement in your name with the offer, you're going to be making a financed offer. On the bright side, when sellers (especially banks) accept a financed offer, they realize that the risks of the deal not closing are going to be significantly higher, and they tend to be more lenient when it comes to other aspects of the deal and re-opening negotiations should there be inspection items that the lender takes issue with.

If you're wondering whether you can get away with offering cash when you actually plan to finance a purchase, here's something to consider: I've seen investors try to pass off financed offers as cash offers on many occasions, and it normally backfires on them. Investors will try to treat a hard-money loan as cash or will try to treat a private loan from a friend or family member as cash, but banks don't see it this way. If you claim to be doing an all-cash purchase when you don't have proof that the funds are in your account at the time of the offer, you stand a good chance of having your offer rejected outright, without further consideration.

In addition, you risk looking like an amateur and reducing your odds of getting future offers considered from that listing agent or that seller.

For what it's worth, it's always bothered me that banks are so concerned when it comes to whether an offer is cash or financed. In a logical sense—and I've made this argument to sellers on several occasions—*every* offer is a cash offer, simply because the seller will always receive a cash payment at the closing, regardless of how the buyer obtained the funds. But from the seller's perspective, a cash offer is preferred over a financed offer, simply because they don't have to worry that the buyer will not being able to get the loan; but, in my opinion, sellers get way too caught up in the terminology as opposed to considering all aspects of the offer.

You may be wondering about whether getting pre-approved for a mortgage loan makes a difference. In my experience, not much.

A pre-approval means that the buyer has submitted their information to the mortgage broker, and based on that information, the numbers appear to work.

In reality though, if the buyer has exaggerated any of the information, or left out any information, or if there is some other circumstance that wasn't considered, it's not uncommon for a loan not to close. For example, a buyer might say (honestly) on their application that they make $100,000 per year; but there are plenty of situations where the details of that information can make it difficult to get the loan. For example, if they've been in that job or industry for less than two years, or if they're self-employed and don't have two years' worth of tax returns yet, or if that $100,000 represents a big increase from the year before—these are all things that won't be verified until later in the process and can derail getting a mortgage. Plus, many buyers simply lie or exaggerate to the mortgage broker up front, hoping they won't get caught.

In general, during times of tight credit, up to 50 percent of loans can fail to close. So as far as the seller is concerned, your offer is either cash or financed—period.

2. Purchase Price

The next big decision you'll need to make is your starting offer price. In Chapter 8, we discussed The Flip Formula, which should have helped you determine what your maximum purchase price (MPP) will be on the property.

You often won't make your first offer at your highest price, instead starting with a low offer that you expect will get negotiated higher. In other situations, you'll want to offer at your MPP right off the bat. Depending on the specific situation, one strategy will likely be more successful than the other.

STARTING WITH A LOWBALL OFFER

For properties that have been sitting on the market for long periods of time (over 90 days) and that haven't seen a recent price drop, the seller has most likely not had any reasonable offers. This means that the seller is going to be more willing to negotiate in order to get the property sold, which oftentimes offers you an opportunity to pick up the property well below the list price, and hopefully well below your MPP. With REOs, even properties that have been sitting on the market for a long time likely won't sell for less than 75 percent to 85 percent of list price, but that doesn't mean you can't open negotiations at 65 percent or 70 percent of list price and work up from there. And with private sellers, you can start negotiations at any price, as long as you're comfortable making a low offer.

When making your first offer on a property that has been on the market for a long period of time, your foremost goal should be to get a counter offer. This indicates that the seller is willing to negotiate. Once you get that first counter offer, you can be reasonably sure that the seller is motivated and will come further off the list price if you continue to negotiate.

Regarding REO offers, in my experience, the seller's first counter-offer will be near or at full price, while the second counter-offer will represent his or her biggest price reduction. For example, let's say a property is listed at $100,000 and you offer $75,000. Oftentimes, the seller will make their first counter-offer near full price; in this situation, the seller may counter at $97,000 or $98,000. You will then make your first counter-offer; I would suggest giving in just a bit more than the seller did, perhaps with a counter-offer of $79,000. The seller's next counter-offer will represent their biggest price drop, perhaps down to $88,000. At this point, you can expect that future counter-offers will be small and that the seller will want to stay close to that $88,000 price. Of course, this is just an example—actual price negotiations will vary wildly based on the property, the seller, and the situation.

STARTING WITH YOUR MAXIMUM OFFER

There are other situations where you're more likely to get a property under contract by making your first offer your highest offer your MPP. This situation commonly arises when buying a publicly marketed property on the MLS that has just been put on the market and is priced very reasonably, especially if there doesn't seem to be a lot of competition.

As an example, I remember looking at the MLS a few years ago just before Christmas. I came across a two-day-old REO listing in a neighborhood where I had already flipped several houses. The list price of the property was about $5,000 below what I knew I'd be willing to pay for it. In other words, it was a great deal. I called the agent expecting that she would already have gotten several offers or at least several phone calls about the property, but she told me that she didn't have any other offers and that the seller was motivated.

The fact that she told me that the seller was motivated indicated that I likely could have submitted an offer below list price, and still have a reasonable shot at negotiating the deal. So, what did I do?

I immediately put in an offer *over* list price!

Why would I put in an offer over list price when I knew there was no competition and the seller was motivated? Because I realized that had I opened up negotiations by putting in an offer lower than list price, the whole negotiation process would drag out for several days. In that time, other investors who had not yet seen the listing—it was Christmas and people were busy doing other things—would have a chance to see it and may start bidding the price up. If that were to happen, the property would likely sell for even higher above list price, and I may not have gotten it.

I knew that putting in an offer slightly above list price would encourage the seller to quickly accept the offer, and even at that price, I was getting a great deal. My above-list-price offer was a very defensive strategy, but certain situations call for being conservative in negotiations instead of being aggressive.

I will often put in an offer at or near my MPP when the property is newly listed, priced competitively, and when I know there will be lots of competition to buy it. And when my MPP is higher than the list price? I have no problem putting in a first offer higher than list price when I know there will be competition and when that higher-than-list-price offer is still a great deal.

"HIGHEST AND BEST"

When dealing with REOs or homeowners in hot markets, expect to frequently hear the term "highest and best." This is the term listing agents use when asking you to submit your best offer on the property. This is often done when the seller has multiple offers and wants to negotiate them all at once. Each bidder will be asked for their best offer and the seller will accept one of them; in some cases, the seller may refuse all of the offers, and instead choose to continue to negotiate with one of the bidders after the highest and best offers are submitted.

Keep in mind that I've seen plenty of cases where the listing agent said there were multiple bidders and asked for my highest and best offer, but I knew—or at least strongly suspected—that I was the only one who had made an offer. For this reason, many investors find the whole "highest and best" strategy to be highly unethical on the part of the seller, especially when it's not true that there are multiple bidders. But you have to remember the seller wants to get as much money as possible from the sale, and highest and best is just one negotiation tactic that will allow him to do that. So, while it may seem unethical—and is certainly frustrating—as an investor, it's just something we need to deal with when offering on REOs.

Here are a couple of key concepts to keep in mind when the seller asks for your highest and best offer:

- Just because you're being asked for your *best* offer doesn't mean that you need to *raise* your offer. If your previous offer is the highest you are prepared to go, or if you suspect that your offer is the only offer and you're willing to take a chance, you can tell the listing agent that your current offer is your highest and best.
- Never go above your MPP just because an agent is asking for highest and best. Even if you know there are other investors willing to bid above your MPP, don't get sucked into feeling like you need to go higher. There are always other properties, and it's certainly better to lose a property than to buy a property and lose money. Remember, with every deal your goal is to make a profit.

3. Earnest Money

The next question you'll need to answer when putting in an offer is how much earnest money you plan to put down on the property. Earnest money is a deposit that you provide along with the offer to show good faith in your promise to purchase. Earnest money is also the security that the seller gets to ensure that you follow through on your contractual commitment; if you back out of the deal after your contingency period(s) are up (in other words, if you violate the contract), the seller may be legally entitled to keep your earnest money deposit.

When dealing with a private seller, the earnest money deposit could be as small as $10 or $100; in some cases, it's not even necessary. There is no significant downside to giving a small earnest money deposit as a buyer, so when buying from private sellers, always shoot for as little as possible. The big advantage to a larger deposit is psychological—a large amount of money paid upfront looks very enticing to a seller and may allow you to negotiate better terms on the rest of the deal, such as a lower purchase price.

When dealing with a bank-owned property, you are going to be required to put down at least $500 in earnest money, or more. Many banks require at least $1,000 in earnest money, and if your offer is an all cash offer, you will often be required to put down 10 percent of the purchase price as earnest money.

Here's a tip for when making an offer on REOs: You will likely be required to provide a personal check for the earnest money at the time the offer is made. Your agent will photocopy the check and attach a copy to the offer. But nearly 100 percent of the time, this check *will not be cashed.* If the bank decides to accept your offer, you will be asked to provide earnest money in the form of certified funds (cashier's check, for example) and your personal check will be returned to you. If you plan to make several simultaneous offers and are concerned about all the personal earnest money checks you'll need to write, ask your agent to use the same photocopy of your check for all the offers. Since this check will almost never be cashed, your agent should have no problem doing this.

4. Closing Costs

A lot of new investors (and new homebuyers) don't realize this, but in some areas of the country and for some price level of houses, it's not uncommon for the buyer to ask the seller to pay some or all of their closing costs for them. This is more common for lower-priced houses and for buyers who are getting loans, as these are the buyers who tend to have the least amount of disposable cash, and they are trying to save their cash as much as possible.

When I'm selling a property, it's not uncommon for my buyers to ask for me to pay up to 4 percent of the sale price towards their closing costs, with some buyers asking me to pay up to 6 percent (the maximum limit that FHA lenders will allow).

So, when you're the buyer, remember that you have the right to ask the seller to offset some of your upfront costs by having them pay part or all of your closing costs for you. That said, keep in mind that when making offers on short sales, the seller generally doesn't have any money to contribute (they can't even pay their mortgage), and the lender generally won't contribute; so, don't expect to get any closing costs in this situation. And when buying REOs, the bank is going to be a lot more accommodating about paying closing costs when the buyer is getting a loan than when they are paying cash, simply because the need for a loan indicates the buyer is in a more worse cash position.

5. Contingencies

A contingency is a statement added to your contract that gives you the right to back out of the deal under specific circumstances. Contingencies are often used by buyers who aren't 100 percent convinced they're ready—or able—to buy the property and want some extra time to "get their ducks in a row."

When making an offer, you'll need to decide if you want to include a contingency, and if so, what specifically the contingency will say. There are several standard contingencies that are used in real estate contracts that you might want to use.

Here are the three most common:

- **Inspection Contingency:**
  - Also known as a "due diligence period" or a "due diligence contingency," this contingency says that the buyer has a set amount of time (often ranging from five to ten days) during which they can do whatever they need to do to ensure that they want to buy the property. This might include inspections, appraisals, or contractor walk-throughs.
  - The way most contingencies are written, if at any time within that inspection period the buyer chooses to back out of the deal for any reason, they can. An inspection contingency is common for anyone who is not intimately familiar with inspecting properties and coming up with rehab cost estimates. The buyer can use this time period to get a full property inspection and get bids from

contractors to do any necessary work. If any surprises turn up, they can then either ask for a discount, ask for repairs, or just back out of the deal.

- **Financing Contingency:**
  - This is one of the most common types of contingencies. It says that your offer is contingent on you being able to procure financing for the property. It will often be specific about the type of financing (FHA, conventional loan, etc.), the terms (interest rate, down payment, etc.), and the time period.

For example, a typical financing contingency might read as follows:

Buyer shall have 20 days from the date of binding agreement ("Financing Contingency Period") to determine if buyer has the ability to obtain a loan with the following terms:

- Loan Amount: 96.5 percent of the total purchase price of the property
- Term: 30 years
- Interest Rate: No Higher Than 4.5 percent
- Loan Type: FHA

This agreement shall terminate without penalty to Buyer if Buyer is unable to obtain the loan described above and notifies seller in writing of this event within the Financing Contingency Period.

Any buyer who is planning to get a loan to purchase a property should include a financing contingency; worst case, your financing will fall through, but you'll still have the option to back out of the deal without penalty.

- **Appraisal Contingency:**
This contingency basically says:
1. If you can't get an appraisal on the property that is at least as high as the purchase price, you can back out of the deal; or
2. If you can't get an appraisal on the property that is at least as high as the purchase price, you can ask the seller to drop the price. If if he or she refuses, you can then back out of the deal.

The appraisal contingency often goes hand-in-hand with the financing contingency, as the lender will not fund a loan if the appraised value of the property comes in below the purchase price.

While there are thousands of other possible contingencies that you might see or use in a real estate contract, these are the most common, and many of the others are based on one of these.

Some others that you might come across at some point include:

- Termite letter contingency
- Lead paint test contingency
- Deed contingency (stipulates what type of deed is expected from the seller at closing)
- Radon testing contingency
- Mold inspection contingency
- Sewer inspection contingency
- Private well inspection contingency
- Homeowner association documents contingency
- Selling another property contingency
- Insurance contingency (stipulates that you can get insurance at a reasonable price)

Rules for Using Contingencies

I have four rules for using contingencies to improve investing success. Following these rules will both help you make strong offers to sellers, as well as help keep you out of trouble by putting your cash at risk before you complete your due diligence process.

RULE #1: THE FEWER CONTINGENCIES USED IN YOUR OFFER, THE MORE ATTRACTIVE YOUR OFFER WILL BE TO THE SELLER.

This is the most important rule of using contingencies. Perhaps it's obvious, perhaps not. Let's look at it from the perspective of the seller:

He wants to sell his property as quickly and as efficiently as possible, and any contingency you put in your offer is an opportunity for you to back out of the deal before it closes. The more contingencies, the more chances for you to back out of the deal.

For that reason, as a buyer, you want to limit your contingencies to only those that are absolutely necessary. I'm certainly not saying to never use a contingency—sometimes they're very important—but don't use more than necessary to protect your interests. And, if you have the ability to use *no* contingencies in your offer, that makes your offer much stronger than any competing offers.

Of course, unless you've had the property professionally inspected or were able to inspect it yourself and are absolutely sure that you want to move forward, you take a risk by not having a contingency in your offer.

So, what I recommend for most people is:

RULE #2: WHEN POSSIBLE, LIMIT YOUR OFFER TO A SINGLE CONTINGENCY.

While it may be reassuring to you to have lots of contingencies in your offer, a single contingency will often provide all the protection you need. In fact, for about 80 percent of the offers I make, the only contingency I use is the inspection contingency; and for the other 20 percent of the offers I make, I have no contingencies at all.

The inspection contingency will give you a fixed period of time—generally five to ten days, depending on how much you think you need—to get everything in order to ensure that you want to, and are able to, move forward with the purchase. During the inspection period, you can complete tasks including getting your property inspection completed, ensuring that you have your financing lined up, creating your scope of work, having your contractors come out to the property to give you bids, and contacting your insurance agent to get quotes.

Remember, while an inspection contingency is technically designed to allow you to back out of a deal if you come across an inspection issue, in reality, if written correctly, you can use this contingency to back out of the deal for many reasons. In the worst-case situation, if the seller asks you why you are backing out, you can always say that your contractor bids came in higher than expected and that your numbers just don't work, even if the real reason you're backing out has nothing to do with inspections or contractors.

By the time you've used up that inspection period, you should know whether you're ready to move forward on the property. If you've come across any concerns (such as structural issues, mold, missed repair costs), you can go back to the seller to request a lower price; and worst case, you can back out of the deal.

Which brings me to Rule #3:

RULE #3: ONLY EXECUTE A CONTINGENCY IF ABSOLUTELY NECESSARY.

I know plenty of investors who will make a lot of offers, each with an inspection contingency. They won't even bother looking at the properties unless they get their contract accepted. While this is a perfectly reasonable way to make lots of offers in a short period of time, it also increases the probability that you'll end up having to back out of one or more of those offers using your contingency.

Perhaps you find that there is more repair work than you needed. Or maybe you find that there is a structural issue that will be costly to fix. Or maybe you determine the layout of the property will make it difficult to sell. Or perhaps you just got too many of your offers accepted and can't afford to buy them all! Regardless, if you're not careful, you'll find yourself using the contingency to back out of deals.

And if you back out of too many deals, you run the risk of getting a bad reputation. If you work with the same listing agents over and over (for example, if you buy REO properties), and you have a reputation for backing out of deals using your contingencies, you'll find that you start getting many fewer offers accepted. Remember, sellers are interested in getting rid of their property as quickly and efficiently as possible, and if they think you're just going to waste their time by backing out of the deal, they won't even bother to accept your offers.

Lastly, if you intend to use your contingency, consider alternatives to just backing out of the contract:

RULE #4: CONTINGENCIES CAN BE NEGOTIATING TOOLS.

Just because you find that the deal isn't working out for you doesn't mean that you need to use your contingency to back out of the deal. You can use that contingency to re-open negotiations with the seller instead.

For example, let's say that during your inspection you find that there are some major plumbing issues in the property that will require an extra $3,000 in plumbing work that you hadn't factored in. Instead of using your contingency to back out of the deal, use it as an opportunity to ask the seller to drop his price by $3,000. Not only do you keep the deal alive, but the seller would likely face the same issue with the next buyer, so one way or the other, he's going to end up eating that $3,000 cost.

Or let's say your financing falls through. Instead of using the contingency to back out of the deal, you can use it to re-open negotiations around seller financing, especially if the seller is a bank.

The key is that even when you use a contingency, you don't have to use it to back out of the deal; you can instead use it to revisit the original deal and try to come to a reasonable compromise that resolves the issue(s) and makes both parties happy.

Negotiating Tips

If you're going to be dealing directly with private sellers, there may be occasions where you'll find yourself in a verbal negotiation. As I mentioned above, I don't recommend verbal offers or negotiation when you're inexperienced, but if the situation arises, you should be prepared.

For those interested, I've actually co-written an entire book on real estate negotiation (*The Book on Negotiating Real Estate*). While I don't have the space to discuss all aspects of real estate negotiating in this book, here are a few negotiating tips that you should be able to put into action immediately.

Tip #1: Let the Other Party Speak First

You'll often hear people say, "Never make the first offer... let the other party do it." This is great advice, but do you know why that will help your negotiating position?

There are two reasons:

1. First, it allows you to define a mid-point in price. Many inexperienced negotiators will find themselves "splitting the difference" in their negotiations. For example, if one inexperienced negotiator starts by asking $200 in the negotiation and another inexperienced negotiator starts by offering $100 in the negotiation, the negotiation result generally will end up somewhere around $150 (the midpoint). This is human nature not to want to give more or less than you're getting, so people tend to increase or decrease their offers by the same amount as the other party.

   But when the other party states their position first, you then have the ability to define the mid-point of the negotiation!

   In the example above, if the seller had stated the $200 ask first, the buyer could easily have offered $60, thereby reducing the mid-point of the negotiation (where they expect to end up) down to $130. On the other hand, had the buyer offered $100 to open the negotiation, the seller could have increased his ask to, say, $260, thereby increasing the midpoint to $180. As you can see, the person who states the first position is at a disadvantage to the person who waits, as the person who waits can define the midpoint, which is often where the price will fall.

2. Second, it's quite possible that the other party's first offer will be better than the first offer you would make. For example, let's say you want to hire a plumber, and your budget is $500 for a particular project. While you could state upfront that you have $500 to spend on the plumbing work in the hopes that the plumber doesn't ask for more than that, what if the plumber was only planning to charge $300? You've now told him that you're willing to pay $500, so he has little reason to quote you anything less than that. By stating your position first, you've given away valuable information to the other party (your maximum price), and he will use that information to extract the most money possible from you.

Tip #2: Stop Talking and Start Listening

One of the strongest maneuvers when negotiating is to keep your mouth shut. Unfortunately, it's also one of the most difficult. People are naturally uncomfortable during a negotiating silence, but this is exactly why you should work to ensure those silent periods occur. If *you're* uncomfortable, you can be sure that the person you're negotiating with is uncomfortable as well. And the common result of this uncomfortable situation is that one party will make a concession to break the awkward silence.

Next time you are negotiating and the person on the other side of the table throws out an offer, make a point to say nothing. Whether it be ten seconds or ten minutes, make the other person break the silence. You'll be surprised to find that he or she will often interpret your silence as anger or disappointment and will break the silence by revising their offer or offering a concession. Master negotiators will use this tactic to get less experienced negotiators to make successively lower offers without ever having to throw out a counter offer themselves.

This may be the most basic—but most useful—negotiating tactic you'll ever employ.

Tip #3: Information Is Power

I'd estimate that in 95 percent of all negotiations between experienced negotiators, the one with the most information pertaining to the negotiation will walk away with the better outcome. When negotiating, it's important to know as much as possible not just about the object of the negotiation but also about the party you're negotiating with and their motives.

Most people tend to assume that negotiation is always about money, but often it is not. Smart negotiators realize that, in many cases, it's more important to *solve a problem* than to offer the most money.

For example, let's say two buyers show up at an open house and both want the house. The first buyer assumes that the seller wants the most money possible, and offers full asking price, but needs two months to close in order to get financing in order, get inspections, etc. The second buyer asks the seller why he is selling, and the seller says that he has received a job offer in another state and needs to move in the next two weeks; the second buyer makes an offer for $10,000 less than asking, but agrees to close in two weeks, and has no financing or inspection contingencies. While the first buyer offered more money, the second buyer likely solved a problem that was more important than the price difference in the offers, all because he gathered some information from the seller before making an offer.

Tip #4: Check Your Ego at the Door

Oftentimes, we assume that the other side is looking for something tangible in the outcome of a negotiation, such as more money or better terms. But a lot of people who pride themselves on their negotiating skills are more interested in having their ego stroked than they are in any real tangible outcome. While some people are going to be all about getting every extra penny in the deal, there are those who will happily give a discounted price—assuming they are still above their minimum threshold—in return for some solid ego stroking.

In real estate negotiation, this might mean telling a contractor how highly recommended he comes; it might mean reminding a potential investor/buyer how good he is at rehabbing on a shoestring budget; or it might mean "confessing" to your wholesaler how much you hate buying from him because he is such a good negotiator. You'd be very surprised how far some sincere flattery will go in getting you a better negotiating outcome. Not only will it encourage the other party to lower their defenses, but they will feel an obligation to "return the favor" in some way.

Make sure you give them a way to return it in terms of a lower price or whatever else you might want.

Remember the last time you negotiated with someone who was really nice? How about the last time you negotiated with a complete a**hole? Which one did you feel better about "sticking it to them?" And which one were you happy to give a break to?

CHAPTER 11
YOUR DUE DILIGENCE

I'm going to start this chapter with a story. Hopefully this story will impart the importance of doing a thorough job of due diligence *every* time you are considering buying a property.

A Cautionary Tale

This is a story about an REO property that we got under contract about a decade ago when we were first starting out. As a little backstory, my wife occasionally looks through the expired listings on the MLS to see if there may be something good that slipped through the cracks and that might be worth trying to negotiate. She found a property that looked like a good deal and was surprised it didn't sell at the listed price prior to expiring, so she called the listing agent to get more info.

The listing agent was confused, and said, "Oh, it's not expired, it's still active and ready to be sold, though we haven't gotten much activity on it recently." Clearly, the agent didn't realize that the MLS listing was incorrect, which explained why there was no activity on the property—no other agents or buyers even realized the house was for sale!

We went to look at it, and it was even nicer than in the pictures. It was clear that at some point after the MLS pictures were taken, the seller (the bank) had come in and painted both the interior and exterior, replaced the carpet, and obviously made some additional repairs. It went from being a decent deal to what seemed like a great deal. Thinking we found a hidden gem lost in the MLS, we quickly put in an offer, and requested three days of an inspection period to do a bit more investigation should our offer get accepted.

Within 24 hours, we received a counter offer just a little higher than our offer price. The agent told us that the property was scheduled for auction, so she needed a response ASAP. We quickly accepted the counter-offer and were excited that we had gotten this practically move-in-ready house for such a great price, and without any competition!

But as I always do when I get a house under contract, I immediately sent my project manager over to see if there were any issues I might have missed on the initial inspection (though on this one I was pretty confident I hadn't missed anything). My project manager was working on a house around the corner, so he went right over.

He called me when he got there, and the first thing he mentioned was a little mound of dirt in the corner of the kitchen. I had seen it during my inspections, and knew that it likely meant termites, but I didn't notice any additional or obvious damage in the area, so I assumed it was a minor termite problem—something we deal with all the time. Luckily, my project manager wasn't convinced it was so minor, and investigated further. When he pushed on the baseboard at the bottom of the wall near the dirt mound, his finger went right through the baseboard!

He kept looking. Apparently, the entire baseboard was destroyed by termites and was only being held together by the fresh coat of paint that had recently been applied. He checked the window sills—completely eaten by termites. He checked the steps in the center of the house—many of the steps were destroyed by termite damage. He went upstairs and found that a bunch of the wood trim on the second level had been destroyed by termites, but again, the damage was not obvious due to the fresh paint keeping the wood from crumbling.

Once he knew what he was looking for, it only took a few minutes to realize that—best case—there was likely $20,000 or more in damage, as many of the walls would need to be ripped out and framing components would likely need to be replaced. Worst case, the house could have such extensive termite damage to the structure that it could be cheaper to just knock it down. And the house was less than 15 years old!

Without ripping out much of the drywall in the house, there was just no way to know how much work was needed or how difficult the damage would be to repair. Needless to say, we used our contingency and backed out of the purchase of the property.

The takeaway from this story is that someone—likely the bank who was selling it—went into the property and did their best to cover up the extensive damage with fresh paint and new trim pieces. And they actually did a good enough job that I missed the warning signs during my inspection. I have a feeling some unsuspecting buyer ended up purchasing this property at the upcoming auction, not knowing until too late what he was facing.

Due Diligence Tasks

The goal of due diligence is to verify all the assumptions you made during your initial evaluation of the deal. In other words, you'll be using this time to ensure that you have all the numbers necessary to make a final go or no-go decision on this project. Much of your due diligence work should have already been started before your offer was made but was not completed to the level of specificity that is required to have made you perfectly comfortable moving forward.

With that in mind, here is what should be done at this point in the purchase process:

1. Get an Inspection

In Chapter 8, we discussed property inspections just a bit. At that point in the process, the goal of the inspections was to be able to generate a list of work items detailed enough to create a decent rehab estimate. You either did the inspection yourself, had another investor help you out, or perhaps worked with a GC to do a cursory walk-through of the property and provide some basic inspection services.

Now that you actually have a property under contract and are considering putting a great deal of cash at risk, it's time to be a lot more formal with your inspections. The goal at this point is to ensure that nothing major was missed during the initial inspections that might have a serious impact on the project schedule, budget or scope, and also to provide a detailed enough report that you can create your scope of work (SOW). You will use this SOW to create your budget and your schedule, so you need it to be complete and accurate, which all goes back to having a full inspection on the property.

When you're new to inspecting a property yourself, I highly recommend spending a few hundred dollars to get a full inspection completed by a well-trained property inspector. To find a good inspector, talk to other investors in your area or even ask a good real estate agent. You may also want to do a little research into how property inspectors in your area are licensed and deemed qualified. For example, in Georgia, where I started my flipping career, there is absolutely no requirement for home inspectors to get licensed or accredited, so basically anyone can adopt the title "home inspector" and start inspecting houses.

While there isn't much in the way of national home inspector accreditation in the United States, the American Society of Home Inspectors (ASHI) is one of the more respected organizations. If you have nothing else to go on when searching for a home inspector, at least find one that is ASHI certified, and you're probably going to do better than just picking a random inspector without any certification.

A good home inspection will cost between $350 and $450, but not only is this an opportunity for you to get a full report of the problem areas of your house, it's also an opportunity for you to start to learn the inspection process on your own. While the inspector is at the property, follow him around and ask *lots* of questions. Most inspectors will follow a similar protocol when walking through a house, and by asking lots of questions about what they are doing, what they are looking for, and what they are finding, you'll begin to get a feel for the process and how to do it yourself in the future. For a few hundred dollars, you'll not only get an inspection report for the property, but you'll get an education to go along with it!

In fact, this process is the basis for my learning to do inspections on my own. After about a half dozen home inspections and a couple of rehabs under my belt, I was comfortable inspecting every aspect of a house other than the foundation or major structural issues. (I'll still call in a professional when there's a problem I'm not comfortable diagnosing myself.) After a few houses, if you pay attention and ask a lot of questions, I promise you'll start to get much more comfortable inspecting and estimating without spending any money.

2. Create a Scope of Work (SOW)

Once you're confident that you have a firm understanding of the condition of the property—what is working and what is not working—the next step of the due diligence is to create a scope of work (SOW). The SOW is the detailed plan from which the entire project will be created. The SOW will determine the budget, drive the schedule, and guide the contractors. In many ways, the SOW is the most important piece of the project—without it, the project can't come together.

What I have to say about the SOW and how to create it is a big chapter unto itself, so I won't try to squeeze that information in here. Chapter 12 has everything you need to know about creating a SOW; feel free to jump to that chapter now (make sure you come back!) or keep reading and you'll get there soon enough.

3. Create a Final Rehab Budget

Once your SOW is finalized, it's time to use it to create a detailed budget. While we talked about putting together a ballpark rehab estimate in Chapter 8, now is the time to create a precise and accurate budget that will help you make a final determination about whether this project makes sense.

Chapter 12 talks about how to use the SOW to generate a detailed budget.

4. Verify Your Resale Value

Back in Chapter 8, we discussed how to do your own comparable market analysis to determine the resale value of the property after it was re-habbed. Now is the time to ensure that you're confident in that value. If this is your first project or you're not very familiar with the area where you're investing, you shouldn't hesitate to hire a professional to help you with this step.

If you can find one or two experienced real estate agents (preferably listing agents) who are familiar with the area to provide you a comparative market analysis (CMA), that's a great first step. If there is any suspicion that the values generated by those agents are not correct (for example, if they are far from what you estimated or if they are vastly different from one another), don't hesitate to hire a licensed appraiser to help determine what the resale value of the property will be.

Run the Numbers Again

With all the information you've generated above, it's now time to run the numbers again with the new—and hopefully more detailed—information that you have. This is the ultimate goal of the due diligence process—to generate the information necessary to determine *once and for all* if you really should go through with the deal.

In this step, we're going to take the data we've generated to determine whether this property will be likely to generate our minimum acceptable profit should we purchase, rehab, and resell it. To determine your profit potential on this deal, we're going to rearrange The Flip Formula we discussed in Chapter 8 and plug in the numbers we generated during due diligence:

Profit =

Sales Price - Purchase Price - Fixed Costs - Rehab Costs

where:

Sales Price is what was determined by your final appraisal or comp analysis

Purchase Price is the contract price on the property

Fixed Costs are the final estimated costs to complete the project, minus your rehab costs

Rehab Costs are the costs to complete the rehab (your rehab budget).

After running the numbers using the data you've collected during your due diligence, you should be able to estimate the profit potential on this deal pretty accurately. If the profit potential on the deal meets the criteria you laid out in Chapter 10, then you have a project worth pursuing.

If the profit potential for this deal doesn't meet your requirements, now is the time to consider other options.

If the Numbers Don't Work

Sometimes you're going to find that the numbers you generated during due diligence indicate that the deal you have isn't really a good deal at the agreed-upon purchase price. How you handle this situation will play a large part in whether you consistently make profits rehabbing houses or whether you end up in situations where you are at risk of losing money.

Too many rehabbers determine during due diligence that the numbers don't really work but are so emotionally attached to the deal that they convince themselves it's a good deal anyway. Perhaps they talk themselves into believing they can sell for more than they originally thought; perhaps they think they can cut rehab costs; or perhaps they think they can get the project done more quickly to reduce holding costs. In nearly all cases, all they are doing is delaying the inevitable problems that come with doing a bad deal.

So, if you find yourself in a situation where you realize during due diligence that the numbers don't work, then what are your options?

They're actually pretty simple:

1. **Ask for a price reduction.** The first course of action is to go back to the seller and request a price reduction. I've found that honesty is the best policy in these cases—just tell the seller that your initial numbers didn't work and provide some support for your realization. For example, if you realized that the resale value is lower than expected, let the seller know about recent comps that impact resale value. If your rehab costs are higher than expected, provide the seller a list of the surprise repairs that you found during due diligence. In my experience, if you can convince the seller that you really did gather new information during due diligence that affects the deal, the seller is going to be more willing to consider a price drop than if you just ask for a discount without any substantiation. For REO deals, the bank will often require inspection reports and/or contractor bids before they consider a price reduction based on repair issues that were found during due diligence; but it's not out of the question that they will consider a price reduction if it's warranted.

2. **Back out of the deal.** If you're unsuccessful at getting a price reduction on the deal, it's time to cut your losses and back out. This can often cause hurt feelings—the seller won't be happy, your agent won't be happy, your contractors may not be happy—but temporary hurt feelings aren't as bad as long-term monetary losses.

Purchase Checklists

As a professional house flipper, one of the big requirements of my business is to scale to the point where—despite often only making $20,000 to

$40,000 per house—my company is able to sustain a significant annual profit. To do this, I focus a lot of energy on creating systems and processes, and I document those systems and processes so that anyone in the company can execute them.

One of the processes I have in place is the set of tasks required to get a property under contract, through due diligence, and then through the final purchase of the property. Because the due diligence period for a typical purchase is only five to ten days, there's a lot to be accomplished in that small amount of time. If anything in the due diligence process is missed, it's very easy to overlook key information that may hurt your project and your profits. Having a good process in place is not just about efficiency; it's also about long-term success.

Here is the checklist I use between the time I get a property under contract to purchase and the time I actually complete the purchase. Keep in mind that this checklist is appropriate for the way I approach due diligence, but everyone is different, and you may need to modify it for your approach.

Property Acquisition Checklist

UPON CONTRACT ACCEPTANCE

ENSURE ACCESS TO PROPERTY:
- ❏ If property is empty, get lockbox code or make copy of key (with owner's permission)
- ❏ Place key(s) in lockbox and install at property (with owner's permission)

IF CERTIFIED FUNDS ARE REQUIRED FOR EARNEST MONEY:
- ❏ Get certified funds from bank
- ❏ Submit earnest money to agent

IF FINANCING THE PURCHASE:
- ❏ Send contract to loan officer
- ❏ Provide loan officer the property information
- ❏ Connect loan officer with RE agent
- ❏ Have loan officer schedule appraisal
- ❏ Make sure loan officer knows anticipated closing date

DUE DILIGENCE

INSPECTIONS:
❑ Turn on utilities for inspection (water, gas, electric)
❑ Schedule termite inspection, if needed
❑ Schedule property inspection
❑ Attend inspection and take notes for SOW
❑ Get final inspection report
❑ Get termite letter/pest inspection report

CONTRACTOR PREP:
❑ Create SOW
❑ Bring in GC or subs for bids
❑ Create materials list
❑ Assemble contractor estimates/bids

PURCHASE DECISION:
❑ Perform final financial analysis using estimates/bids
❑ Make go/no-go decision on purchase

UPON CONTINGENCY FINALIZATION

FINAL PURCHASE PREP:
❑ Get closing date from lender/agent
❑ Arrange builder's risk insurance policy

If financing:
❑ Connect insurance agent with loan officer
❑ Follow up on appraisal
❑ Get pictures/video
❑ Create budget
❑ Create schedule
❑ Assemble contractor team

PRIOR TO CLOSING

FINAL LOAN AND CLOSING PREP:
❑ Obtain and review HUD-1 closing statement

If financing:
- ❏ Obtain and review "Good Faith Estimate"
- ❏ Ensure loan is ready for closing
- ❏ Get certified funds for closing
- ❏ Determine how to hold title

UPON CLOSING

DAY OF CLOSING:
- ❏ Get keys
- ❏ Get GC and sub-contractor contracts signed
- ❏ Arrange GC and sub start dates

CHAPTER 12
CREATE YOUR SOW

I mentioned it in the last chapter, but wanted to highlight it again here because it's so integral to successful flipping:

> Your scope of work (SOW) document is the single most important component of your project. It is the roadmap that will allow you and your contractors to get from the purchase of a property to a quality renovation that will make you money. Your SOW will help you develop your budget and your schedule and will help you create and carry out your entire renovation plan.

You must be willing to spend the time and energy it takes to put together a comprehensive SOW for every project you undertake, and this chapter will teach you how to do that.

With that said, let's talk about what a SOW is.

Your SOW is *the specific list of tasks* that will be completed as part of the renovation. In theory, you should be able to hand your SOW to your contractors, walk away, and have the renovation go as planned without any further instruction. Of course, that won't be the case in real life, but that's what you should be striving for.

There is no common format for a SOW. They range from a one-page spreadsheet to 100 pages of detailed specifications. Personally, I like my SOWs to be short and sweet, but to contain enough detail to help me generate my budget and schedule, and to let my contractors know exactly what will need to be done on the project.

In this chapter, I will build a SOW for a fictitious project. This fictitious project may not be an actual house I'm working on, but the SOW we create (and then the follow-on budget we generate) will be very realistic. Because I like to name my projects, I'm going to call this example project The Demonstration House, or The Demo House for short.

Determining How Much Renovation You Need

The $64,000 question of rehabbing is what renovation tasks are parts of your scope of work and what are not. Because every market, every neighborhood, and even every house is going to be different, there is no one right answer to this question. The key to successful rehabbing is to optimize the work done and the costs, and to find the "sweet spot" where the property will sell quickly but where you won't be spending more money than necessary.

While I can't tell you exactly what renovation work you need to do in your market and on your houses, let me walk you through how we approach *our* houses; perhaps this will give you an idea of how to think about this very important concept and hopefully will help you determine what you should and shouldn't be focusing on with your houses.

In our business, we often focus on entry-level houses geared towards first-time homebuyers, most of whom are blue collar. Because our buyers are generally moving from an apartment or rental house, they aren't expecting any frills or upgrades. They are accustomed to builder-grade fixtures, basic flooring, and laminate countertops. They don't need upgrades. But what they do get excited about is anything *new*.

They've gotten used to using old and dirty appliances, and they've always had to wonder if the carpets their kids were playing on were cleaned prior to their moving in. They've become accustomed to seeing a little bit of grime in the showers of their rental units and have never had the pleasure of soaking in a perfectly clean and brand-new tub. So, when they see that everything in the house is brand new, they don't care that it's not granite; they don't care that it's not hardwood; they don't care that it's just a soaking tub and not a whirlpool.

What they care about is that they're getting "all NEW flooring, FRESH designer paint, NEW kitchen with 42" cherry cabinets, NEW countertops and NEW stainless appliances including washer and dryer, all NEW lighting fixtures, all NEW plumbing fixtures."

The reason that sentence above is in quotes is that it is taken directly from one of our house listings. This is what gets our buyers excited. When you think about it, their attitude makes perfect sense. From their point of view, appliances and furnishings need not be expensive, but they need to be new, and they're willing to pay for that. We don't waste their money on things they don't care about.

In the interior of our houses, we'll ensure that all cosmetic components are either brand new or look brand new; we might keep existing fixtures if they're in very good condition. On the exterior of our houses, we'll replace any rotted or worn siding to match the rest of the house, and then paint, so the buyers won't be able to tell what siding was replaced. We won't do anything with concrete or asphalt unless it's a safety concern or such an eyesore that it will impact the sale of the house. We'll replace any doors or windows that need it, but if they are in good shape, a coat of paint will make them look new.

Again, I can't tell you exactly what you should and shouldn't be doing as part of your renovation, but to say it simply, you want to do the minimum amount of work that will still allow you to fetch your maximum resale value. You do this by focusing *only on the features your buyer will really want.*

At the same time, you must ensure that there are absolutely no safety concerns with your property and you should strive to ensure that the product you create is something that you're proud to stamp your name on. Remember, it's very possible to earn great profits as an investor and still get a great reputation. Strive to do both.

Over-Rehabbing

Many new investors want to do more work than is necessary on their properties. They think to themselves, "I wouldn't want to live in this house unless it had X, Y, and Z." What they don't realize is that they are usually not the target buyer, and generally speaking, their wish list is much more than what their typical buyers will expect at that price point.

While it's commendable to want to do more work than necessary on your houses, the extra money you're spending over and above what it will take to sell at your ARV is just money that's coming out of your eventual profits. You're probably thinking, "But if I spend more on the rehab and do some nice upgrades, perhaps I'll sell for more than ARV!" The problem with that reasoning is that it can be very difficult to get your property to appraise for more than ARV—cosmetic work plays a relatively small role in the appraisal—and most of your buyers will only be able to pay up to the appraised value for the property.

I'm a big believer in doing things that will set you and your properties apart from the competition, but I prefer to do things that won't cost a lot of money. For example, great staging, great customer service, and being flexible and easy to work with are all things that will set you apart from others who are selling in your market; and the cost of these things is minimal compared with expensive renovation upgrades you might be considering.

Now, that said, if you want to do one or two things to set your renovation and your property apart, go for it. Perhaps put in an upgraded shower massager, mount a large flat-screen TV above the fireplace, or put in a grand chandelier in the entryway. As long as you don't spend too much on any one feature and as long as you don't throw in too many of these expensive upgrades, there's nothing wrong with doing a little something to set your finishes apart from your competition.

Under-Rehabbing

While over-rehabbing is a major problem that will cut into your profits, under-rehabbing is a much worse problem, as it will impact your ability to resell your property, eliminating your profits altogether. Again, there is no magic formula for what should be done as part of your renovation, but you're going to want to ensure that your property has at least the same level of finish as your competitors.

Do all your competitors have granite countertops? If so, you probably don't want to use laminate tops. Do all your competitors have hardwood in the main living areas? If so, you probably don't want to carpet your living room.

Another thing to keep in mind during your renovation is that when you install something new, everything around it will look older. If you put in new countertops but don't replace the cabinets, the cabinets will suddenly look shabby. If you put in new carpet in the master bedroom, the existing carpet in the other bedrooms will look dingy in comparison. If the paint is fresh, the old light switches, outlets, and covers will look old and grimy.

As I mentioned above, I like to ensure that everything in my renovations is either new or looks new. And this is the reason: If there is anything that's old, it will look much worse just because it is in the presence of things that are new. It's very difficult to do a true "paint and carpet" rehab, as the new paint and new carpet will make the existing cabinets, light fixtures, plumbing fixtures and appliances look old and outdated.

Again, I'm not saying you need to do all the same thing in your renovations as we do in ours, but make sure you keep in mind how the things you *don't* replace will look when sitting next to the things you *do* replace.

The 25 Renovation Components

In my BiggerPockets book, *The Book on Estimating Rehab Costs*, I talk about the 25 components of a typical renovation project. I will use the methodology I discuss in that book here in this chapter (and the next) to create my SOW and budget for The Demo House.

The following comprise the ten exterior components, 11 interior components, and four general components that go into evaluating a rehab and creating my SOW.

EXTERIOR COMPONENTS	INTERIOR COMPONENTS	GENERAL COMPONENTS
1. ROOF	11. DEMO	22. PERMITS
2. GUTTERS/SOFFIT/FASCIA	12. PLUMBING	23. MOLD
3. SIDING	13. ELECTRICAL	24. TERMITES
4. EXTERIOR PAINTING	14. HVAC	25. MISCELLANEOUS
5. DECKS/PORCHES	15. FRAMING	
6. CONCRETE	16. INSULATION	
7. GARAGE	17. SHEETROCK	
8. LANDSCAPING	18. CARPENTRY	
9. SEPTIC SYSTEM	19. INTERIOR PAINTING	
10. FOUNDATION	20. CABINETS/COUNTERTOPS	
	21. FLOORING	

The reason that I prefer to break up my SOW into three parts (exterior, interior, and general components) is that it helps me track patterns among my projects to help make estimating renovation costs much easier. For example, I find that many of my properties have a very similar interior SOW, but the exterior and complex pieces tend to vary a lot in scope and cost. I can often just cut-and-paste the interior SOW from a past (similar) project, even though I have to do the exterior and complex pieces from scratch.

By breaking out the interior SOW and budget separately, I tend to find that I can build the interior budget very quickly, because it will be similar to previous projects. Then I can focus my energy on the exterior and complex renovation components. Also, I have a very specific order in which I examine the interior of the property and then examine the exterior of the property. I prefer to think of each of the three major areas (interior, exterior, and complex components) as their own separate process.

Scope of Work: The Demo House

My goal here is to lay out the process I go through for every project I encounter in order to create my SOW, and my renovation budget. Using our fictitious house, I will go through the same process I use on-site to build my SOW, examining each of the 25 renovation components one by one.

The Demo House: Overview

The house we'll use in this example is a foreclosure. A traditional style built in 1999, it's got 1,500 square feet, 3 bedrooms, 2 baths, and an 800-square-foot unfinished basement, of which we plan to finish 600 square feet (leaving the rest as an unfinished utility room). The basement will be one large recreation room and won't have a bathroom. The house is in pretty good condition, though to resell, we'll plan to do an entire cosmetic renovation on the interior and spruce up the exterior.

The Demo House: Exterior

For building the SOW for the exterior of the property, I like to start from the top of the structure and work my way down. This means examine the roof first, then the gutters, the trim and siding, and working my way down to the components on the ground.

1. ROOF

The house was built in 1999, so the roof is about 20 years old. Given that a typical roof will last about 30 years, we may want to get a roofing company to do an inspection. If there is extreme wear and tear or damage from tree limbs or other types of impact, it should be replaced. But in this case, let's assume the roof is in pretty good condition with at least five years of life left on it. Instead of replacing it, we'll just have our roofer walk the roof, perform standard roof maintenance, and replace old pipe boots.

ROOF MAINTENANCE	ROOFER TO WALK THE ROOF, PERFORM STANDARD ROOF MAINTENANCE, REPLACE OLD PIPE BOOTS, ETC.

2. GUTTERS/SOFFIT/FASCIA

The soffit and fascia (the wood behind and above the gutters) are in decent shape around the house, though there are about ten feet of wooden fascia board that appears to have some termite damage or wood rot. We'll replace that section prior to painting.

The aluminum gutters on the house are in good condition, and just need to be painted. There is a 15-foot run of gutter on the back of the house that is rusted through, so we'll replace that section of gutter during the rehab.

There is a tree overhanging the roof of the property, and this has caused a lot of debris to fall into the gutters. We'll either have our roofer or our gutter professional clean the gutters as well.

CLEAN GUTTERS	ROOFER TO CLEAN THE GUTTERS.
REPLACE GUTTERS	ROOFER TO REPLACE A 15' SECTION OF ALUMINUM GUTTER.
REPLACE SOFFIT/FASCIA	CARPENTER TO REPLACE A 10' SECTION OF FASCIA.

3. SIDING

The house was built with a composite wood siding that is in relatively good shape, though it could use a good pressure washing. Some of the boards around the base of the house are starting to deteriorate from moisture, and another section of the house was apparently damaged by a falling tree branch. Overall, about 100 square feet of siding needs to be replaced; we'll use a cement board siding that matches nearly perfectly for the replacement.

PRESSURE WASH	PAINTERS TO PRESSURE WASH THE EXTERIOR PRIOR TO PAINTING.
PATCH SIDING	CARPENTER TO REPLACE 100 SQUARE FEET OF EXISTING SIDING WITH CEMENT BOARD SIDING.

4. PAINTING

We paint both the interior and the exterior of the property. While the exterior paint on The Demo House is in good shape, the fact that we need to replace some of the siding and trim means that the new siding will need to be painted, and to avoid the difficulties of matching 20-year-old faded paint colors we'll just paint the whole thing. We'll also paint the trim and gutters. We'll use a three-color paint scheme (siding, trim, doors/shutters).

PAINT EXTERIOR	PAINTERS TO PAINT THE ENTIRE EXTERIOR USING A THREE-COLOR PAINT SCHEME.

5. DECKS/PORCHES

There is an existing concrete porch on the house, but most of the other houses in the neighborhood have back decks. To match the surrounding properties, we're going to build a basic wood deck that can be accessed from the first floor living room. Our new deck will be 12' wide by 12' long.

BUILD DECK	CARPENTER TO BUILD A DECK APPROXIMATELY 144 SQUARE FEET IN SIZE.

6. CONCRETE

There isn't any concrete work to be done on this project.

N/A	N/A

7. GARAGE

As typical on a 20-year-old foreclosure house, both garage doors are dented up pretty badly, so they'll need to be replaced. One of the garage door openers is in good shape and is working properly, but the other one is not functional and will likely need to be replaced.

REPLACE GARAGE DOOR	GARAGE DOOR COMPANY TO REPLACE (2) 8' GARAGE DOORS.
REPLACE DOOR OPENER	GARAGE DOOR COMPANY TO REPLACE (1) GARAGE DOOR OPENER.

8. LANDSCAPING

We have some basic landscaping to do at this project. The lawn desperately needs to be cut, bushes need to be trimmed, there is a large (~45' tall) oak tree that has branches overhanging the roof and obstructing the view of the house, and there are two dead trees in the wooded part of the backyard that need to be removed (both relatively small with plenty of clearance to bring them down).

LAWN MAINTENANCE	LANDSCAPER TO CUT THE LAWN.
TRIM BUSHES	LANDSCAPER TO TRIM THE BUSHES.
TRIM TREE	TREE COMPANY TO TRIM 45' TALL OAK TREE.
REMOVE TREE	TREE COMPANY TO REMOVE (2) MEDIUM SIZED TREES IN BACK YARD.

9. SEPTIC SYSTEM

The house is on public sewer, and there is no septic system. No work to be done here.

N/A	N/A

10. FOUNDATION

Luckily, there are no moisture or mold issues with this house.

N/A	N/A

The Demo House: Interior

11. DEMO

We'll be doing a complete cosmetic renovation, so we'll need to demo the flooring, the cabinetry, the light fixtures, the plumbing fixtures, and appliances. It looks like we can salvage the master bath Jacuzzi tub and stand-up shower, but the tub/shower combo in the second bathroom is stained and cracked—we'll need to demo and replace that one. We'll also need a roll-off dumpster to dispose of all the debris. The roll-off dumpster will also be used for all the exterior repair debris and the basement finishing debris, so we'll want to go with a larger size to avoid having to get a second dumpster later in the project.

ROLL-OFF DUMPSTER	DUMPSTER COMPANY TO PROVIDE A 30-YARD ROLL-OFF DUMPSTER.
DEMO LABOR	CARPENTERS (WHO GENERALLY DO OUR DEMO) TO DEMO THE INTERIOR HOUSE ON THE FIRST DAY OF WORK.

12. PLUMBING

This house has two bathrooms: The master bathroom has a double vanity, a stand-up shower, and a Jacuzzi tub; and the secondary bathroom has a single vanity and a tub/shower combo.

The house has several plumbing-related issues. The water heater is original to the house, and any water heater over ten years old should be replaced. There was obviously a leak under the master bathroom soaking tub, as there is a big water stain on the ceiling in the living room directly below the master bath. The water pressure is extremely high, so we'll need to replace the pressure regulator valve ("PRV"). As I noted above in the demo section, we're replacing the cracked tub in the second bathroom. And, of course, we'll need to do all the finish plumbing work, including replacing the sinks, faucets, toilets, and tub/shower hardware.

REPLACE PRV	PLUMBER TO REPLACE THE PRV.
REPLACE WATER HEATER	PLUMBER TO REPLACE THE WATER HEATER. WE'LL PROVIDE THE WATER HEATER AND EXPANSION TANK.
INSTALL/REPLACE TUB	PLUMBER TO SET THE NEW TUB. WE'LL PROVIDE THE THREE-PIECE FIBERGLASS TUB AND SURROUND.
INSTALL/REPLACE SINK	PLUMBER TO INSTALL (3) BATHROOM VANITY SINKS AND HOOK UP THE DRAIN LINE TO THE KITCHEN SINK INSTALLED BY THE GRANITE COMPANY. WE'LL PROVIDE THE BATHROOM VANITY SINKS.
INSTALL/REPLACE FAUCET	PLUMBER TO INSTALL (1) KITCHEN FAUCET AND (3) BATH SINK FAUCETS. WE'LL PROVIDE ALL THE FAUCETS.
INSTALL/REPLACE SHOWER/TUB HARDWARE	PLUMBER TO REPLACE (1) SHOWER-ONLY TRIM KIT, (1) JACUZZI TUB TRIM KIT AND (1) SHOWER/TUB COMBO HARDWARE SET WITH MIXER.
INSTALL/REPLACE TOILET	PLUMBER TO REPLACE (2) TOILETS. WE'LL PROVIDE THE TOILETS.
INSTALL DISHWASHER	PLUMBER TO INSTALL THE DISHWASHER. WE'LL PROVIDE THE DISHWASHER.
FIX LEAK	PLUMBER TO FIX THE LEAK UNDER THE MASTER JACUZZI TUB.

13. ELECTRICAL

The electrical in the house is in good shape and we currently have 200-amp service, which should cover all our electrical needs. But, since we'll be finishing the basement, we'll need to add a new circuit for all the basement outlets and fixtures. The new basement circuit will be wired to six new outlets and eight new can lights, with a new 3-way switch to control the can lighting.

In total, the house has 14 lights that need to be replaced and four fans that need to be replaced. Also, the bathrooms don't have GFCI outlets, so we'll be upgrading those. And we'll be replacing all the outlets and switches throughout the house, as the existing ones look old and grungy.

ADD NEW CIRCUIT	ELECTRICIAN TO ADD (1) NEW CIRCUIT FOR THE BASEMENT ELECTRICAL.
ADD NEW OUTLET/BOX	ELECTRICIAN TO ADD (6) NEW OUTLETS IN THE BASEMENT.
UPGRADE OUTLET TO GFCI	ELECTRICIAN TO UPGRADE THE (2) BATHROOM OUTLETS TO GFCI.
ADD NEW SWITCH	ELECTRICIAN TO ADD (1) NEW 3-WAY SWITCH IN THE BASEMENT FOR THE CAN LIGHTING.
INSTALL CAN LIGHT	ELECTRICIAN TO INSTALL (8) CAN LIGHTS IN THE BASEMENT.
INSTALL LIGHT	ELECTRICIAN TO REPLACE (14) LIGHTS. THIS INCLUDES: (8) DOME LIGHTS FOYER/ENTRY LIGHT DINING ROOM CHANDELIER KITCHEN TRACK LIGHT BATHROOM VANITY LIGHTS WE'LL PROVIDE THE LIGHT FIXTURES.
INSTALL FAN	ELECTRICIAN TO REPLACE (4) FANS, INCLUDING: (2) LARGE ROOM FANS (2) SMALL ROOM FANS WE'LL PROVIDE THE FANS.
REPLACE OUTLETS AND SWITCHES	ELECTRICIAN TO REPLACE ALL (42) OUTLETS AND SWITCHES THROUGHOUT THE HOUSE.

14. HVAC

The HVAC appears to have been replaced in the past few years. But, while the furnace is in great condition and can be kept, the outside air conditioning unit (the compressor/condenser) was stolen and needs to be replaced. We'll get routine maintenance performed on the existing furnace and will replace the compressor/condenser.

The HVAC contractor says that the existing indoor evaporator coil won't work with the new compressor, so the evaporator coil will need to be replaced as well. In addition, there is some duct work in the attic that has been disconnected and damaged; the HVAC contractor will repair or replace the ductwork and charge hourly for that work. It appears the previously installed compressor was a 2.5-ton unit, but with the additional square footage being added to the basement, the HVAC contractor recommends upgrading to a 3.5-ton unit.

REPAIR DUCTWORK IN ATTIC	HVAC CONTRACTOR TO REPAIR THE DAMAGED DUCTWORK IN THE ATTIC. HE WILL TREAT THE DUCTWORK REPAIRS AS A SERVICE CALL AND WILL CHARGE HOURLY. HE EXPECTS THE WORK TO TAKE ABOUT TWO HOURS.
HVAC MAINTENANCE	HVAC CONTRACTOR TO PERFORM INSPECTION AND ROUTINE MAINTENANCE ON EXISTING FURNACE.
REPLACE A/C COMPRESSOR AND EVAPORATOR COIL	HVAC CONTRACTOR TO REPLACE THE COMPRESSOR/ CONDENSER, AND ASSOCIATED EVAPORATOR COIL.

15. FRAMING

We'll be finishing the basement in this house, which will be the extent of the framing we need completed. The basement will consist of one large 20' × 30' room, which is a total of 100 linear feet of framing.

FRAME WALLS	CARPENTER TO FRAME 100 LINEAR FEET OF WALL SPACE.

16. INSULATION

We'll need insulation for two parts of this job. First, we'll be finishing some basement space, and by code requirements, will need to install batt insulation along all the exterior walls in the finished space. Second, there is very little insulation in the attic, so we'll be blowing loose-fill insulation in the attic to bring it up to code.

For the basement, we are building one big room, about 20' × 30' in size. That's 100 linear feet of wall space, and we'll have studs every 16", meaning we'll have about 75 studs and about 75 cavities between the studs to fill. Each cavity is 8' tall, so we'll have about 600 linear feet (75 × 8') of wall cavity to fill with batt insulation.

The attic is about 900 square feet in size, and we'll need loose-fill insulation blown throughout the entire space.

INSTALL INSULATION	INSULATION CONTRACTOR TO INSTALL 600 LINEAR FEET OF BATT INSULATION.
INSTALL INSULATION	INSULATION CONTRACTOR INSTALL 900 SQUARE FEET OF LOOSE-FILL INSULATION.

17. SHEETROCK

The existing sheetrock in the house is in good condition. Most of the sheetrock prep work will be standard stuff done by the painters as part of their bid/work. The two exceptions are the new sheetrock that will be installed in the basement and the sheetrock repair that will be required after the plumber fixes the leak below the master Jacuzzi tub. In my area, smooth walls are standard (no texture), so I won't be applying any texture to the walls or ceiling in the basement.

The finished basement area will be one large room—20' × 30'—with an 8' ceiling. Total square footage of new sheetrock will be about 1,400 square feet.

PATCH SHEETROCK	SHEETROCK CONTRACTOR TO PATCH HOLE IN LIVING ROOM CEILING.
INSTALL NEW SHEETROCK	SHEETROCK CONTRACTOR TO INSTALL AND FINISH 1,400 SQUARE FEET OF NEW SHEETROCK.

18. CARPENTRY (DOORS, WINDOWS, TRIM)

There is definitely some basic carpentry work to be done on this house. Two of the three exterior steel doors are pretty banged up and need to be replaced. All the interior doors are old, hollow-core doors that are flimsy and don't look very attractive, so we'll replace those with new pre-hung 6-panel doors.

Most of the windows are in good shape, though two of them have fogged glass, indicating the seal has failed and air has gotten between the panes. We'll replace those two windows.

As for trim work, we'll need to install new baseboard around the entire finished basement (about 100 linear feet) and new quarter-round molding around the hardwood floor on the main level (about 120 linear feet). We'll also need some casing around the two new basement doors (about 20 linear feet) and some additional trim in the basement to cover the exposed circuit panel (about 10 linear feet). Since we won't be trimming out the entire house, we'll likely pay the carpenter hourly for this work; I estimate about a day (eight hours) of work to complete the trim-out.

INSTALL DOOR	CARPENTER TO INSTALL (2) EXTERIOR DOORS.
INSTALL DOOR	CARPENTER TO INSTALL (14) INTERIOR DOORS.
REPLACE WINDOW	CARPENTER TO REPLACE (2) WINDOWS.
FINISH TRIM	CARPENTER TO INSTALL APPROXIMATELY 250 LINEAR FEET OF TRIM.

19. INTERIOR PAINTING

We'll paint the entire interior of the house with a three-color paint scheme (walls, ceiling, trim). This will include 1,500 square feet of existing painted walls and about 1,400 square feet of freshly installed sheetrock, which will require priming prior to painting.

PAINT INTERIOR	PAINTERS TO PAINT ENTIRE INTERIOR WITH THREE-COLOR PAINT SCHEME.

20. CABINETS AND COUNTERTOPS

The cabinets are probably in salvageable shape, but since we're doing a full cosmetic rehab on the rest of the house, old cabinets will stick out and draw negative attention. Plus, with kitchens and baths selling houses, we want all the cabinets, vanities, and countertops to provide a "wow" feature for the house. We'll go with 42" semi-stock cherry cabinets, matching bathroom vanities, granite countertops in the kitchen, and, to save a little money, we'll put laminate countertops in the bathrooms.

Our cabinet supplier did all the measurements and the kitchen came out to about 20 linear feet of kitchen cabinets, a 30" single vanity in the main bath and a 60" double vanity in the master bath. Based on the layout of the kitchen cabinets, we'll need about 50 square feet of granite for the kitchen countertops.

INSTALL KITCHEN CABINETS	CABINET INSTALLER TO SUPPLY AND INSTALL 20 LINEAR FEET OF 42" SEMI-STOCK CHERRY CABINETS.
INSTALL BATHROOM VANITIES	CABINET INSTALLER TO SUPPLY AND INSTALL: (1) 30" BATHROOM VANITY (1) 60" BATHROOM VANITY
INSTALL COUNTERTOPS	GRANITE INSTALLER TO TEMPLATE FOR, SUPPLY, AND INSTALL APPROXIMATELY 50 SQUARE FEET OF MID-RANGE GRANITE.
INSTALL COUNTERTOPS	CABINET INSTALLER TO SUPPLY AND INSTALL LAMINATE COUNTERTOPS FOR THE (2) BATHROOM VANITIES.

21. FLOORING

This house currently has carpet and vinyl throughout. To help it stand out from our competitors, we'll be installing solid oak hardwoods (site finished) throughout the main level, carpet in the upstairs bedrooms and hallways, and vinyl in the bathrooms. We'll also install carpet throughout the newly finished basement area. Lastly, we'll install carpet on both sets of stairs—going up to the second level and down to the basement.

INSTALL VINYL/ LINOLEUM	CARPET INSTALLER TO INSTALL 14 SQUARE YARDS OF VINYL. WE'LL PROVIDE THE VINYL.
INSTALL CARPET AND PAD	CARPET INSTALLER TO INSTALL 130 SQUARE YARDS OF CARPET AND PAD. WE'LL PROVIDE BOTH.
INSTALL SOLID HARDWOOD (SITE FINISHED)	HARDWOOD INSTALLER TO INSTALL AND FINISH 900 SQUARE FEET OF OAK HARDWOODS.

The Demo House: General Components

22. PERMITS

On this house, we'll need to get the basement finishing permitted. Inspections will include framing, insulation, electrical, and then a final inspection prior to completion of the project. I'll have my architect do the basement drawings and apply for the permits, and have my GC attend the three inspections—the electrical inspection can be done with the others.

Because I only need my GC to pull permits and inspect the job for compliance, I'll pay him a flat fee. Legally, he'll oversee the job site, but he'll spend minimal time at the site other than to ensure that things are being done legally and to code.

PERMIT DRAWINGS	ARCHITECT TO DO PERMIT DRAWINGS AND APPLY FOR PERMITS.
PERMITS	ARCHITECT TO GET PERMITS REVIEWED/APPROVED BY PERMIT OFFICE.
INSPECTIONS	GC TO ATTEND (3) INSPECTIONS.
GC FEE	GC TO PULL PERMITS AND SIGN OFF ON WORK.

23. MOLD
Luckily, there are no moisture or mold issues with this house.

N/A	N/A

24. TERMITES
As with most of our houses in this area, there is indication of termite infestation. Luckily, it doesn't appear that there is any major damage, just a few baseboards that need to be replaced. To avoid additional damage, we'll have our pest control company treat for termites and provide a clean termite letter.

TERMITE INSPECTION	PEST COMPANY TO PERFORM TERMITE INSPECTION AND PROVIDE BID FOR TREATMENT.
TERMITE TREATMENT	PEST COMPANY TO TREAT EXISTING TERMITES WITH CHEMICAL BARRIER.
TERMITE LETTER	PEST COMPANY TO PROVIDE CLEAN TERMITE LETTER.

25. MISCELLANEOUS

In all of our houses, we'll do things like replace all the outlet and switch covers, install mini blinds, replace doorknobs and deadbolts, and install door stops. Additionally, in this house, we'll be replacing all of the kitchen appliances, including the refrigerator, range, dishwasher, and microwave.

MISCELLANEOUS TASKS	HANDYMAN TO PERFORM ALL MISCELLANEOUS TASKS AROUND THE PROPERTY, INCLUDING REPLACING ALL THE OUTLET AND SWITCH COVERS, INSTALLING MINI BLINDS, REPLACING DOORKNOBS AND DEADBOLTS, INSTALLING DOOR STOPS, ETC. HE WILL ALSO PERFORM PUNCH LIST WORK AT THE END OF THE PROJECT AND COMPLETE ANY REQUIRED INSPECTION REPAIRS.
APPLIANCES	PURCHASE ALL NEW KITCHEN APPLIANCES, INCLUDING THE REFRIGERATOR, RANGE, DISHWASHER, AND MICROWAVE.
HOUSE CLEANING	HOUSE CLEANER TO CLEAN THE PROPERTY POST-RENOVATION.

The Demo House: Putting It All Together

If we combined the SOW tasks above into a single spreadsheet, here is our SOW for The Demo House:

COMPONENT	TASK
ROOF	ROOF MAINTENANCE
GUTTERS/ SOFFITS/FASCIA	CLEAN GUTTERS REPLACE 15' OF ALUMINUM GUTTER REPLACE 10' OF WOOD SOFFIT
SIDING	PRESSURE WASH EXTERIOR REPAIR/REPLACE 100 SF OF CEMENT SIDING
EXTERIOR PAINTING	PAINT EXTERIOR W/3-COLOR PAINT SCHEME
DECK	BUILD 12' × 12' WOOD DECK

GARAGE	REPLACE (2) 8' GARAGE DOORS REPLACE (1) GARAGE DOOR OPENER
LANDSCAPING	CUT LAWN TRIM BUSHES TRIM LARGE OAK TREE REMOVE (2) DEAD TREES IN BACKYARD
DEMO	30-YARD DUMPSTER DEMO INTERIOR FOR COSMETIC RENOVATION PORTA POTTY FOR (2) MONTHS
PLUMBING	REPLACE PRV REPLACE WATER HEATER (40 GALLON) INSTALL PRE-FORM FIBERGLASS TUB INSTALL (3) VANITY SINKS CONNECT KITCHEN SINK DRAIN INSTALL (1) KITCHEN FAUCET INSTALL (3) BATHROOM FAUCETS REPLACE (1) SHOWER TRIM KIT REPLACE (1) JACUZZI HARDWARE SET REPLACE (1) SHOWER HW SET W/MIXER INSTALL (2) TOILETS INSTALL DISHWASHER FIX LEAK ABOVE LIVING ROOM
ELECTRICAL	ADD NEW CIRCUIT FOR BASEMENT ADD (6) OUTLETS IN BASEMENT UPGRADE (2) BATHROOM OUTLETS TO GFCI ADD (1) NEW 3-WAY SWITCH IN BASEMENT INSTALL (8) CAN LIGHTS IN BASEMENT INSTALL (14) LIGHTS THROUGHOUT HOUSE: (8) DOME LIGHTS (1) FOYER/ENTRY LIGHT (1) DINING ROOM CHANDELIER (2) KITCHEN TRACK LIGHTS (2) BATHROOM VANITY LIGHTS INSTALL (4) FANS: (2) LARGE ROOM FANS (2) SMALL ROOM FANS REPLACE (42) OUTLETS AND SWITCHES
HVAC	REPAIR DUCTWORK IN ATTIC STANDARD MAINTENANCE ON FURNACE REPLACE COMPRESSOR/COIL WITH 3.5-TON UNIT

FRAMING	FRAME LINEAR 100' OF WALL IN BASEMENT
INSULATION	INSULATE BASEMENT W/600' OF BATT INSULATE 900 SF OF ATTIC TO R-32
SHEETROCK	PATCH SHEETROCK IN LIVING ROOM HANG AND FINISH 1,400 SF OF SHEETROCK IN BASEMENT
CARPENTRY	INSTALL (2) EXTERIOR DOORS INSTALL (14) INTERIOR PRE-HUNG DOORS INSTALL (2) REPLACEMENT WINDOWS INSTALL 250 LINEAR FEET OF TRIM
INTERIOR PAINT	PAINT INTERIOR W/3-COLOR PAINT SCHEME
CABINETS/ COUNTERTOPS	INSTALL 20 LINEAR FEET OF 42" CHERRY CABINETS INSTALL VANITIES TO MATCH KITCHEN (1) 30" SINGLE SINK (1) 60" DOUBLE SINK INSTALL COUNTERTOPS 50 SF OF SANTA CECELIA GRANITE LAMINATE TOPS FOR BATHROOM VANITIES
FLOORING	INSTALL 14 SY OF ROLLED VINYL INSTALL 130 SY OF CARPET AND PAD INSTALL AND FINISH 900 SF OF #1 OAK
PERMITS	PERMIT DRAWINGS (~10 HRS OF WORK) PERMITS FROM COBB COUNTY WAIT TIME FOR (3) INSPECTIONS GC FEE FOR PULLING PERMITS
TERMITES	PERFORM TERMITE INSPECTION PERFORM TERMITE TREATMENT (CHEMICAL BARRIER) PROVIDE CLEAR TERMITE LETTER
MISCELLANEOUS	PUNCH LIST AND GENERAL WORK TASKS PURCHASE AND INSTALL APPLIANCES: REFRIGERATOR GAS RANGE DISHWASHER MICROWAVE CLEAN HOUSE AT COMPLETION OF RENOVATION

CHAPTER 13
CREATE YOUR BUDGET

Building Our Budget

For those just starting out in this business, building a budget is perhaps the most daunting of tasks. New rehabbers believe that estimating their rehab is the hardest part of the business. In actuality, the hardest part of this business is what you did in the previous chapter—putting together your SOW. Once you have your SOW in place, estimating costs are as easy as plugging in estimates for each of your tasks or getting contractor bids to determine a more formal and accurate estimate.

Budget: The Demo House

In the previous chapter, we created a SOW for The Demo House. That SOW was created using the methodology described in *The Book on Estimating Rehab Costs*, and at the end of that guide, I listed my actual costs in my area for each of the renovation tasks.

Because The Demo House is located in my area and because my contractors will be doing the renovation, getting an estimate on the renovation costs for The Demo House is as easy as plugging in my cost estimates for each of the tasks in the SOW.

I do that on the next several pages. You'll notice that I like to round any labor amount under $50 up to $50, and any amount between $50 and $100 up to $100 (many contractors can't afford to drive to the house if the job isn't worth at least $100). I also round all estimates up to the nearest $5, as I like round numbers.

COMPONENT	TASK	LABOR	MATERIALS	TOTAL
ROOF	ROOF MAINTENANCE	$225.00	$0.00	$225.00
GUTTERS	CLEAN GUTTERS	$250.00	$0.00	$250.00
	REPLACE 15' OF ALUMINUM GUTTER	$150.00	$0.00	$150.00
	REPLACE 10' OF WOOD SOFFIT	$100.00	$0.00	$100.00
SIDING	PRESSURE WASH EXTERIOR	$150.00	$0.00	$150.00
	REPLACE 100 SF OF CEMENT SIDING	$250.00	$0.00	$250.00
EXTERIOR PAINT	PAINT EXTERIOR W/3-COLOR SCHEME	$2,375.00	$0.00	$2,375.00
DECK	BUILD 12' × 12' WOOD DECK	$2,750.00	$0.00	$2,750.00
GARAGE	REPLACE (2) 8' GARAGE DOORS	$1,050.00	$0.00	$1,050.00
	REPLACE (1) GARAGE DOOR OPENER	$250.00	$0.00	$250.00
LANDSCAPING	CUT LAWN	$50.00	$0.00	$50.00
	TRIM BUSHES	$50.00	$0.00	$50.00
	TRIM LARGE OAK TREE	$200.00	$0.00	$200.00
	REMOVE (2) DEAD TREES IN BACK YARD	$200.00	$0.00	$200.00

DEMO	30-YARD DUMPSTER	$450.00	$0.00	**$450.00**
	DEMO INTERIOR FOR COSMETIC RENOVATION	$600.00	$0.00	**$600.00**
	PORTA POTTY FOR (2) MONTHS	$160.00	$0.00	**$160.00**
PLUMBING	REPLACE PRV	$175.00	$0.00	**$175.00**
	REPLACE WATER HEATER (40 GALLON)	$150.00	$350.00	**$500.00**
	INSTALL PRE-FORM FIBERGLASS TUB	$250.00	$500.00	**$750.00**
	INSTALL (3) VANITY SINKS	$120.00	$90.00	**$210.00**
	CONNECT KITCHEN SINK DRAIN	$40.00	$0.00	**$40.00**
	INSTALL (1) KITCHEN FAUCET	$50.00	$85.00	**$135.00**
	INSTALL (3) BATHROOM FAUCETS	$150.00	$120.00	**$270.00**
	REPLACE (1) SHOWER TRIM KIT	$60.00	$75.00	**$135.00**
	REPLACE (1) JACUZZI HARDWARE SET	$60.00	$75.00	**$135.00**
	REPLACE (1) SHOWER HW SET W/MIXER	$120.00	$120.00	**$240.00**
	INSTALL (2) TOILETS	$160.00	$200.00	**$360.00**
	INSTALL DISHWASHER	$80.00	$0.00	**$80.00**
	FIX LEAK ABOVE LIVING ROOM	$100.00	$0.00	**$100.00**

ELECTRICAL				
	ADD NEW CIRCUIT FOR BASEMENT	$125.00	$0.00	$125.00
	ADD (6) OUTLETS IN BASEMENT	$450.00	$0.00	$450.00
	UPGRADE (2) BATHROOM OUTLETS TO GFCI	$60.00	$0.00	$60.00
	ADD (1) NEW 3-WAY SWITCH IN BASEMENT	$125.00	$0.00	$125.00
	INSTALL (8) CAN LIGHTS IN BASEMENT	$520.00	$0.00	$520.00
	INSTALL (14) LIGHTS THROUGHOUT HOUSE:	$700.00	$0.00	$700.00
	(8) DOME LIGHTS	$0.00	$80.00	$80.00
	(1) FOYER/ENTRY LIGHT	$0.00	$60.00	$60.00
	(1) DINING ROOM CHANDELIER	$0.00	$65.00	$65.00
	(2) KITCHEN TRACK LIGHTS	$0.00	$45.00	$45.00
	(2) BATHROOM VANITY LIGHTS	$0.00	$60.00	$60.00
	INSTALL (4) FANS:	$240.00	$0.00	$240.00
	(2) LARGE ROOM FANS	$0.00	$130.00	$130.00
	(2) SMALL ROOM FANS	$0.00	$40.00	$40.00
	REPLACE (42) OUTLETS AND SWITCHES	$210.00	$0.00	$210.00

HVAC	REPAIR DUCTWORK IN ATTIC	$100.00	$0.00	**$100.00**
	STANDARD MAINTENANCE ON FURNACE	$125.00	$0.00	**$125.00**
	REPLACE CONDENSER/ COIL W/3.5-TON UNIT	$2,800.00	$0.00	**$2,800.00**
FRAMING	FRAME 100 LINEAR FEET OF BASEMENT WALL	$800.00	$400	**$1,200.00**
INSULATION	INSULATE BASEMENT W/600' OF BATT	$510.00	$0.00	**$510.00**
	INSULATE 900 SF OF ATTIC TO R-32	$950.00	$0.00	**$950.00**
SHEETROCK	PATCH SHEETROCK IN LIVING ROOM	$50.00	$0.00	**$50.00**
	HANG AND FINISH 1400 SF IN BASEMENT	$1,350.00	$0.00	**$1,350.00**
CARPENTRY	INSTALL (2) EXTERIOR DOORS	$100.00	$400.00	**$500.00**
	INSTALL (14) INTERIOR PRE-HUNG DOORS	$560.00	$840.00	**$1,400.00**
	INSTALL (2) REPLACEMENT WINDOWS	$140.00	$250.00	**$390.00**
	INSTALL 250 LINEAR FEET OF TRIM	$250.00	$250.00	**$500.00**
INTERIOR PAINT	PAINT INTERIOR W/3-COLOR PAINT (1500 SF)	$2,875.00	$0.00	**$2,875.00**
	PAINT NEW SHEETROCK (600 SF)	$960.00	$0.00	**$960.00**

CABINETS	INSTALL 20 LINEAR FEET OF 42" CABINETS	$900.00	$3,000	**$3,900.00**
	INSTALL VANITIES TO MATCH KITCHEN	$0.00	$0.00	**$0.00**
	(1) 30" SINGLE SINK	$50.00	$150.00	**$200.00**
	(1) 60" DOUBLE SINK	$80.00	$350.00	**$430.00**
	INSTALL COUNTERTOPS	$0.00	$0.00	**$0.00**
	50 SF SANTA CECELIA GRANITE	$2,000.00	$0.00	**$2,000.00**
	LAMINATE TOPS FOR VANITIES	$200.00	$0.00	**$200.00**
FLOORING	INSTALL 14 SY OF ROLLED VINYL	$100.00	$100.00	**$200.00**
	INSTALL 130 SY OF CARPET AND PAD	$520.00	$800.00	**$1,320.00**
	INSTALL AND FINISH 900 SF OF #1 OAK	$2,750	$2,750	**$5,500.00**
PERMITS	PERMIT DRAWINGS (~10 HRS OF WORK)	$450.00	$0.00	**$450.00**
	PERMITS FROM COUNTY	$200.00	$0.00	**$200.00**
	WAIT TIME FOR (3) INSPECTIONS	$180.00	$0.00	**$180.00**
	GC FEE FOR PULLING PERMITS	$500.00	$0.00	**$500.00**

TERMITES	PERFORM TERMITE INSPECTION	$0.00	$0.00	$0.00
	PERFORM TERMITE TREATMENT (CHEMICAL)	$900.00	$0.00	$900.00
	PROVIDE CLEAR TERMITE LETTER	$65.00	$0.00	$65.00
MISC	PUNCH LIST AND GENERAL WORK TASKS	$1,000	$1,000.00	$2,000.00
	PURCHASE AND INSTALL APPLIANCES:			
	REFRIGERATOR	$0.00	$600.00	$600.00
	GAS RANGE	$0.00	$450.00	$450.00
	DISHWASHER	$0.00	$300.00	$300.00
	MICROWAVE	$50.00	$150.00	$200.00
	HOUSE CLEANING POST-RENOVATION	$250.00	$0.00	$250.00
			TOTAL:	$48,855

As you can see, our rough estimated budget for this project is just under $49,000.

Remember, this is only a rough estimate, and I would highly recommend that if this is your first or second project, you tack on a healthy "surprise" line-item to this budget. Personally, I would round the estimate up to $55,000 until I could get actual contractor bids, but new investors might want to round to $60,000 or more if this is your first project.

While this estimate may be good enough to help you do your initial analysis, you'll want to ensure that you have actual contractor bids before you complete your due diligence and commit to the project.

CHAPTER 14
CREATE YOUR SCHEDULE

While poor scheduling probably won't cost you lots of money or cause your project to fail, a good schedule will certainly help reduce stress, reduce the total hold time of your project, and allow you to keep holding costs to a minimum. It will also send the message to your contractors that you know what you're doing and that you value their time.

There are three parts to a good schedule:

1. Correct order of tasks.
2. Understanding and planning for dependencies.
3. Realistic time frames.

Below, I'm going to walk you through the order in which you'll likely want to schedule and complete your rehab. This will include all the major renovation components we've discussed in the previous chapters, as well as many minor components and considerations as well.

For each piece, I will discuss the dependencies that you should be aware of and will give a rough idea of the time frames involved. You'll want to work with your contractors to ensure that there are no special dependencies for your project and also to define actual realistic time frames given your specific SOW.

I like to think of a typical property renovation as occurring in four stages. Each stage consists of several exterior components and several interior components. For a specific project, you may not need every component—in fact, you may not need every stage. But, by thinking about renovations in these terms, you can get an idea of what parts of the project need to happen in what order, and you can start to understand the dependencies each component has on the others.

The table below indicates the four stages of renovation and the components that make up each stage. In the following section, I'll go into more detail on each component, including the dependencies it has on other components and the average time frame it will take to complete each component as part of a typical renovation.

STAGE 1: IMMEDIATE CONCERNS	STAGE 2: ROUGH WORK	STAGE 3: UNFINISHED WORK	STAGE 4: FINISH WORK
EXTERIOR/INTERIOR:	EXTERIOR:	EXTERIOR:	EXTERIOR:
1. SURVEYS, PLANS, PERMITS	9. SITE PREP/CONCRETE	21. DECKS/PORCHES	29. EXTERIOR PAINT
2. DUMPSTER/PORTA POTTY	10. EXTERIOR FRAMING	22. GARAGE	30. LANDSCAPING
3. FOUNDATION REPAIR	11. WINDOWS	INTERIOR:	INTERIOR:
4. WATERPROOFING	12. SIDING/TRIM	23. FIREPLACE	31. INTERIOR PAINT
5. MOLD REMEDIATION	13. ROOF	24. INSULATION	32. CABINETS/COUNTERTOPS
6. TERMITE/PEST CONTROL	14. GUTTERS/SOFFIT/FASCIA	25. INSULATION INSPECTION	33. FINISH ELECTRICAL
7. TREE REMOVAL/GRADING	INTERIOR:	26. SHEETROCK	34. FINISH PLUMBING
8. SEPTIC	15. DEMO	27. DOORS	35. FINISH HVAC
	16. FRAMING/SUBFLOOR	28. CARPENTRY/TRIM	36. FLOORING
	17. ROUGH ELECTRICAL		37. TILE
	18. ROUGH PLUMBING		38. APPLIANCES
	19. ROUGH HVAC		39. MISC/PUNCH
	20. ROUGH INSPECTIONS		40. FINAL INSPECTIONS

Scheduling Components

Stage 1: Immediate Concerns

The first set of tasks you'll want to tackle are those things that will keep your rehab from moving forward and those things that present immediate threat of additional damage or cost to your property. These items should be tackled immediately upon starting renovations, and except in rare circumstances, these items should be completed before moving on to any components in Stage 2.

1. SURVEYS, PLANS, AND PERMITS

If you're going to need any architectural plans, drawings, surveys, or designs, now is the time to have them completed. And, if you're going to need permits from the city, county, or local authority, you'll want to get those issued prior to beginning any other work on the property. If you start work on the property without the proper permits, you risk getting your project shut down and getting fined.

- **Dependencies:** You likely won't be able to pull permits until you have closed on the purchase of your property. The permit office may require proof of ownership prior to issuing permits.
- **Time frame:** Between one day and six months. Drawings and plans can take weeks or months to complete for a complex project, and some local building authorities can take weeks or months to review plans and issue permits. Talk to your GC and local building department to get an idea of how long the process is likely to take for your specific project.

2. DUMPSTER AND PORTA POTTY

Once you have the necessary permits in hand, if you plan to be doing any significant amount of cleanup or cleanout, it's time to get a dumpster delivered. And if you expect that you won't have usable toilets for your contractors, get a porta potty delivered onsite to ensure that your contractors don't need to leave the job every time they need to go to the bathroom.

- **Dependencies:** None.
- **Time frame:** Most dumpster and porta potty companies can arrange delivery within 24 hours and will deliver within a few hour time frame.

3. FOUNDATION REPAIR

Even when done correctly, foundation repair has the potential to cause damage to other parts of the structure. For example, leveling the house can damage sheetrock or even crack framing members; and doors will often need to be re-hung after foundation work. Also, foundation issues can cause safety concerns for those in and around the property. For those reasons, any structural work should be done at the beginning of the project.

- **Dependencies:** Foundation work shouldn't be initiated until the property has been evaluated by a licensed structural engineer and all permits have been issued.
- **Time frame:** Depending on the scope of the work, it could be anywhere from a couple of hours to several weeks or more.

4. WATERPROOFING

If you have a water intrusion or moisture problem in your house, now is the time to fix it. Water is one of the biggest threats to a property, and the longer the problem lingers, the more you will spend in remediation and cleanup. Waterproofing could be as simple as repairing openings in the roof or siding; or could be as complicated as excavating around foundation walls and sealing them around the exterior of the structure.

- **Dependencies:** None.
- **Time frame:** One to five days, depending on the problem and the scope of the solution.

5. MOLD REMEDIATION

Once any waterproofing has been completed and water intrusion has been stopped, it's time to clean up any mold that may have developed from past water problems. A licensed mold remediation company can remove damaged materials and sheetrock, remediate the remaining mold, and dehumidify the problem areas to prevent mold from continuing to grow.

- **Dependencies:** Waterproofing must be completed prior to mold remediation.
- **Time frame:** Two to ten days, depending on the scope of the problem, the level of humidity, and the remediation techniques employed.

6. TERMITE AND PEST CONTROL

If your house has termites, rats, mice, or any other infestation, you'll need to get rid of them prior to starting your rehab; otherwise, you'll be fixing problems while the little critters are just recreating them. Anything from termites to ants to roaches to rats to bats can be handled by a local pest control company in just a few hours.

- **Dependencies:** None.
- **Time frame:** Less than one day.

7. TREE REMOVAL AND GRADING

We're still in the "remove all possible catastrophes" phase of the project, so if there are any dead trees on the property that might be in danger of falling on your house, or if there is any major grading that needs to be done to control water drainage, you should get a good heavy equipment landscaping company to take care of the job.

- **Dependencies:** None.

- **Time frame:** One or two days.

8. SEPTIC
If your property has septic issues, get them addressed and corrected prior to completing any plumbing work on the interior or any landscaping on the exterior, as septic work can impact both.
- **Dependencies:** None.
- **Time frame:** One to five days.

Stage 2: Rough Work
Once all the plans and permits are issued and all major threats to the integrity of the property are mitigated, it's time to move on to the "rough" components of the renovation. On the interior of the property, "rough" generally refers to the framing and any components within the walls; on the exterior, I use the term "rough" to denote any work required to complete an addition and those parts of the structure that are integral in ensuring that the interior of the property is protected from the elements.

9. SITE PREP AND CONCRETE
If you'll be doing an addition to the property, the first step will be to prepare the site for the new structure and pour (or lay) your new foundation. While you're dealing with the concrete for the new foundation, now is a great time to deal with any other concrete issues, including replacing steps or walkways, or pouring footers for decks or other structures.
- **Dependencies:** If you are pouring a new foundation, you will likely need a building inspection prior to moving on to the next component.
- **Time frame:** One to five days, depending on scope and weather conditions.

10. EXTERIOR FRAMING
If you'll be doing any exterior framing, tackle that next. The most common circumstances in which you'll be doing exterior framing will be when putting on an addition or when repairing or retrofitting existing framing; for example, repairing termite damage or installing doors or windows that didn't previously exist.
- **Dependencies:** If you're putting on an addition, you'll need your foundation work to be completed and inspected prior to framing. If you

are repairing or adding new exterior framing, you will likely need a building inspection prior to moving on to the next component.

- **Time frame:** One day to two weeks, depending on scope.

11. WINDOWS

Windows should be installed after the framing is complete (your framing should have accounted for any window work that needed to be done) but before siding and trim. Siding and trim needs to be installed around the new windows, so you'll want your windows in place before that work is started. Also keep in mind that windows can take several weeks to manufacture and be delivered, so order early if you need new windows.

- **Dependencies:** Windows should be done *after* framing and *before* siding and trim.
- **Time frame:** One or two days, though keep in mind there will be long lead times for window manufacturing.

12. SIDING AND TRIM

Once the framing is done and windows are installed, you can repair or replace your siding. For a new addition or a complete re-siding of the house, you'll want to install your sheathing and house wrap first, then your siding and then your trim.

- **Dependencies:** Siding and trim should be completed after framing and windows are installed.
- **Time frame:** One day to three weeks, depending on scope of work. If the entire house is being re-sided, you should expect the work to take at least a week, and closer to two or three weeks.

13. ROOF

If you're putting on an addition, the roof installation will take place after the framing and siding; if you're retrofitting an existing roof (repairing or replacing), this work can be done pretty much any time during the rough exterior work. One thing to keep in mind: You won't want to do any other exterior work at the same time as the roofing, as roofers will be throwing debris to the ground, which can endanger other contractors working around the house.

- **Dependencies:** Depending on your jurisdiction and the scope of work, you may need a building inspection after completing your roofing work.

- **Time frame:** One to three days to replace a roof.

14. GUTTERS AND SOFFIT AND FASCIA BOARDS

Once the integrity of the roof is ensured, it's time to make sure the gutters and downspouts are in good condition and are appropriately transporting water off the roof and away from the property. Because the gutters are attached to the soffit and fascia boards, those should be repaired at the same time as the gutters.

- **Dependencies:** Wait until roof is repaired or replaced.
- **Time frame:** One to two days.

15. INTERIOR DEMO

On the interior of the property, the first task after dealing with all the immediate concerns is to do demo. This may involve removing flooring, old cabinets and countertops, old light fixtures, old appliances, plumbing fixtures, water heater, and any other components that will be replaced during the renovation. It's best to demo everything at once, as you'll find that your dumpster will fill up quickly and you'll want to get the majority of trash into the dumpster as quickly as possible before it fills up.

- **Dependencies:** None.
- **Time frame:** One or two days.

16. INTERIOR FRAMING AND SUBFLOOR

Once demo is complete, the first order of business on the interior of the house will be the framing and any subfloor carpentry. This includes building walls, securing floors, and repairing damage to existing framing—for example, from termites or poor construction. Any load-bearing framing members should have been designed by a structural engineer and should be built based on the approved drawings and plans.

- **Dependencies:** None.
- **Time frame:** One day to one week, depending on scope.

17. ROUGH ELECTRICAL

Rough electrical includes things like replacing the panel, upgrading the service, replacing circuit breakers, running new wiring, and installing new outlet and switch boxes. You will want to do the rough electrical before moving on to other rough components, simply because the electrician may need to turn off the electricity to complete this portion of the work, and your other contractors may not be able to work without electricity.

- **Dependencies:** None.
- **Time frame:** One day to one week, depending on scope.

18. ROUGH PLUMBING

Once the rough electrical is completed and the power is restored, you'll want to do your rough plumbing. Rough plumbing will involve replacing the main line, if necessary, replacing any supply or drain lines, setting new tubs and showers, and perhaps replacing the water heater (though some plumbers will do this as part of the finish work). Again, the reason for bringing in the plumber before the other rough components is that the other contractors (especially the HVAC professional) may need water or gas to complete their work.

- **Dependencies:** May need working electrical.
- **Time frame:** One day to one week, depending on scope.

19. ROUGH HVAC

Once the power is restored and water and gas are available, you can bring in your HVAC company to repair or replace ductwork, install a new furnace, and perhaps install a new A/C condenser (though some HVAC companies will do this as part of the finish work). I like to have my HVAC company complete as much as possible during the rough work, especially in the winter and summer. If the HVAC system is working, my other contractors can work in comfortable conditions.

- **Dependencies:** Will need working electrical and may need working gas.
- **Time frame:** One to three days, depending on scope.

20. ROUGH INSPECTIONS

Depending on the scope of the interior renovations, you may need one or more inspections during the rough stage of work. Specifically, you may need a rough framing inspection, a rough electrical inspection, a rough plumbing inspection, and/or a rough HVAC inspection prior to moving on to Stage 3 of renovation.

- **Dependencies:** Inspections will require the completion of the associated rough work.
- **Time frame:** One to five days, depending on how your jurisdiction works.

Stage 3: Unfinished Work

Now that the major exterior components and the interior mechanicals are completed, it's time to start working on what I call the "unfinished work." On the exterior, this includes the decks and porches, and any work that needs to be done on the garage. In the interior, this includes everything required to get all the walls closed up and all the basic carpentry.

21. DECKS AND PORCHES

In the previous phase of exterior work, we did everything necessary to ensure that the structure was sound and there was no water or pest intrusion. Now it's time to focus on the exterior entryways and exit-ways. This includes front and back decks and porches. Any concrete work was likely done back in Step #9, so at this time, you're probably focused strictly on carpentry. One thing to keep in mind: You'll want to ensure that whoever is working on the interior still has access, so don't tear out all the entryways at once.

- **Dependencies:** None.
- **Time frame:** One day to one week.

22. GARAGE

If you need to replace any garage doors or garage door openers, install any insulation, sheetrock, or firewalls, or do any carpentry to finish off a garage space, now's the time. We'll be doing all the insulation and sheetrock work on the interior during this phase, so the same contractors should focus on the garage at the same time.

- **Dependencies:** None.
- **Time frame:** One day to one week.

23. FIREPLACE

If your fireplace needs to be cleaned or repaired, it's best to do this early in the process. While there's usually no reason why this work can't be done later in the renovation, it can be a dirty job, and once you start putting your house back together, you'd prefer it to get cleaner, not dirtier. Also, in some cases, to do work on the fireplace will require some sheetrock to be removed, and you'll want this work to be complete before you start fixing sheetrock.

- **Dependencies:** None.
- **Time frame:** One or two days, depending on scope.

24. INSULATION

If you have exterior walls that are opened up, you need to ensure that they are insulated properly. Oftentimes, your sheetrock crew can also do some basic insulation; but if it's a major job, you'll want a dedicated insulation company that can get the job done quickly and most likely for less money than a non-specialty contractor.

- **Dependencies:** Completed framing and mechanical inspections.
- **Time frame:** One or two days.

25. INSULATION INSPECTION

Most jurisdictions will require a separate insulation inspection after the insulation is put in and before the walls are closed up. Make sure that you schedule the extra time between insulation and sheetrock to cover this inspection, especially if your sheetrock crew will be doing the insulation—they'll need to know that they can't just move ahead to sheetrock once the insulation is done.

- **Dependencies:** Insulation complete.
- **Time frame:** One day to one week, depending on jurisdiction.

26. SHEETROCK

Once you've had your insulation inspection, it's time to close up the walls. Hopefully, your sheetrock professionals have already gotten the materials on site. If it's a large sheetrock job, they probably had to have special equipment to deliver and place the sheetrock. Depending on the temperature, the humidity and other factors, sheetrock times can vary greatly. A small job may be able to be completed in two days while a large job with unfavorable temperatures or humidity conditions could take up to two weeks or more. This is one part of the construction where having a specialty crew will save you lots of time—a good sheetrock crew will complete a large job in much less time than a handyman who installs sheetrock or a typical painting crew that does some sheetrock work.

- **Dependencies:** Passed insulation inspection.
- **Time frame:** Two days to two weeks, depending on size of job and temperature and humidity conditions.

27. DOORS

Once the sheetrock is completed (hung, taped, mudded, and sanded), your handyman or carpenters will hang all the doors. A good carpenter can hang a door in 20 minutes; a not-so-skilled handyman can take an hour or two. So, the time it takes to hang your doors will vary based on how many you have to hang and the proficiency of your contractor doing the work.

- **Dependencies:** None.
- **Time frame:** One or two days.

28. CARPENTRY AND TRIM

Once the doors are in, your carpenter can move on to trim-out. This will include all the door and window casings, baseboard installation, any cosmetic trim (columns, custom wood-work), building a fireplace mantle, etc. To install all new trim in a typical single-family house can take up to a week, so make sure you plan accordingly.

- **Dependencies:** None.
- **Time frame:** One day to one week.

Stage 4: Finish Work

We're now getting to the fun part of the project. The house is finally starting to look like a house again, and now it's time for all the finish work. These are the things that are referred to as the "cosmetics," and consist of everything from paint to flooring to cabinets to fixtures, and everything else that makes your house look custom to your tastes. If you're doing a small rehab, it's quite possible that your entire renovation is limited to work in this stage, and this is the part of the project where things can either move very quickly (if you schedule well) or can drag on for a long time (if you don't).

29. EXTERIOR PAINT

If you have a good paint crew, they're going to tackle interior and exterior paint at the same time. And they will want the run of the house while they're doing their job. I try to never schedule any other contractors while my painters are working on the exterior or the interior of the house. Painting can take a while, and it's messy; and by allowing my painters to have the house to themselves, I find that the entire process goes much faster and more smoothly.

- **Dependencies:** You don't want to schedule any other contractors while the painters are working on or in the house.
- **Time frame:** Two to five days, depending on whether the painters are focused on the exterior or are completing the interior at the same time.

30. LANDSCAPING

Some rehabbers like to do the landscaping at the beginning of the project. In certain situations, this can be a good idea. For example, when the yard looks so bad that the neighbors or building inspectors are complaining, or when you're trying to pre-sell the property and you want the curb appeal to be great as soon as possible. That said, in most situations, I prefer to do the landscaping at the end, for several reasons. First, you won't have to worry about other contractors messing up the landscaping that was already completed. And second, if you have a long project, any landscaping that was done at the beginning may already start to look overgrown again. For these reasons, I prefer to do landscaping as one of the final rehab tasks.

- **Dependencies:** Everything else on the exterior of the house should be done.
- **Time frame:** One day to one week.

31. INTERIOR PAINT

When it comes to interior paint, cabinets, countertops, and flooring, every rehabber has their preferred order in which to complete things. Personally, I've found that painting first is more optimal in a lot of ways than painting later in the process. The downside is that you'll have to have the painters come back to do touch-up work after the rest of the finishes are complete, but the upside is that you won't have to worry about getting paint all over your new cabinets, floors, or fixtures. It's a worthwhile trade-off in my opinion and this is how we've done things for several years now. Also, as mentioned earlier in Step #29, you are going to want to give your painters the run of the house while they are completing their work.

- **Dependencies:** None.
- **Time frame:** One day to one week, depending on whether the painters are focused on the interior or are completing the exterior at the same time.

32. CABINETS AND COUNTERTOPS

Once the painting is completed, it's time to get your cabinets installed. This should include your kitchen cabinets as well as your bathroom vanities and any other cabinetry going into the house. If you're using laminate countertops or pre-molded countertops, those will be installed at the same time as your cabinets. If you're getting custom stone countertops (granite, for example), cabinets need to be installed before you can get the countertops "templated." Once the template is complete, it will take one to three weeks until the cabinets are ready to be installed; in these situations, you'll want to move forward with the rest of the project and then tackle countertop installation when the countertops are ready. Keep in mind that until the countertops are installed, you won't be able to complete final plumbing and may not be able to complete final electrical, so be prepared to have your plumber and/or electrician come back later in the project to handle these final details.

- **Dependencies:** None.
- **Time frame:** One or two days.

33. FINISH ELECTRICAL

Once the paint is done and the cabinets are installed, I'll move forward with the finish electrical, plumbing, and HVAC work. For electrical finish, all lights and fans will be installed, all outlets, switches, and plates will be replaced and, the garbage disposal will be installed.

- **Dependencies:** Can be done simultaneously with plumbing and HVAC finish work.
- **Time frame:** One to three days.

34. FINISH PLUMBING

While finish electrical is being done, you can also be tackling finish plumbing. This includes installation of the sinks, faucets, shower/tub hardware, etc.

- **Dependencies:** Can be done simultaneously with electrical and HVAC finish work.
- **Time frame:** One to three days.

35. FINISH HVAC

While the finish electrical and plumbing are going on, your HVAC company can be completing all the final HVAC work, including installing new registers/returns and installing the condenser and/or furnace if this wasn't done during the rough HVAC portion of the job.

- **Dependencies:** Can be done simultaneously with electrical and plumbing finish work.
- **Time frame:** One or two days.

36. FLOORING

I like to save flooring for the end of the project. This is because contractors are sometimes very messy (including their shoes) and having lots of foot traffic through the property after the flooring is installed can make the new flooring look old. By putting in flooring at the end, there's less chance of the new flooring getting destroyed or needing to be cleaned again before buyers start coming through the house.

- **Dependencies:** I prefer to do flooring as close to the end of the project as possible.
- **Time frame:** One to three days.

37. TILE

There are several places around the house where you may need to do custom tile work. If you are tiling a shower, this was probably done as part of Step #18 (rough plumbing), but everything else will be done towards the end of the project. This includes tile floors, tile surround around bathtubs, a backsplash above the kitchen countertops, and tile around a fireplace or on a fireplace hearth. Assuming you'll be using a specialty tile contractor, you'll want to get him or her to do all the custom tile work at once, to avoid having to pay him or her to come back several times.

- **Dependencies:** Generally done towards the end of the project.
- **Time frame:** One to three days.

38. APPLIANCES

Appliances should be installed after the kitchen floors are done, after the cabinets and countertops are installed, and towards the end of the project where they are less likely to get dinged up or even stolen. You may need your plumber to install your dishwasher, fridge (water line) and/or gas stove, in which case there was nothing wrong with getting the appliances installed during finish plumbing; just make sure that your flooring is down prior to the appliances going in, as you can't easily move a dishwasher or fridge once it's installed.

- **Dependencies:** Should be completed after kitchen flooring, kitchen cabinets, and countertops.
- **Time frame:** Less than one day.

39. MISCELLANEOUS/PUNCH LIST

Once everything is substantially completed, you'll want to do a thorough walk-through and inspection of the property. You can either do this on your own, with your GC, or with your subs, whichever you prefer. Your goal will be to identify everything that wasn't completed (or completed properly) during the rehab and get it fixed. This is the point where you'll want your painters to come back to repair any sheetrock that got dinged and touch up the paint where necessary.

- **Dependencies:** After your walk-through and inspection.
- **Time frame:** One to three days.

40. FINAL INSPECTIONS

After you and your contractors have verified that everything was properly completed during the rehab, it's time to get your final building inspections completed. This will likely include final electrical, plumbing, HVAC, and deck inspections. If all is good, the building department should issue your certificate of occupancy ("CO"), and you'll be ready to list your house for sale.

- **Dependencies:** All renovation work complete.
- **Time frame:** One day to one week, depending on jurisdiction.

Scheduling Rules of Thumb

After several years of scheduling projects and learning the hard way what does and doesn't work, I want to provide you some basic rules of thumb that I use when creating a renovation schedule. These may or may not work for you, but they certainly work for us.

1. Do as much work as possible before the renovation starts. A lot of investors consider the project started the day they purchase the property. I like to start renovations the day we purchase the property (or the day after), so I try to get as much of the preliminary work out of the way before I even close on the purchase. This can include architectural drawings, cabinet measurements, termite inspections, and mold inspections. While I won't order materials until we own the house (that's an expensive mistake if the house doesn't close for some reason), I will often order anything that has a long lead time for delivery.

2. Pack in as much work in the first week as possible. A lot of what a good rehabber does is psychological, especially when it comes to managing your contractors. If you want them to feel a sense of urgency on the project, you need to project that sense of urgency to them. A good way to do this is to have as much activity going on at the property the first week of work as possible. This tells your contractors that you're serious about getting stuff done and will encourage them to push through the project.

3. Schedule your renovation to the day, not the week. Many rehabbers will create a schedule that lays out what they want to accomplish on a week-to-week basis. I prefer to lay out my schedule on a day-to-day basis, for three reasons.

First, as I mentioned earlier, it gives my contractors a sense of urgency. They realize they can't put things off to the end of the week, like they do with a weekly schedule.

Second, if you slip a task on a weekly schedule, you've now slipped a week; but if you slip a task on a daily schedule, you may have only slipped one or two days.

Lastly, scheduling to the day (and keeping the schedule updated when things slip or change) ensures that your contractors know when they are expected to be on site and can never use ambiguity in the schedule as an excuse for not showing up.

4. Group your inspections together. I like to pack as many building inspections together at once as possible. For example, I'll wait for all of my rough work to be done, and then order my rough electrical, rough plumbing, and rough HVAC at the same time (and may do the final framing inspection the same day as well). The reason for this is that inspections are disruptive, and contractors can waste a lot of time sitting around waiting for the inspector. I'd rather get it all done at once to minimize the disruption and the waiting.

5. Finish the exterior of the property as quickly as possible. While you may not be trying to sell your house before it's completed, generating interest and anticipation is always a good thing. Some rehabbers will spread out their exterior repairs over the duration of the project (exterior repairs generally take less time than interior repairs), and some will put off the exterior repairs to the end, preferring to focus on the interior. Personally, I'll try to knock out the exterior work in the first week or two, which will get the neighbors talking and may also get my phone ringing (we like to put a "COMING SOON!" sign with our phone number when the project starts).

6. Wait as long as possible to install your flooring. Perhaps I'm more anal than others (no doubt I am), but I really, really, really hate putting in new flooring and then having my contractors trample all over it with their dirty shoes and grimy tools. I will usually install all the flooring the last week of the project, and very often the last day of the project. Once the flooring is in, I keep strict control of the house, and ensure that anyone entering knows to take off their shoes and wipe their feet.

7. Expect the last 10 percent of the project to take a long time. One of the biggest takeaways for many first-time flippers is how long it takes to complete the final renovation punch list. These final details can often take a week or more, even though each individual item should be quick to complete. Make sure you schedule plenty of time at the end of the project to complete your punch list.

Schedule: The Demo House

In the previous two chapters, we used The Demo House as an example of how to create a scope of work and how to estimate a budget. Earlier in this chapter, I discussed the methodology for creating a schedule. Next, I use this methodology to create a hypothetical schedule for The Demo House. While this schedule may seem jam-packed, this is the schedule I would implement if this were a real house I was undertaking.

For anyone working on their first or second project, this schedule would extend out a few more weeks, but I wanted to give you an idea of what can be packed into a six-week project when planned efficiently.

Note that for the schedule on the following pages, I assume there was some work done upfront, including all the architectural plans, cabinet measuring, and termite inspections.

WEEK	AREA	CONTRACTOR	START	DAYS	TASK
1	GENERAL	GC	M	1	DAY 1: PERMIT FILING/PERMITS
	EXTERIOR	ME	M	1	DAY 1: DUMPSTER DELIVERED
		ME	M	1	DAY 1: PORTA POTTY DELIVERED
		TERMITE	M	1	TERMITE TREATMENTS
		ROOFER	M	1	ROOF MAINTENANCE
		ROOFER	TU	1	GUTTERS/SOFFIT/FASCIA
					CLEAN GUTTERS

WEEK	AREA	CONTRACTOR	START	DAYS	TASK
1					REPLACE 15' OF GUTTER
					REPLACE 10' OF SOFFIT
		LANDSCAPER	M	2	LANDSCAPING:
					MOW LAWN
					TRIM BUSHES
		LANDSCAPER	TU	2	TREE WORK:
					TRIM OAK TREE
					REMOVE TREES
		GARAGE PROFESSIONAL	TU	1	GARAGE:
					REPLACE GARAGE DOORS
					REPLACE OPENER
	INTERIOR	DEMO CREW	M	1	DEMO
		CARPENTER	M	3	FRAME BASEMENT
		ELECTRICIAN	TH	2	ROUGH ELECTRICAL (BASEMENT):
					INSTALL NEW CIRCUIT
					INSTALL NEW OUTLET BOXES
					INSTALL NEW SWITCH BOX
					INSTALL CAN LIGHTS
		PLUMBER	TU	3	ROUGH PLUMBING:
					REPLACE PRV
					REPLACE WATER HEATER
					INSTALL TUB
					FIX LEAK

WEEK	AREA	CONTRACTOR	START	DAYS	TASK
1		HVAC	TU	2	ROUGH HVAC:
					REPAIR DUCTWORK
					FURNACE MAINTENANCE
					REPLACE COMPRESSOR/COIL
2	EXTERIOR	PAINTER	M	1	REPLACE 100 SF OF SIDING
		PAINTER	M	1	PRESSURE WASH
		PAINTER	TU	4	PAINT EXTERIOR
	INTERIOR	GC	M	1	INSPECTIONS:
					ROUGH ELECTRICAL
					ROUGH PLUMBING
					ROUGH HVAC
					FRAMING
		CARPENTER	TU	1	INSTALL INSULATION IN BASEMENT
		GC	W	1	INSULATION INSPECTION
		CARPENTER	W	3	CARPENTRY:
					INSTALL EXTERIOR DOORS
					INSTALL INTERIOR DOORS
					REPLACE WINDOWS
3	EXTERIOR	CARPENTER	M	4	BUILD DECK
	INTERIOR	SHEETROCKER	M	5	PATCH SHEETROCK IN LIVING ROOM
					SHEETROCK BASEMENT
4		INSULATION	M	1	BLOWN INSULATION IN ATTIC

WEEK	AREA	CONTRACTOR	START	DAYS	TASK
4	INTERIOR	PAINTER	M	4	PAINT INTERIOR
		CABINET INSTALLER	F	1	CABINETS:
					INSTALL KITCHEN CABINETS
					INSTALL VANITIES
					INSTALL VANITY TOPS
5	INTERIOR	GRANITE INSTALLER	M	1	TEMPLATE FOR KITCHEN GRANITE
		ELECTRICIAN	M	5	FINISH ELECTRICAL:
					UPGRADE OUTLETS TO GFCI
					INSTALL ALL LIGHTS
					INSTALL ALL FANS
					TRIM OUT CANS
					REPLACE ALL OUTLETS/ SWITCHES
		PLUMBER	M	5	FINISH PLUMBING:
					INSTALL VANITY SINKS
					INSTALL BATHROOM FAUCETS
					REPLACE TUB/SHOWER HW
					INSTALL TOILETS
					INSTALL DISHWASHER
		CARPENTER	M	2	INSTALL TRIM (OTHER THAN HARDWOODS)
6	INTERIOR	GRANITE INSTALLER	M	1	INSTALL GRANITE

WEEK	AREA	CONTRACTOR	START	DAYS	TASK
5		PLUMBER	TU	1	FINISH PLUMBING:
					HOOK UP KITCHEN SINK DRAIN
					INSTALL KITCHEN FAUCET
		CARPET INSTALLER	M	1	INSTALL CARPET/VINYL
6		HARDWOOD		3	HARDWOOD INSTALLATION & FINISH:
			TU		INSTALL HARDWOOD
			W		STAIN HARDWOOD
			TH		FINAL COAT OF FINISH
		CARPENTER	F	1	BASEBOARDS/MOLDING FOR HARDWOODS
		HANDYMAN	F	1	PUNCH LIST:
					WALK-THROUGH REPAIRS
					INSTALL APPLIANCES
		GC	F	1	FINAL INSPECTIONS:
					DECK INSPECTION
					FINAL ELECTRICAL
					FINAL PLUMBING
					FINAL HVAC
					CERTIFICATE OF OCCUPANCY

CHAPTER 15
HIRING CONTRACTORS

You have your SOW, you have your budget, and you've put together a first pass at the schedule. Now it's time to start building another team. This is the crew of contractors whom you will entrust to turn your investment into something you can sell for a nice, big profit.

In down real estate markets (like the market most of us saw between 2008 and 2012), finding and managing good contractors is easy. The lack of demand for construction work means that only the great contractors survived the downturn with their businesses intact—if you find any random carpenter or painter who is making money in a down real estate market, and it's likely they have good business acumen, know their trade, are reliable, and are fairly priced.

When I started in this business in 2008, during the Great Recession, I barely needed to keep an eye on my contractors. I never had to wonder if my contractors were actually working when they said they were working, and I never worried that they were going to charge me for work that didn't really need to be done. Most importantly, they cared about future business, so it wasn't hard to build long-term relationships that lasted years—and dozens of projects.

But things change quickly when the real estate market changes. Many contractors are opportunistic, and when there is a lot of demand for construction professionals, finding a skilled and trustworthy crew of contractors is by far the most difficult part of this business. Think about it: It doesn't take much to buy some tools and call yourself a contractor, so for many people who don't have the skills to do anything else, when demand is high and there is easy money to be made, they decide to start swinging a hammer. As you can imagine, this is especially true for trades that don't require much formal training or licensing, like painters, carpenters, and handymen.

Long story short, when the real estate market is hot, contractors will give you headaches. They won't show up when they say they will, they will come and go as they please, and the really bad ones will do their best to separate you from your hard-earned cash without completing the job. Unless you enjoy herding cats—the kind of cats looking to rip you off and take advantage of you—managing contractors is likely going to be the least fun part of this business for you.

Even in a market where good contractors were plentiful, it took me about two years before I started to figure out what to look for in a reliable contractor, how to find one, and how to keep them motivated and working hard.

In the following pages, hopefully I can teach you some of what took me years to learn. While there's no doubt you'll find yourself in the midst of bad contractors at some—or many—points in your rehabbing career, hopefully you'll be able to recognize them more quickly than I first could, and you'll be prepared to act to rectify the situation.

The Spectrum of Contractors

Contractors run the gamut from jack-of-all-trade types (handymen) to high-end specialized artisans, and everything in between. I remember on my first flip, when I spent weeks interviewing contractors and getting bids. Strangely, I was getting bids ranging from $18,000 all the way up to $70,000 for the exact same scope of work! I never imagined I would see such a wide range of bids, and I couldn't figure out what was going on. Especially considering that I was only getting bids on labor costs, not materials, which I specified and priced separately.

This is what I soon realized:

There are several different types of contractors and contracting services, and each is unique in what they have to offer and what you'll pay. If I had to categorize them, I would define three major types of contractor. The differences in these three categories of contractor account for the differences in price and have a large impact on the amount of work the investor will be required to contribute. As you might suspect, as you move from the more expensive contractor services to the less expensive contractor services, the amount of effort that you as the investor must contribute will increase proportionately.

Here are the three buckets of contractors you'll find:

1. General Contractors

The term "general contractor" is used in two ways, in my experience. From now on, I am going to differentiate "general contractor" from "General Contractor" (note the capitalization). A general contractor is someone who has the ability to tackle a lot of different aspects of a rehab project; most general contractors are good at carpentry, sheetrock, basic electrical, basic plumbing, basic HVAC, and other general areas of home renovation and rehab. This type of general contractor might be referred to as a "handyman," though if he is licensed and highly experienced, he's likely a lot more than just that.

When I use the term General Contractor (or "GC"), I am referring to someone who has all the skills of a general contractor, but also manages all the aspects of the renovation that he doesn't actually execute himself. A GC will often hire subs (contractors with specific skill sets) to come in to handle the work that he is either not skilled enough to complete or too busy to complete. For example, GCs will often hire plumbers, electricians, roofers, and foundation experts to cover those aspects that require specific expertise.

Not only does a GC hire the necessary subs, but he will often manage the schedule, the project budget, and all the payments as well (if you want him to). For big projects, the GC might spend all his time managing schedules, budgets, and subs, and therefore might not have time to do any of the work himself. The GC is also responsible for ensuring that his subs are properly licensed and insured, to protect you and your investment (as well as to protect himself).

As you can see, having a GC makes your job as an investor very easy; you hire one person, you pay only him, and everything just gets done. At least this is the theory; in actuality, there are plenty of bad GCs out there, and if your GC isn't any good, you may need to be very hands-on and manage him to make sure he's getting the job done, which dilutes his value tremendously.

The benefit of a good GC is obvious—he does your scheduling, budgeting, and management jobs for you. The downside to working with even the best GC is that he will charge you for all this extra work he does. If he hires a plumber for $1,000, he'll charge you $1,200 for that plumber's work, because he had to find, hire, manage, and take responsibility of the performance of the plumber. (Likewise with all the other sub-contractor trades.) The GC is also managing the schedule and ensuring that the project is on budget, so there will be extra overhead charges for that. In all, having a General Contractor manage your project can cost you an additional 10 percent to 30 percent on your rehab labor costs.

2. Turnkey (Specialty) Services

If you don't like the idea of paying someone to manage your schedules and hire subs for you, you can do this work yourself. But you still need to hire contractors to do the actual rehab work.

When hiring and managing your own contractors, you have a couple of options. The most common—and most reliable—is to hire specialty contractors who are licensed, insured, and can manage themselves and their team. If you don't know anyone, Google the specialty contractor you want, such as electrician or roofer, or go on a site like Angie's List.

Specialty contractors range from the big names such as Terminix (pest/termite) and Roto-Rooter (plumbing) to the 70-year-old local electrician who's been contracting for 50 years and now just does it to keep busy. There are thousands of these kinds of specialty contractors in your area, and they all have one thing in common: They hold the licensing credentials and insurance requirements mandated by the state for their specialty profession.

While these professionals may not be the cheapest—they spent a lot of time and effort getting the experience necessary to get their licenses and credentials and want to get paid for their efforts—they will get the job done without you having to "babysit" them or watch their every move. That said, you'll still have to call them, get estimates, schedule their time, and make sure they have access to the property and the information they need. These are the types of things that a General Contractor would normally do, and that you would be paying to have done for you if you used one.

One of the major drawbacks to working directly with specialty contractors is that *you* will be responsible for managing schedules and ensuring that the rehab progresses in the most optimal fashion.

For example, if you hire a painter to come to the house before the cabinet installer and the flooring professionals, you'll likely pay less for painting, as the painters don't have to spend as much time protecting the new materials from getting paint on them. If you do it the other way around—bring the painter in *after* the cabinets and floors are completed—you'll find that the rehab takes longer and is more expensive. While a GC will know these sorts of things and can keep a rehab moving along quickly, you might not, and getting that first-hand experience of having to re-sheetrock a wall because you had your sheetrock contractor work before your plumber can be both frustrating and expensive.

I would consider an experienced handyman to be part of this specialty contractor group. As I'll discuss later in this chapter, a good handyman may be the most important of all contractors in your arsenal.

3. Freelance Workers

The cheapest—but most time intensive for you—solution for getting a rehab done is to hire what I call "freelance workers." These are people who might have some experience in some aspects of rehab, but don't have enough expertise and experience that you should trust them to complete even individual parts of a project without management and constant supervision. Whereas a licensed (turnkey specialty) plumber can be trusted to hook up a faucet while you head to lunch, you would want to stick around to manage and instruct a freelance worker who was doing the same thing.

Freelance workers are often called "unskilled laborers," because while they work very hard, they don't have the expertise to know how to solve tough problems themselves. They'll look to you to do that, so you need to have the knowledge and expertise to solve those problems. For example, a freelance worker might be happy to install carpet or lay tile for you but may not know how; it would be up to you to demonstrate proper technique and then ensure that he is following it and getting the job done correctly. Even if he does know how to complete the job, it's unlikely that the result will look nearly as professional as his skilled counterpart.

Freelance workers are, by far, the cheapest labor costs for a rehab, but will require the most time, effort, expertise, and patience from you.

Many investors will choose a combination of these three types of contractors for their project. They may choose to hire a GC for the large projects that they couldn't handle themselves, and then use a combination of turnkey service contractors and freelance workers for the smaller projects. It's all a matter of balancing the cost, time, and effort required to get a job done.

The Value of a Great Handyman

Notwithstanding the three groups of contractors above, you should try to find a great handyman to help you out. A great handyman is the perfect combination of freelance worker with many of the skills of a turnkey specialist. He can do a lot of the stuff the turnkey specialist contractors can do, but at a fraction of the price. For example, you'd probably pay a plumber about $50 to replace a faucet and an electrician about $70 to replace a light fixture; a handyman would charge you about $30 for each of these items.

In fact, a handyman can do a lot of things, including basic plumbing, electrical, carpentry, painting, drywall, and flooring. Additionally, some handymen have been around the business for decades and can even help you with your rehab estimates and help you find great subs.

Just don't get into the habit of trying to use a handyman for things where you need a specialist. For example, no matter how good he is, you don't want your handyman to replace your roof or rewire your house (though many will say they can). And for things where the quality of finish is really important, like hardwood floor installation, you want to entrust the work to a seasoned professional who will be more attentive to detail.

Also, keep in mind that most handymen aren't going to be licensed in any trade and probably won't carry insurance. While the lack of license often isn't a big deal—assuming he won't be doing anything that requires a license in your state, such as permitted work—the lack of insurance creates a much bigger risk. If you don't require your handyman to get insurance, you are potentially setting yourself up for a lawsuit should he be injured on the job or should he injure someone else.

All the negatives aside, if you can find a great handyman who is reliable and trustworthy, he'll be worth his weight in gold.

Creating Your Rehab Team

Now that I've discussed the various tiers of contractors and the trade-offs you'll have dealing with different types of contractors, you're probably wondering how I manage my own rehabs and what I recommend for you as a new investor.

While I'm happy to recommend how I think you should do things and share how I do things, don't assume these are the best ways. Every rehabber is going to be in a different situation, and what's best and most beneficial for one investor may not be for another investor. For example, an investor who has a full-time job is going to require much more trustworthy and self-sufficient contractors than someone who has the time to be on site all day managing workers. Always consider what's best for you and your situation when deciding how to handle your rehabs, and don't let anyone tell you what you should or shouldn't be doing.

How I Recommend You Manage Your Rehabs

If you've never managed a rehab before, you have a lot more to learn than you think. Between day-to-day management, budgeting, scheduling, and dealing with any required local inspectors, there are a lot of things that can go wrong; and even when they don't go wrong, they rarely go optimally. While you could jump in with both feet and try to do everything yourself the first time out, if you go this route, be prepared for your project to take longer than expected and likely cost more than you planned.

Unless you have some renovation management experience, for your first few renovations, my recommendation would be to bring in a GC who is accustomed to working with investors. There are two ways that you can structure the financial arrangement between you and your GC:

FIXED-PRICE BID

The most common financial arrangement you'll have with your GC—and the one I highly recommend early on in your career—is to have the GC provide a fixed price upfront for all the work based on your detailed SOW. This price will cover all the subcontractor work, the GC's fees, and the permitting fees—basically a comprehensive price for the entire rehab. This price can be negotiated, of course, but once it's agreed, the GC should be willing to commit to the price and sign a contract agreeing to that price before work begins.

During the renovation, situations may arise where you'll want or need the GC to do additional work that you both agree on. When that happens, the GC will prepare a *change order*, which is a formal addition to the fixed-price contract that adds in the new work and the additional price that you will negotiate for the additional item(s).

Fixed price bids can be a double-edged sword. If the renovation is less costly than the GC estimated, you'll end up paying more than you could have; but if the renovation is costlier than the GC estimated, you'll end up getting a great deal. The best-case scenario is that the GC will provide an accurate estimate up front, creating a fair deal for both sides.

COST-PLUS PAYMENT

The other common financial relationship between investors and GCs is what's called "cost plus." The way this typically works is that the GC will do everything he does with the fixed-priced bid, but instead of giving you a price upfront for all the work, he simply passes on the costs of his subs and materials directly to you, with no markup. In addition, you'll pay a flat fee to the GC for his efforts—management, scheduling, and expertise. This is the GC's profit.

Using the cost-plus model is a great way to ensure that you don't over-pay a GC who tends to overestimate rehab costs or who adds a big mark-up to all his subcontractors and materials. On the other hand, you won't know the actual cost of the project until after the end, as the GC doesn't get invoices from his subcontractors until work is completed.

If you go the cost-plus route, I highly recommend you ask your GC to provide bids from his subcontractors *prior* to renovations beginning. This will ensure that the subcontractors don't try to increase their prices just because you'll be paying instead of the GC. The GC will have more leverage than you will if the price comes in high, and subcontractors are less likely to try to take advantage of your GC than to take advantage of you.

How I Manage My Rehabs

Given that I've completed over 150 renovations and have up to five going at any given time, many people are curious how I manage my projects.

Like I recommend you do, I went the GC route on my first several renovation projects, and it worked out pretty well. If I knew everything back then that I've been telling you here in this chapter, it would have worked out much better. Though, I didn't feel that I had enough control over my projects—I didn't pick the subs, I didn't make the schedule, and I didn't negotiate the prices for the work. Given my type-A personality, farming everything out to a GC didn't suit me. Don't get me wrong—doing it this way for the first several projects was a tremendous learning experience and allowed me to get my rehabs completed on schedule and on budget, but I was ready to take more control of my projects.

Unfortunately, even after several projects, I didn't have the construction experience necessary to be comfortable hiring and managing the subs directly, but I knew I needed more control. To give me that control, I broke my projects up into two areas, management and contracting, and structured my business in a way that allowed me the control I wanted without requiring me to be the construction expert.

Here's how I've managed most of my projects the past decade and how I still manage my projects to day:

MANAGEMENT

Every rehab is going to require some level of day-to-day management. As we discussed above, the two most common ways to handle management are to: (1) hire a GC, who in turn deals with all the management issues; or (2) manage the project yourself, in which case you are responsible for dealing with all the issues that pop up.

And, as we've discussed, the benefits of the GC route are that you won't need to be on site all day, every day to handle the issues; you won't have to hire and oversee the subs yourself; and you know that the person in charge has construction background and experience. The downsides to using a GC are that you'll pay more than if you manage the project yourself and you don't have nearly as much control over the subs and their prices.

I actually decided to go a third route for management that combines many of the benefits of a GC with the control of self-management: I hired a full-time project manager to be my eyes and ears for all my rehabs. My project manager's job is to essentially replace the GC: Interview contractors, get bids, negotiate prices, schedule work, verify that quality is maintained, ensure that we stay on budget, write checks for completed work, procure materials, and basically keep me informed about everything that I might need to know without me having to visit the property every day.

My project manager is probably just as expensive as a GC, but because I know and trust him, and because much of his salary is based on profit sharing, I can be sure that the right decisions are always being made for the project. While a GC is going to be interested in doing more work to generate more income, my project manager would rather save time and money, as he gets a percentage of any additional profits.

Also, because my project manager is only working on our projects, he is always accessible, and he knows how we do everything, right down to the paint colors we use and the materials we choose. My project manager is an extension of me, and in fact, most of my contractors consider *him* the boss, because he's the one they deal with on a daily basis.

I've had several project managers in several states, and they generally know as much about our business as I do. I can always trust them to make the right decisions every time there is an issue because, again, their goal is to maximize profits, part of which they keep. Because my project managers have authority to write checks and hire and fire contractors, the contractors we use have a lot of respect for them and treat them like the boss, which frees me up to focus on bigger business issues.

While the option of having a full-time project manager may not be feasible when you're first starting out, once you get a few rehabs under your belt and are working on more than one project at a time, you may find the hiring a full-time project manager costs about the same as hiring a GC on every project, but with many benefits over a GC.

CONTRACTORS

Because I no longer have a GC to provide all the subs for our jobs, I have the opportunity to hire the specific subs I want to handle the various aspects of our renovations.

One of the big decisions we've made that has made our lives much easier in this business is to hire much of our rehab work out to one company, which is responsible for most aspects of the renovations.

Specifically, they handle all of the following:
- Basic carpentry (handrails, decks, subfloor, doors, basic framing, and repairs)
- Painting (interior/exterior)
- Sheetrock repair and replacement
- Basic electrical
- Basic plumbing
- Installing carpet and vinyl
- Installing flooring trim
- Exterior repairs (siding replacement, soffits, fascia, trim)
- Pressure washing
- Gutters

They are essentially contractors who handle all aspects of the project that don't require state licensing, permits, or highly specific repair work.

Here is the list of other contractors that we bring in as needed:

- Licensed HVAC contractor
- Licensed plumber
- Licensed electrician
- Roofer
- Expert carpenter (for bigger/more intricate jobs)
- Cabinet supplier/installer
- Window company (supplier/installer)
- Countertop/tub refinisher
- Sheetrock installers (for very large jobs)
- Hardwood floor installer

For a typical project, our contractor crews will do about 75 percent of the work. They are the first on the job (they do demo), the last on the job (they do the punch list) and are there almost every day in between.

While the contracting crews have a scope of work for each job (and gets paid by the job), they know that their job is to make the house look perfect, whatever it takes. For example, if they're hanging drywall and notice that some framing has rotted or has termite damage and my project manager and I can't be reached, they won't wait around for us to tell them what to do—they will fix it, let us know about it at the earliest convenience, and, if it was more than a $50 fix or so, they charge it to us at the end. If it's a cheap fix, they may not even tell us about it until it comes up in conversation later. Also, if they notice something needs to be fixed that we didn't initially ask them to fix, they'll just do it, as they know it has to be done eventually.

Most people are probably thinking, "I wish I could find contractors who are willing to do more than necessary and will go out of their way to fix things they haven't been asked to fix!" In a hot market, employing a crew like this isn't cheap; we're paying as much for this crew of contractors as we'd pay for specialty contractors doing the same work. But, the benefit is that they are trustworthy and hardworking, and they make our lives much easier and less stressful.

Another nice thing about having a general crew who does most of the work is that you don't need to deal with a lot of scheduling issues. Not only do they know what to do and in what order, but there are always little nuances to scheduling that now take care of themselves. For example, if you repair sheetrock and paint early in the project, you will find that there's often a lot of touch-up needed after the flooring, cabinets, and the light fixtures go in. But if you hold off on repairing sheetrock and painting until later in the project, you need to be a lot more careful about not messing up the stuff you've already done.

If you're looking to go this route, don't hesitate to find a great general handyman with a large network. While our crew is several guys, we've achieved the same result with one carpenter who had a list of other contractors he could bring in to help and support him.

Most importantly, don't hesitate to go through 100 contractors to find three or four good ones. Don't settle for mediocre. If someone does a decent (but not spectacular) job on a project, it's tempting to keep him around as you know you'll at least get decent performance on future jobs; but I'd rather cut him loose and try to find someone who is better than decent.

Last thing I'll say on this topic: When you find a great contractor, treat them like gold. It's took us years to find a great group of subs, and all the effort that went into it was well worth it.

Finding Your Contractors

Even if you plan to use a GC for your first few projects, at some point you're going to find yourself looking for subcontractors on your own.

Here are my top six suggestions for finding great contractors:

1. **Recommendations from other investors.** The bulk of your contractors should come from other investors who are already successful in this business. These may be investors in your local network, investors you meet at local Real Estate Investors Association (REIA) meetings, or even investors you can network with over the internet on popular investor-focused websites. Successful investors have become successful in part because they've built strong teams of high quality, inexpensive contractors, and in many cases they're happy to share those contractors with other investors. Seek out these other successful investors and ask them for all their contractor recommendations.

2. **Recommendations from great contractors.** Something I've noticed in this business: Great contractors tend to know other great

contractors. This makes sense, of course—if you're in the service industry and are great at what you do, you're not going to want to tarnish your reputation by hanging out with those who will make you look bad. Additionally, a great contractor isn't going to want to risk his business relationship with you by referring someone who hurts your business. So, when you find a great contractor, make a point to ask about every other great contractor he knows. Even if you aren't currently looking for a particular trade, use it as an opportunity to build your list.

3. **Home Depot at 6:30 a.m.** If you want to find great contractors, hang out where they hang out. Most contractors spend time at the big box stores (Home Depot, Lowe's), but the really good contractors are there first thing in the morning. These are the contractors who have jobs pre-scheduled—they're not sitting by the phone all day waiting for a call—they're diligent and hard-working enough to get out of bed early, and they are efficient enough that they're buying supplies before the start of the job as opposed to having to leave the jobsite midday to make a materials run. When you see contractor trucks roll up to your local Home Depot or Lowe's at 6:30 a.m., start chatting up the workers, and exchange business cards.

4. **Well-run project sites:** Part of my job entails spending a decent amount of time in the car driving between houses. When I'm driving, I'm always on the lookout for houses undergoing renovation. If it looks like an investor job, I'll stop. I'll talk to the contractors and ask if they're working for an investor. If so, I'll ask if I can have a look around. If the quality looks good and the crew is working diligently, I'll start asking about their pricing or what they're charging for this job. In about ten minutes of looking around and chatting with the crew, I can get an idea of whether these are people I'd want on my jobsite or not. If so, I'll get their information and give them mine. I've actually found a lot of my long-term crew by this very method.

5. **Builder supply houses:** If you're looking for a skilled tradesman (electrician, plumber, HVAC), one of the best places to find them is where they buy their materials. And the good ones don't generally buy their stuff at the big box stores like Home Depot. Instead, they buy from local suppliers, as they know they'll get better prices and better service. So, if you want to find these good contractors, start

hanging out at the supply houses. Here's the catch—many of the busy contractors will just call in their orders, so you may not actually catch them at the store. But it's the busy ones you want to find, as they are the ones who are in demand. So, my recommendation is to introduce yourself to one or two of the employees in the sales department and ask them who they recommend. Some places have a policy not to give recommendations, in which case, you can ask who some of their bigger clients are instead; you'll get the same names even though you asked a different question.

6. **New home subdivisions.** When I started doing new construction, I came to the realization that builders tend to get the best contractor prices, especially when they're doing volume work and building lots of houses at once. Not to mention, builders are using licensed and insured contractors as well. These days, when I'm looking for contractors, I'll drive through subdivisions as they are being built out. In many cases, I'll see the contractors they're using just by looking at the trucks in the neighborhood; in other cases, I'll walk into the houses, introduce myself to the contractors and ask if they're looking for additional work. Sometimes you'll find that they work exclusively for the builder, but often they're either freelance contractors who will work for anyone, or they work exclusively for the builder but sneak side jobs on the weekends.

Despite how highly recommended a contractor may come, it's important to *always check references*. It's amazing how many rehabbers will ask contractors for references but will never actually check those references before hiring them! You don't necessarily need to interview past clients of the contractor, but at least take a look at the work that was done. For example, if your contractor is a painter or a roofer, it should be fairly easy to obtain a list of addresses the contractor worked on, and then just drive by the exterior of the house to see the quality of work.

Perhaps the contractor has work currently going on. (And if they don't, you need to wonder why not!) Will they allow you to stop by and check out the crew, check out the progress, and evaluate the safety precautions the crew is taking?

Worst case, if you have any doubts, you should call previous clients of the contractor. Ask them pointed questions about how well the contractor maintained the schedule, the budget, and the overall quality of the work.

Lastly, ask the client if they would hire the contractor again. The answer to this question will tell you everything you need to know.

Better, Faster, Cheaper

There's a popular saying in the technology industry:

"Better, Faster, Cheaper: Pick Two"

Basically, the idea was that you can build something at 1) higher quality, 2) in less time, or 3) for less money—but you can't do all three of those simultaneously. At best, you can optimize for two of them, in which case it was generally the third that would suffer. For example, when building a new piece of software, you can build it better and faster, but it will cost more to do so; or you can build it fast and cheap, but the quality will likely suffer.

This principle applies to many aspects of business and life and is certainly true when it comes to contractors and real estate renovation. While there are some contractors who churn out only high-quality work, some contractors who are tremendously efficient and always on schedule, and some very reasonably priced contractors, you won't normally find a contractor who is all three of these things. In fact, the "better, faster, cheaper: pick two" principle is very alive and well when it comes to contractors.

For that reason, I recommend determining up front which two of these three aspects of your renovation you are most concerned with, and then expect that you might need to compromise on the third. In my case, I'm unwilling to compromise on quality, and with my margins being relatively small on many of the houses I flip, I'm rarely willing to risk my budget. So, if I want to ensure that I have contractors focused on quality and price (better and cheaper), I must be willing to compromise on schedule (faster).

My project manager and my general contractors have some amazing qualities: They know construction and building codes in great detail, the GC's workers produce high quality results, and their prices are reasonable compared to other similarly qualified workers. But because we often have many projects going on at one time, my crew is often not very good at keeping on schedule. But I've decided upfront that I'm willing to trade that aspect of my projects knowing that I'm nearly always going to hit my budgets and that the results will be top-notch.

My suggestion to anyone new to this business is to decide up front which two of these three things are most important to you and focus your contractor selection toward optimizing those two things. Then be prepared to compromise on the third, as you're unlikely to find contractors who can deliver all three.

Your Contractor Paperwork

For anyone planning to get into this business (even as a hobby), let me recommend that you have a consistent contract regimen with every contractor you work with, regardless of whether it's a $500 project or a $50,000 project. The risks are the same, and the amount of effort to mitigate that risk is really not too great. With that in mind, here are the documents that I require every one of my contractors to sign before they start on a project:

IRS Form W-9

A W-9 is an IRS form that is used to collect information about your contractor (name, address, Social Security number, etc.) that can be used at the end of the year to create and issue tax forms to the contractor and to the IRS. Without the W-9, you risk not being able to get in contact with the contractor at the end of the year to provide him with a statement of earnings for the year. You also run the risk of having no proof of independent contractor relationship with the contractor and may end up paying payroll taxes for that contractor on any wages you paid him.

Some people figure that they'll be able to collect the contractor's information at some point in the future, but remember, a contractor may be just as happy if you can't file tax information about him, so it may actually be more difficult to collect this data after the contractor has completed your job. A W-9 only needs to be filled out once (and kept on file); it's best to have this filled out by the contractor prior to handing him his first check.

Independent Contractor Agreement

This is a big one and should be created and signed before each project begins and with each contractor you will be paying. The independent contractor agreement lays out the contractual relationship between you and the contractor. Besides containing all the details about the specific project at hand, it clarifies that the relationship between you and the contractor is **not** employer-employee, but instead an independent contractor relationship. This is very important, both from a legal and a tax perspective. From a legal perspective, it provides you some protection against things like workman's comp suits. And from a tax perspective, it will likely save you quite a bit of money in payroll taxes that you'd otherwise pay if the contractor were considered an employee.

Plus, as I mentioned, the independent contractor agreement lays out the specific contractual terms for the project at hand. For example, the contract specifies such things as:

- List of specific services to be performed.
- Compensation terms.
- Terms around who provides tools, materials, etc.
- Penalties assessed for missing deadlines.
- Insurance obligations.
- Description of how change orders are done.

This is the primary contractual document between you and your contractor(s) and may contain some or all of the following documentation pieces I discuss below.

Scope of Work

This document may be included as part of the independent contractor agreement or it may be a separate document referenced by the independent contractor agreement. The scope of work is what we put together in Chapter 12.

To protect yourself, the SOW should be as detailed as possible, and should even contain specific information about the materials to be used and where to procure them. If you ever go to court against this contractor for failure to complete his job, the judge will want to see the SOW and compare it to the job performed. The more specific the SOW is, the more likely the contractor will live up to expectations, and if it should ever go to court, the more likely you are to convince a judge that the job was not properly completed.

Payment Schedule

This document may also be included as part of the independent contractor agreement or it may be a separate document (and again, referenced by the independent contractor agreement). The payment schedule clearly defines the milestones the contractor needs to hit to get paid, and exactly how much he will get paid at each milestone. What the payment schedule looks like is up to you and your contractor, but suffice it to say, you should be looking to pay as little as possible until a substantial percentage of the job is complete (and of course, the contractor will likely want as much money as possible upfront and early in the project).

When you work with a contractor for the first time, you may find the need to have many payment milestones. For example, here is the payment schedule I try to use when I work with a contractor for the first time:

- Milestone #1: 10 percent paid when these documents are signed.
- Milestone #2: 20 percent paid after the first day of work is successfully completed.
- Milestone #3: 30 percent paid after half the work is completed.
- Milestone #4: 30 percent paid after substantial completion of the project.
- Milestone #5: 10 percent paid two weeks after substantial completion of the project.

Paying 30 percent at the beginning of the project generally appeases the contractor and withholding 40 percent until the end of the project usually encourages the contractor not to slack off or leave your project for another job. Certainly, after working with the same contractor on several jobs, you'll want to make things simpler by consolidating to just a couple milestones (if not a single milestone); perhaps 50 percent upfront and 50 percent at the end of the project.

Insurance and Indemnification Agreement

This form is used to ensure that the contractor provides a reasonable amount of insurance (both liability and worker's comp) for both himself and any of his subcontractors, employees, or agents. This form also obligates the contractor not to sue you for any actions that he or his crew might take. This is a document that ensures the contractor will take responsibility for his crew's actions and also will provide adequate insurance should there be an accident on the job site.

A lot of people will not use this particular document, but remember, all it takes is one lawsuit to put an end to your business and your savings.

Lien Waiver

A lien waiver is a document signed by the contractor at the end of the job stating that they have been paid everything due to them. By signing this document, they are agreeing not to file a mechanic's lien against your property. (A mechanic's lien is a claim made against your property's title and can keep you from being able to sell it until the lien is cleared.) Make sure that your contractor(s) sign a lien waiver prior to getting their last payment. And refuse to provide payment until the lien waiver is signed, especially if you don't have a good relationship with that contractor.

Other Documents to Collect

The documents above are the primary documents you need to have signed when working with any contractor. In addition to these documents, you should collect some important information from the contractor and keep it on file in case any legal issues arise later.

Other documents you could get a copy of include:

- Proof of license
- Proof of liability insurance
- Proof of workman's comp insurance
- References

Employee or Independent Contractor?

In this chapter, we've talked a lot about hiring people to work on your properties. But there is something very important to add to any discussion about those who do work for you: While it may be clear in your mind that each of these people is an independent contractor (IC) and not an employee, it's very important that the IRS agrees with you. If the IRS determines that the people who are doing work for you are actually employees, it could end up costing you dearly. Not just in terms of extra tax payments—which would amount to about 15 percent of the total amount paid in wages plus responsibility for unemployment wages—but also in terms of risk to your business.

For example, if a roofer working as an IC for one of your properties falls off the roof, they are responsible for their own medical costs. But if the courts determine that they were actually an employee at the time of the fall, you might be responsible for paying the medical costs, disability, and even potentially death benefits to the family!

So, what can you do to ensure that the IRS and the courts also recognize your workers as ICs and not employees? Keep in mind that the IRS and the courts will use a number of different criteria to subjectively make the determination, so your job is to ensure that you do as many of these things as possible for your independent contractors:

- **Independent contractor agreements.** First and foremost, make sure you have a contract that specifically calls out the independent contractor relationship you have with your contractor. If you plan to hire a lot of ICs, it's worth the time and cost of getting a contract attorney to create a sample agreement that you can use for all your projects and all your contractors.
- **Separate entity.** Encourage your ICs to set up a separate corporate entity under which they do business. If they have their own LLC or corporation under which they provide services, they are less likely to look like your employees to the IRS.
- **Invoices.** Have your ICs invoice you at regular intervals from their corporate entity. Being able to show invoices to the IRS will support your claims that the workers are ICs and not employees.
- **Sub-contractors.** Independent contractors are allowed to hire out the work you contract them to do. If you specifically state that your contractors must do the work themselves, you are likely to be viewed as their employer. Your ICs can hire sub-contractors and bring in additional labor.
- **Work for others.** If possible, ensure that your ICs do contracting work for someone (or better yet, many someones) other than yourself. If a worker receives 100 percent of their income from you, they are more likely to be classified by the IRS as one of your employees.
- **Tools.** Ensure that your contractors provide all their own tools for the job. If you provide the tools (or other materials, for that matter), the IRS will be more likely to look upon you as an employer.
- **Instructions.** Employees are required to adhere to instructions about how, when, and where to work; independent contractors are not. If you tell your workers how to do their job and when to do their job (i.e., you require them to work 8 a.m.-4 p.m. daily), they may be classified as employees.
- **Right to fire.** Make sure that if you fire an IC, you do so for a reason that has clearly violated your independent contractor agreement. You can fire an employee for any reason, but you can only fire an IC based

on contractual obligations and responsibilities.

- **Training.** Never provide any type of training for your ICs. While employees are permitted to receive training from an employer, if you provide training to your ICs, they will look like employees to the IRS.

CHAPTER 16
MANAGING YOUR REHAB

By now, you should have your SOW, your budget, and your schedule all ready to go, leaving you well-positioned to start your rehab off on the right foot. But managing a rehab will rarely go as smoothly as you hope or expect. Usually, your schedule is a bit too aggressive, your budget is a bit too small, and there are at least a few things that you've forgotten or missed on your SOW.

If you're not prepared, these things can quickly snowball out of control and your six-week project can easily turn into a 10-, 12-, or even 20-week project. In fact, even under the best circumstances, it's easy for a rehab to get off track. After nearly 100 renovations, in mid-2012 we undertook our first out-of-state project. Our partner on the project was an experienced rehabber who had nearly 300 successful projects under his belt at the time. Between the two of us, we had nearly 400 rehabs worth of experience. We carefully selected our contractors, we had a detailed SOW, a conservative budget, and a realistic schedule.

But despite our extensive experience and diligent preparation, things didn't go smoothly on that first out-of-state project.

We were nearly 20 percent over budget, our schedule almost doubled from eight to 15 weeks, and by the end of the project, our SOW was completely different from when we started. Because we didn't spend enough time ensuring that our new crew of contractors would work well together and knew what was expected of them, things spiraled out of control quickly, and it was a constant struggle to keep the project from getting derailed completely.

Luckily, the experience from the other projects we'd done allowed us to (barely) get through the renovation, but it just reinforced to us how important it is to stay in control of your project at all times. Through the rest of this chapter, I want to provide some pieces of wisdom on keeping your project under control from start to finish.

Don't Lose Days

When we first started in this business, our typical rehab took about six to eight weeks. The same rehab today takes about three to four weeks. The bulk of the time savings is due to the fact that we no longer have days where our rehab is completely empty, with no work going on.

On our first few projects, it wasn't uncommon for two or three days to go by without anything getting done. There were lots of reasons for this, from poor scheduling (I didn't let my contractors know up front when I would need them) to slow decision-making (it would take two days to pick out light fixtures we wanted to use) to poor management of my contractors (they wouldn't show up and I'd put up with it). All the reasons for lost days were completely my fault, and once I took control of my projects, things started to move a lot faster.

These days, all my contractors know the schedule up front. On day one, we post our schedule in a prominent location in the property, so contractors always know when they are expected to be working and when they are expected to have their tasks completed. If a schedule has to be shifted around, the contractors notify us immediately and we get everything rescheduled. If a contractor can't be there on a specific day that they're scheduled, we'll rearrange the schedule to get another contractor in that day. And we encourage our contractors to talk to each other and communicate when there are issues or delays. We *never* like to have a house sitting empty for 24 hours.

In terms of materials, we know at the beginning of the project when we're going to need things, and we ensure that the needed materials are onsite before they are needed. The contractors know what materials we will provide and what materials we expect them to provide, and if there is ever any confusion over materials and a contractor doesn't have what he needs, he knows that he's empowered to buy it himself and I'll always reimburse him.

Lastly, in terms of managing contractors, I don't put up with contractors who don't show up when they're scheduled to work. I understand that things will sometimes come up and that other jobs can run over, but if a contractor is consistently late or doesn't show up for an entire day at a time without letting me know, I'll happily replace him. Remember, it's *your* jobsite, and you must maintain control of it. If your contractors know that they can walk all over you, they absolutely will.

Successfully working with contractors requires mutual respect. It's your job to clearly define expectations and to ensure that you provide materials and payments as promised; it's their job to show up as promised and to communicate with you clearly and honestly. A smooth rehab requires both sides to keep up their end of the bargain.

Plan Your Schedules Upfront

This goes along with my points from above. Having a schedule planned out ahead of time isn't just good for you and your project, but it's also good for keeping your contractors happy. Contractors only get paid when they're working, and if your failing to plan ahead causes your contractors to lose days of work, they will be much less motivated to finish the job or to work for you in the future.

I go out of my way to ensure that my project schedules are geared towards optimizing my contractors' time. For example, my painter has a large crew that can come in and tackle both the interior and exterior painting in about three days. They are like a well-oiled machine—once they get going, they hardly stop to eat or sleep until the job is completed. But the entire process will get derailed if they can't work on the interior and the exterior simultaneously or if they need to share the property with other contractors while they're working. When that happens, their job can take twice as long, and everyone gets frustrated.

So, to optimize their time, I make sure that I don't schedule them to start working until both the interior and the exterior are ready for paint and I'll never have other contractors working in the house while they are. By doing this for them, not only are they happy and optimizing their working (earning) time, but I'm happy as well because my project is moving along as quickly as possible.

As I alluded to above, one thing I like to do at the beginning of a complex project is to create a schedule, print it on a large piece of paper, and post it at the jobsite. This way, the contractors always know when they're scheduled to be on the job and there's never any confusion. It also allows the contractors to coordinate amongst themselves and ensure that my project manager is aware of the schedule as well.

Schedules shouldn't just be posted on the wall of the house, they should also be included in the contracts you have with your contractors. While the schedule in the contract doesn't necessarily need to be as detailed as the schedule you create for the project, it should at the very least have a start date and an end date.

Prepare for Dependencies

One of the quickest ways to derail a project is to not properly coordinate two contractors who are dependent on each other to complete their jobs.

For example, we will often bring in our electrician at the beginning of the job to upgrade the electrical service or replace the electrical panel. From a scheduling standpoint, since the electrician will be confined to one area of the house while doing this, it would seem reasonable that you could also have other contractors in the house working at the same time. But the electrician will generally need the power turned off while completing a service upgrade, and that means that other contractors won't be able to use their power tools and may not have much light. This can be frustrating for your contractors if they weren't prepared ahead of time.

Sometimes, contractors can't get into the house for some period of time—for example, while the hardwood floors are still wet or while the tub refinisher is working with caustic chemicals. Even situations where one contractor is working inside, and another is working outside can cause problems; for example, if your plumber is fixing the main line outside and needs the water turned off at the same time your sheetrock professionals need water to do their job inside.

Any time you have a situation where one contractor may be waiting for another contractor or one contractor can't complete his work because of what another contractor is doing, you risk frustrating your crew and derailing the renovation. If you're new to rehabbing and don't have a GC to help you coordinate these types of dependencies, you should be conservative and only schedule contractors one at a time, or only when you know they won't get in each other's way. Once you get more experience, and once your contractors get accustomed to working together, these are things that can be planned for upfront and that your contractors should even be able to resolve together when situations arise.

Know Who Supplies What Materials

Some rehabbers want full control over their money and materials, and will provide everything themselves, from lumber to roofing materials to light fixtures and plumbing fixtures. Some rehabbers are just the opposite: They want their contractors to supply everything, so they don't have to deal with it. When it comes to your rehabs and how you deal with materials, you need to decide what is right for you.

Here's how I do it:

For the major trades (plumbing, electrical, HVAC, roofing, carpentry, paint, siding), I have my contractors provide all defined *building materials* and include them in their bid. Building materials include things like lumber, nails and fasteners, sheetrock/tape/mud, paint, roofing materials, concrete and mortar, etc.

I provide all the *finish materials*: light fixtures, plumbing fixtures, appliances, doors, doorknobs, switches and plates, etc.

When it comes to the specialty trades, I have a separate arrangement with each contractor. For the cabinets and countertops, I have a contractor who provides the cabinets and countertops that I specify, and he installs them. Likewise, for garage doors and openers; I have a garage door company that will supply what I specify and install it themselves. And also, for hardwood flooring—I specify the type of wood and then I hire someone to take care of materials and installation. For carpet, I get great carpet prices from my supplier, so I'll provide carpet material and my contractor only provides labor.

The reason we like to provide all finish materials is that we want to have full control over the look of our final product. We want to ensure that the finishes we use will appeal to our customers and that all the finishes coordinate well with each other. For example, if white kitchens and brushed nickel fixtures are popular these days, we don't want our contractors choosing brown cabinets and gold faucets. Most contractors aren't good interior decorators or designers, so don't leave this important job up to them.

You should discuss and negotiate with your contractors before work begins to ensure that it's clear who is supplying which materials. In general, remember that if the contractor is going to supply materials as part of his bid, and it's up to him what materials to use, he will generally use whatever is most inexpensive. This might be fine for things like lumber and fasteners, but again, you don't want your finishes to be decided on price alone.

Note that for the materials we provide, I like to get most of the stuff from one store (Home Depot is our go-to place), and I'll have the store deliver everything at the same time right to the project. This gives us the control we want but allows us to keep the time and effort of shopping for and delivering the materials to a minimum.

Never Pay Ahead of the Work That's Been Completed

Many contractors will tell you that they can't start on your project until you pay them some amount of the total cost upfront. Then, they'll have you continually pay them throughout the project to ensure that you've always paid more than the work that has been completed at that point in time.

This is backwards! If your contractors ever walk off the job or fail to show up for work, you've paid more than you've received in work, and *you lose money*. Instead, your contractors should be working *ahead* of your payments, not the other way around. This way, if the contractor chooses to not show up, he's done at least some of the work for free and *he loses money*.

Of course, most contractors are smart enough to not want to take the risk of you not paying and will refuse to do work ahead of their payments. Now you've reached an impasse—the contractors won't work if they're not paid and you won't pay before the work is completed.

The solution is to offer to pay in many small installments. For example, in the most extreme case, you can pay the contractor at the end of every day for the work that was completed that day, or even at the beginning of the day for the work to be completed that day. This ensures that the contractor never has to worry about losing more than a day's pay to an unscrupulous investor who doesn't pay, and you can ensure that if the contractor ever doesn't show up, you're not out any money. As you and the contractor learn to trust each other, the time between installment payments can increase.

Certainly, there will be cases where the materials are a considerable portion of the total contractor cost—such as getting a roof replaced or sheetrocking an entire house—in which the contractor will rightly want some payment upfront to ensure he's not buying a bunch of materials he never gets paid for. In these cases, I like to agree to pay for the materials upfront, but I insist on making my payment directly to the material supplier instead of handing the contractor a big check for the materials. Again, this will protect both sides, and as you build trust, you can modify these arrangements to suit both parties.

Make Sure You Visit the Jobsite

Best case, you or someone on your management team will be on site at any time a contractor is working on the property. Unfortunately, this isn't always realistic, and if you have a trusted crew that you've worked with in the past, this may not even be necessary. But if you're not going to be at the property full time, make sure you at least check in a couple times a day—and make them surprise visits.

Too many investors will let their contractors know exactly when they plan to be at the property. For example, they'll meet the cabinet installer at 9 a.m. to let him in the house, and then say, "I'll be back at 2 p.m. to check up and see if you need anything." While this won't matter with good contractors, if you have a bad one, you've now given him the information he needs to slack off for the next couple hours or go finish up another job down the street. He knows he just needs to be back by 2 p.m. to avoid getting caught not doing his job.

I know this sounds far-fetched, but there are many contractors who overbook their schedules, and will use any opportunity they can to make it seem like they're in two places at once. The really bad ones will not just screw up schedules by doing this, but they will also take investors for extra money by pretending to be working on a job when they are not. You want to be sure that your contractors are working when you're not around, and more importantly, you want to be sure that they're working on *your* project.

To avoid problems, don't tell your contractors when you'll be visiting the site, and don't consistently show up at the same time. For example, if you stop by at noon during your lunch break, every once in a while, you should take a late lunch, just to keep your contractors on their toes. Or send a friend over to check on progress every once in a while, if you can't do it yourself.

At First Sign of Trouble, Don't Hesitate to Fire a Contractor

While it may be a pain in the butt to have to find a replacement mid-project, it's much worse to have to deal with a bad contractor for any amount of time.

The biggest mistake I see rehabbers make is not getting rid of bad contractors quickly enough. They will rationalize that the contractor will get better (trust me, they get worse, not better), or that the project is almost over, and they'll just not hire the contractor in the future.

In most cases, if the contractor is not getting the job done early in the project, things will just get worse as the project wears on. Plus, a bad contractor will not only hurt his part of the project but will also affect the morale of the rest of the crew, who are just trying to finish up, so they can move onto the next job.

Contractors are like dating partners—they are going to be on their best behavior early on in the relationship. If they don't treat you well at the beginning, they aren't going to miraculously get better later on. And because the last 10 percent of any renovation project is going to be the most tedious and time consuming, these bad contractors will tend to leave you high and dry when you need them most.

Let me leave it at this: If you have any doubts about a contractor, go find another one. There are plenty of great contractors out there, and it's not worth your frustrations to stick with one who's not performing.

CHAPTER 17
AGENT OR FSBO?

Okay, you've successfully managed your contractors through the rehab on your property. You're now one step closer to collecting your paycheck. Let's get this house sold!

While I prefer to use a licensed real estate agent to sell my properties (for me, this wonderful person would be my wife), there are also some situations where selling your property yourself—commonly called "for sale by owner" or FSBO—makes sense.

In this chapter, I'm going to discuss the value of having a great real estate agent, what types of tasks that agent should accomplish for you, and when you might find that doing it yourself is the preferable alternative. In general, all this information is going to be more important in a buyer's market—where houses are more difficult to sell—but having a great listing agent is important in any market.

The Value of a Good Agent

First, it's important to understand the role of an agent when it comes to selling your investment property. While selling an investment property isn't all that different from selling any other piece of real estate, there are some unique aspects.

For example, your property may be vacant, so much more care needs to be taken to maintain upkeep and ensure showings are done well. Second, because buyers will often have questions about repairs that were made and upgrades that were done on a rehabbed property, the agent needs to understand the basics of renovation and the details of your particular renovation.

All that aside, let me break down the three main areas that I use to evaluate a listing agent to determine if they are good enough to try to sell my deals:

1. Listing and marketing
2. Negotiating
3. Getting to the closing table

Listing and Marketing

The first responsibility of the listing agent is to actually put your property on the MLS (list it) and to get the word out to every potential buyer that it's available and awesome (market it).

Here are some of the things you should be looking for from an agent when it comes to listing and marketing your property:

- **Accurate pricing.** One of the most important aspects of being a listing agent is the ability to accurately determine how much a property will sell for. Overestimate, and you run the risk of not getting any offers, letting the listing get "stale," and keeping the investor from making their profit. Underestimate, and you're leaving money on the table that should be going into the seller's pocket. Great agents know how to accurately price a property; even better agents can tell you how much longer or shorter the property will sit if you adjust your price, allowing you to do your own cost-benefit analysis on the pricing decision.
- **Effective sales message.** Anyone can write a few grandiose words about your property and throw up a half-dozen average pictures. A great agent recognizes that the listing is the premium opportunity to make an excellent first impression on your buyers. The goal is to get them excited about seeing the property just from looking at the listing. If they're excited about seeing the property and have a day or two to look forward to it, they start building up an emotional attachment in their head. So, while they may be out looking at a number of properties before yours, yours is the one they're looking forward to. A great agent knows how to write listing copy to really connect with buyers and knows how to take pictures (or hire someone to take pictures) that present a "wow" factor in the listing.
- **Getting showings.** For $300, you can list your property yourself on the MLS using a flat-fee listing service. So, don't fool yourself into believing

that you need an agent to get you onto the MLS, or that an agent is good just because they get you showings based on your MLS listing. Great agents have a network of other agents with whom they work each time they get a new listing in order to market the property and find targeted buyers. If you can expect to get five or ten showings the first weekend just from listing the property on the MLS, you should expect 20 to 30 showings if you have a great agent.

- **Preparing for showings.** Great agents don't leave things to chance. For example, in our business (where my wife is the agent for our properties), we keep each house on a portable alarm system. One reason we do this is to protect our investment. But the bigger reason is that we want to ensure that buyers' agents *must* call us and let us know *before* they show the property. (Our listing asks for 30 minutes notice, so we can turn off the alarm.) This gives us time to send one of our employees over to the property to turn on the lights, open the blinds, verify the temperature, refill the scented air-fresheners, make sure there are flyers and blank contracts on the counter, and make sure there is no trash in the yard. This ensures that every single showing makes the best possible first impression on the buyer.

- **Soliciting offers and getting feedback.** Any agent can tell you that you had ten showings over the past week. A great agent knows how each of the showings went, what the buyer and her agent liked and (more importantly) *didn't* like about the house, whether an offer is forthcoming or not, and any other information pertinent to the sale. How does your agent do this? Simple... they pick up the phone and call the buyer's agent for feedback a couple hours after the showing. I can't tell you the number of investors I speak with who say they can't get an offer, and when I ask what negative things the buyers have noticed, they say, "How would I know?"

- **Evaluating progress.** Not every showing is going to result in an offer. Hopefully, if the property is priced correctly, you'll get an offer within the first three or five showings, but sometimes, even that doesn't happen. When that doesn't happen, the important task is to find out why. A great agent will be able to use the market data and feedback they've gotten to determine this. Does the property need a price drop? Does it need a fence around the back yard to shield the trash in the neighbor's yard? Does it just need more time and a couple more showings?

Negotiating

Negotiating is the second major area where you'll want to evaluate an agent. While there are several aspects of selling real estate that require strong negotiation skills, I'm going to focus on two.

The first is negotiating an initial contract with a buyer. I know a lot of investors who think they are great negotiators and who insist on doing offer negotiations themselves. But in reality, as the seller, you are probably not as well suited to negotiate your own property sale as someone who is less emotionally connected and vested in the property. There are two risks that an emotionally invested person faces when negotiating their own deals:

1. **Overvaluing the Deal**

   By overvaluing the deal, I mean that many sellers believe their properties are worth more than they actually are; or are too emotionally invested in the property to recognize a fair offer.

   For example, it's the first weekend on the market for your newly rehabbed property, and you're just waiting for that full-price offer from the first person who walks through. Surprise! The first buyer makes an offer $20,000 below the list price. You're positive the house is worth full price, so you counter with full price. The buyer increases his offer to $10,000 below list. Again, you counter with full price. The buyer, annoyed that you're not willing to even budge, walks away.

   Perhaps this was a good move on your part, and you'll be getting that full-priced offer on the next showing. Or perhaps you lost the only offer you'll end up getting for the next six weeks. A great agent would be able to put that specific offer into perspective for you and may have been able to save you that deal.

   For example, perhaps $10,000 less than list price was a great offer, and you just couldn't see it because you were blinded by excitement. Or perhaps the agent would have seen some aspect of the deal—other than price—that you could have conceded to the buyer without dropping the price. Regardless, the fact that you were so excited about the first weekend on the market and a potential sale may have clouded your judgment when it came to negotiating that offer. A great agent wouldn't let that happen.

2. **Undervaluing the Deal**

   On the opposite end of the spectrum are those investors who are willing to give up too much in the negotiation because they don't recognize the value of their property. (I've fallen into this trap myself.) These are the sellers who get an offer the first weekend at $20,000 below list price and want to jump on it. Perhaps they don't even want to present a counteroffer for fear of losing the buyer.

While these sellers will often get their houses sold quickly, they tend to leave a lot of money on the table that could have gone right into their pockets. A great agent will let you know when you're selling yourself short, and will push you to get more, even if it adds a little risk. In fact, many investors are cautious of negotiating, overestimating the risk of losing a deal. In some cases, a great agent will remind you that the buyer is expecting a counter-offer, and if you accept without making one, he may wonder what's wrong with the property if you're willing to give it up so easily!

So, when it comes to negotiating an offer, a great agent is invaluable. Not only is a great agent a strong negotiator, but a great agent is also able to convince you when you're not thinking clearly when it comes to your negotiating tactics.

The second piece of the negotiating puzzle that great agents help with is after the inspection and at the end of the due diligence period.

Oftentimes, the buyers will come back with a list of "demands"— perhaps repairs, additions (like a new fence), or even a decrease in the agreed-upon price of the house. A great agent has been through this process many times and knows when a buyer is just fishing for concessions and when a buyer is seriously at risk of walking away from the deal if he doesn't get what he wants.

Getting to the Closing Table

Getting your property under contract is one thing, but actually getting to the closing table is another. Especially in markets where lending is tight, buyers are flaky, and good real estate professionals are in short supply, a high percentage of deals risk falling out of escrow if the agents don't do their jobs well.

Here are some things we do in our business to ensure that each property gets to the closing table. Even the best agents may not be as persistent as this (and that's not necessarily a bad thing), but the best agents will do as much of this as necessary to get the deal closed:

- **Get appraisals ordered.** A great agent will get in touch with the buyer's mortgage broker/lender within a few days of getting a contract. The first order of business is getting an appraisal ordered, and great agents will make sure that gets done quickly. If it takes two weeks to get the appraisal, and then the appraisal comes in low and the contract needs to be renegotiated, that's two weeks wasted. I make sure an appraisal is ordered within 48 hours of the contract being signed. If it takes longer than that, I will suspect that the broker or the buyer is lying about how qualified the buyer is to buy, and often means they want more time before they have to pay for that appraisal.

- **Be present for the appraisal.** When the real estate market is hot, and banks are confident about lending on real estate, most appraisals will indicate that the house is worth whatever the purchase price is, or more. But in down real estate markets where credit is tight, and banks are skittish and conservative, it's not uncommon for appraisals to come in below the purchase price—sometimes far below. In down markets, one of the most important aspects of your sale may be getting the appraisal to come in at the contract price. A great agent will either be present for the appraisal or arrange for you to be present, with comps in hand to provide to the appraiser. We will even take the agent lockbox off the door so that if the appraiser shows up without anyone telling us, he needs to call us to get in. When an appraiser calls us from the property, we tell him we have the key and we'll run right over. Luckily, we're usually informed beforehand, so we can be there waiting for him and ready to provide any necessary information. Appraisals can make or break a deal, and again, a great agent leaves nothing to chance.

- **Be present for the inspection.** I would never expect my agent to be present for a buyer's inspection (and neither should you), but a great agent will recommend that you be there and will do everything she can to get the buyer to agree to it. This way, you will know beforehand what the buyer is likely to come back with when requesting repairs. More importantly, if the inspector brings up something that you think may be confusing to the buyer (and that you think might concern the buyer unnecessarily), you can ask leading questions right then and there to get the inspector to clarify and make the buyer feel more comfortable. Of course, if the buyer really doesn't want you there, you should respect his wishes and not go.

- **Get the closing scheduled.** This seems like an easy item, but in reality, it's a big one. The average agent will wait until a few days or a week before the contract closing date to schedule a specific closing date and time. A great agent recognizes that a firm date and time slot will help everyone stay on schedule. Our process is, within 48 hours of the contract being finalized, we call the closing attorney and get the closing put on the calendar. While this date may change (hopefully get pulled in sooner!), when you have something actually scheduled, it makes people focus on hitting that date. Trust me, you'll get much more cooperation from the lender when you say, "Are we still on schedule for August 18 at 3:30 p.m.?" than if you say, "Are we still going to hit mid-August for this closing?"

- **Communicate.** Great agents over-communicate. There shouldn't be more than 72 (preferably 48) hours that go by while you're under contract that your agent doesn't call or email you. Even if it's only to say, "Nothing new... everything on track." If your agent knows that they are going to have to give you a status report every few days, it means they also know that *they* have to get the status at least every couple days. Whether that means calling the broker, the processor, the buyer's agent, or the closing attorney, a great agent keeps in touch with everyone, all the time.

These are my basic criteria for a real estate agent, and those that do most, or all of these things well, are the agents you want on your team. Not only will they make you more money on each deal, but they will save you countless hours, countless headaches, and countless sleepless nights.

Keep these things in mind as you continue to read this chapter and as you consider whether you want an agent to represent you or if you prefer to try to sell your houses yourself.

When to Consider "For Sale by Owner"

I very rarely recommend to investors that they should attempt to sell their property "for sale by owner" (FSBO), but there is one situation when I believe not only is a real estate agent not needed, but when a real estate agent probably will do more harm than good. And that's when you plan to resell your property to another investor as opposed to a retail buyer/owner-occupant.

When reselling to an investor, there are many marketing avenues available to you that will be better than the MLS—these include online classified sites such as Craigslist.org, real estate investor association meetings, local wholesalers who have buyers, and just general networking with other investors who may be interested in the property or know someone else who might be. While listing on the MLS may still be advantageous (see the next section on "flat fee listings"), I don't believe that working with the typical real estate listing agent will be to your advantage when your target buyer is an investor.

The reason for this is that most traditional real estate listing agents don't understand how investor buyers analyze a deal, and very few real estate agents in general speak the language of real estate investing. Using a typical real estate agent to market your properties to investors will more likely scare them off than attract them.

All that said, if you really need help marketing your property to investors, try finding a couple of buyer's agents who specialize in working with investors. While these agents probably won't want to list the property for you, they very well may have an investor in their network who is looking for properties. The other advantage to going directly to the buyer's agents is that you will only have to pay one side of the commission on the deal, as you're not paying an agent to list and market the property.

Flat Fee Listings

Over the past decade, brokerages have popped up that specialize in helping sellers get their properties listed and marketed on the MLS for a very low cost—usually a fixed price between $250 and $750. These brokers are often called "discount brokers," and their fixed price listing services are usually referred to as flat fee listings.

Flat fee listings differ from traditional "full service" listings in that the flat fee listing service generally only includes the MLS listing. If the seller wants additional services, they have to pay for those. Those additional services may include:
- Sign in yard
- Realtor lockbox
- Photographs of property for listing
- Taking phone calls from buyers and agents
- Open houses
- Negotiating help

- Contract preparation
- Closing coordination

After all these additional costs, the seller is paying much more than the low price they initially thought they were paying. In fact, I've heard some flat fee listing services claim that—in total—the average seller who uses a flat fee listing will pay about 7 percent of the sale price in commissions and fees. This is 1 percent *more* than the typical commission structure for a full-service listing. In other words, flat fee listings often cost sellers more, not less!

In addition, in my experience, buyer's agents don't typically like dealing with listings that are flat fee, and often steer their buyers away from any properties listed with a flat fee or discount broker.

There are many reasons for this:

1. The big flat fee brokerage in my area (one of the most successful brokerages in the country, incidentally) is known for very poor service. Many agents don't like to deal with them or their clients.

2. Sellers who use flat fee listing services are often less responsive than a listing agent, which makes sense because a listing agent has the job of being responsive. Agents with serious buyers don't like to have to deal with non-responsive sellers or listing agents.

3. Showings can sometimes be difficult, as there aren't always agent lockboxes on the houses, and agents have to speak with the homeowner who may sometimes be difficult.

4. Homeowners like to follow the agent and buyer around. Buyer's agents and buyers *hate* like this.

5. Buyer's agents realize that they may have to do some seller handholding through the process if the flat fee lister doesn't provide any backend support. Buyer's agents are already doing lots of brokerage work to help their buyer, so they don't want to have to do the listing agent's job as well.

If you decide to sell through a flat fee service, you may lose some potential buyers who will never get to see your house.

CHAPTER 18
STAGING

Staging involves preparing a home for resale by making it look attractive through furniture layout, accessories, color, and design. For rehabbers who are trying to sell vacant houses, staging involves bringing in furniture, pictures, and beds to make the house appear to be lived in, which will give buyers an emotional connection to the home and help them envision what it might look like once they move in. Additionally, staging can help highlight the great features of a house while minimizing the less attractive features. For example, staging can help define a large empty space and also help make a small space appear much larger than it is.

My wife and I are both big fans of staging our properties. While it's hard to provide any quantitative data to support it, we're both convinced that our decision to stage each and every one of our properties has contributed to our success in this business. It's not uncommon for buyers and their agents to tell us that the staging was not only what attracted them to the property in the first place (they saw the pictures on the MLS), but that the staging effectively sold the house.

In this market, I don't believe that staging will necessarily help you command higher prices for your rehabs, but I do believe it will help you get your properties sold much more quickly than without staging. And any time you can reduce the number of days your property sits on the market, the more money you'll put into your pocket and the less stress you'll have in this business overall.

If you decide you want to stage your property, you'll need to decide upfront whether you want to hire a stager to handle everything or whether you want to do it yourself. A professional stager brings a lot of experience and expertise, but if you have a good eye for design, understand color palettes and complementary colors, and are a good bargain shopper, why not try doing it yourself to save some money? That said, staging is about detail, and if you don't have the skill to do it yourself, find someone who can, or bring in a professional who can get it all done quickly and stress-free.

Deciding Whether to Buy or Rent Furniture

If you plan to do your staging yourself, at some point you're going to have to decide whether you would prefer to rent the furniture from a furniture rental store or whether you'd prefer to buy the staging furniture outright. This is an important question that will have many ramifications. If you purchase furniture, you'll need to deal with moving and moving costs and will potentially have to deal with storage and storage costs. Moving and storage of furniture adds extra overhead to the process that may not make sense if you only plan to rehab one or two properties per year. But if you plan to undertake at least four projects per year, you may find that—from a financial perspective—it's worth owning your own furniture.

If you're a savvy shopper, it should only take one to two rehabs before it becomes more economical to buy furniture for your staging as opposed to renting it. The big question will be what to do with the furniture between projects. Most people will store the furniture in a storage unit, which increases the cost of having the furniture and also increases the cost of moving the furniture. We try to do two things to reduce our costs and moving expenses:

1. When we have extra furniture that we know we won't need for several months, we will either do staging for other investors or rent the furniture out to other investors. Not only does this keep storage and moving costs down, it actually allows us to make money on our staging furniture. In fact, I would be willing to bet that we've made more money on our staging furniture by staging and renting to others than we've spent on the furniture in the first place. It's a second income stream for us!

2. If you have at least one project going at all times, you can always store extra furniture in the basement or garage of a house that is currently undergoing renovation. If you can accomplish this, you can eliminate the need for a storage unit, and if you will eventually

use the furniture in the house it's stored in, you can reduce moving costs as well.

Another advantage to owning your staging furniture is that often-times, buyers will want some of the furniture as part of the house purchase. Sometimes we sell furniture piecemeal (for example, a buyer asks to buy the couch in the living room); in those cases, we nearly always sell the piece for more than what we paid. And sometimes a buyer will ask for a bunch of furniture, and we'll negotiate it into the purchase price of the house; perhaps we'll offer to throw in all the furniture for a full-price offer. The higher selling price almost always outweighs the cost of the specific furniture we're losing, so this is another opportunity to make extra cash on the project.

Top 16 Staging Tips

There are plenty of good books on staging and how to prepare your house for sale, but there are also some tips and tricks that we've learned by staging over 150 houses in the past several years. While every tip may not work in every house, being able to pull out the right trick at the right time can often help turn an average room into an awesome room.

1. Clean!

This really should go without saying, but unfortunately, in my experience, it often doesn't. Before you ever even think about showing your property, you should have a professional cleaner come in and clean your house top to bottom. When buyers think of a rehabbed house, they think "new," and it's your job to satisfy that expectation.

2. Buy Small and Light

The first rule of staging furniture is to find pieces that are both light-weight (you'll be moving it often) and small (makes the rooms look bigger). Surprisingly, it's difficult to find either of these things, but if you shop around, they can be found. My wife gets most of our staging materials at four places: American Signature Furniture, a small, locally-owned furniture shop called Furniture Land, Walmart, and Craigslist. In fact, most of the furniture comes from Craigslist and most of the accessories come from Walmart.

We used IKEA for many items in the first house, but quickly realized two problems: Things that are put together *inside* a room can be tough to get *out* of the room, and IKEA furniture is *heavy* (think industrial-strength-particle-board-heavy!).

3. Bargain Hunt

Now that we have over a dozen sets of staging furniture, we've learned how to purchase for an entire house (furniture, accessories, pictures, etc.) for about $2,500.

My wife will often buy things that are discontinued, pieces of larger sets where other pieces are damaged, and items with small scratches or imperfections. She even has salespeople from stores call her when they have "small and cheap" stuff available, as they know what she does and what she's looking for.

4. Fake Beds

For things like beds, instead of a mattress, you can use two box springs or a box spring under a blow-up mattress. With the comforter on top, you can't tell it's not a real bed (see picture below), but it's much cheaper and much easier to move than a real bed. Be prepared, though, to rebuild it every time a buyer sits on it, which is about three times a week!

5. Reds and Browns

We like to color coordinate each set of furniture, picking one or two colors that will bring the entire house together. The colors we use will depend on the characteristics of the house (lighting, color of the floors, color of the cabinets), though we've found that buyers are especially fond of deep reds and brown. Most of our houses now incorporate red and brown.

6. Use Staging to Hide Flaws

Staging is a great way to hide any minor defects that buyers might otherwise fixate on.

For example, in a recent bathroom remodel there was a cracked tile behind the magazines and under the plant. We made sure the buyers knew about them after the contract was signed (so they could back out if it was really a deal-breaker), but it kept the buyers from focusing on it when they first viewed the house.

Here's another example—in this room, there was a small, oddly shaped nook that most buyers would think is wasted space. Instead, we found the perfect sized desk that highlights its potential use as an office space:

7. Use Staging to Highlight Positives

Staging is a great way to highlight the best characteristics of a property as well.

For example, whenever we sell a house with a large master bedroom, we like to highlight the size of the room by including a sofa and table:

8. Use Window Treatments

We like to make rooms feel taller and windows look larger than they actually are with clever curtain positioning. In the house in the picture below, the ceilings were only about seven feet high; but with the positioning of the curtain rods well above the windows, it draws the buyer's eye farther upward, emphasizing the height of the room and making the ceilings appear much taller than they actually were:

9. Lots of Light

Buyers love light and bright. It's simple to bring more natural light into your rooms while visually increasing the size and prominence of your windows by positioning curtains on the right and left sides of the window trim, rather than covering the windows themselves. This frames the windows and makes them appear significantly larger and more substantial than they actually are, which is really appealing to buyers.

Here's an example:

10. Even More Light

While natural light is best, any light will help. Keep your eyes open in stores like Home Depot, Lowe's and Target for three-sets of lamps on the clearance shelves and use them wherever you can in the house you're staging. We've picked up a few sets of three—including a floor lamp and two table lamps—for around $20 a set! It's not uncommon for the houses we stage to have ten or more lamps throughout.

Even better, if you or your agent have time to get to the house before your buyers arrive for a showing, brighten up your rooms by turning on every single light in that house, even if it's already sunny outside. This little trick, combined with all the sunlight shining in through your properly staged windows, inspires buyers and leaves them with a cheerful and happy (instead of doomy and gloomy) feeling. Cheerful and happy translates to a buyer being a heck of a lot more willing to write up a contract!

11. Glass Tables

It's no secret that larger spaces generate higher sales prices. So, to show off all that space that exists (or doesn't really exist) in great rooms, living rooms, and dining rooms, use glass top tables. This is also a great way to highlight new hardwood floors.

12. Use Mirrors

We like to use lots of mirrors. It allows the buyer to see themselves in the house. Don't go overboard—stick with simple and classy and you won't go wrong.

13. Protect Your Carpet

If you've installed new carpet in the house, put down plastic carpet protector. Not only does it keep the carpet from getting stained, but buyers will note the effort to protect the carpet indicates that we took extra care when renovating. Another advantage to protective carpet plastic is that you can use it to strategically define the "flow" and walkways through the house, which establishes a clear path for buyers to follow.

14. Use Rugs

While we're talking about the floor, remember that area rugs are an awesome way to add visual interest with splashes of color, define and anchor your furniture to create specific spaces in large rooms, add a sense of warmth to tile and vinyl floors, and draw attention to your newly finished hardwoods or newly installed carpeting.

Area rugs don't have to be expensive to be effective; in fact, most of our area rugs come from seasonal clearance sections at home improvement and big box stores. When used in the right context, area rugs are like artwork accents for your floor!

15. Three Is the Magic Number

When it comes to art and design, three is a very common number. Having three items on a table, three pictures on a wall, or three pillows on a couch, tends to be visually appealing. When in doubt, use groupings of three in your staging.

16. Two Sets of Staging

We'll often stage each house twice. The first time, we're staging for our pictures. We'll arrange furniture and accessories in a way that allows us to get the best shot of the room possible, without worrying about the balance of the entire room. For pictures, we need to show all the highlights of the room (windows, nice lighting fixtures, etc.) all in a small area. But, for our final staging, we want the room to be balanced, which will often require us to move stuff around after the pictures are taken.

CHAPTER 19
BUYER DUE DILIGENCE

If you've done everything right up through this point, it probably didn't take too long to get an offer and negotiate a contract on the sale of your house. But, there's still a lot that needs to happen before you get to the closing table.

The two biggest hurdles to clear for most house sales are the buyer's inspection and the buyer's appraisal. In this chapter, I'm going to touch on how to manage and control both of these processes. I'm also going to discuss some of the big "gotchas" to look out for when dealing with your buyer's financing, as financing issues will be the No. 1 reason your deal may not work out the way you plan.

Preparing for the Buyer's Inspection
The buyer will likely schedule his inspection within a few days of the contract being signed. This is your last opportunity to make sure the house is in pristine condition, that everything is working properly, and that there are no outstanding safety concerns that an inspector might flag. While it's important to have verified that all repairs were completed properly prior to the house being listed for sale, it's doubly important that you do a final inspection at least 24 hours prior to the inspector arriving, so that you can identify any issues and get them fixed prior to inspection.

For my rehabs, I have created a checklist of items that I will run through after the rehab is complete and prior to the inspector visiting the property. While this checklist won't cover everything that the inspector is looking for, it will cover the basics; if the inspector finds that you didn't complete the basic repairs in a quality manner, he'll be especially scrutinizing when looking at the more complex issues.

Also note that the checklist I provide in the next section is relevant to the types of properties and renovations that we do—feel free to add, delete, or modify items in this checklist to suit your particular properties and circumstances.

Final Walk-Through/Inspection Checklist

ELECTRICAL
- ❏ Panel inspected and well-labeled (and at least 150 amps)
- ❏ All outlets/ switches/ covers new or clean
- ❏ All outlets tested, including GFIs
- ❏ GFIs in kitchen, baths, exterior
- ❏ All lights/ switches tested
- ❏ Fans are working, secure, and not noisy or wobbly
- ❏ Garbage disposal works
- ❏ Garbage disposal electrical wiring is insulated (wiring not exposed)

PLUMBING
- ❏ Main line checked (meter doesn't spin when water is turned off at main house shut-off)
- ❏ No interior leaks (meter doesn't spin when water is turned off at main house shut-off)
- ❏ PRV is working (pressure between 40-80 psi)
- ❏ Hot water works
- ❏ Expansion tank on H20 Heater
- ❏ No faucet leaks
- ❏ Hot/Cold correct for all faucets, including showers/ tubs
- ❏ Drain stoppers work in all sinks and tubs
- ❏ All toilets flush easily (handles don't need to be held)

HVAC
- ❏ HVAC maintenance completed, A/C units charged and furnace cleaned (new filter)
- ❏ Thermostat working
- ❏ Insulation on exterior line running from A/C compressor to house

- ❏ Drip pan installed under furnace
- ❏ No obvious damage to ducting (in attic or anywhere else ducting is exposed)

APPLIANCES
- ❏ Stove tested (if gas, verify no leaks)
- ❏ Dishwasher tested and no leaks
- ❏ Washing machine tested (drain full machine to ensure quick drain)
- ❏ Dryer vent hooked up and secure

DOORS/ WINDOWS
- ❏ All doors open and close easily
- ❏ Exterior doors lock/ unlock easily
- ❏ All windows open and close easily (including double-hung opening)
- ❏ All windows lock/ unlock

FLOORING
- ❏ No major squeaks in subfloor
- ❏ Transition strips secured and look good
- ❏ Carpet protection in place

GARAGE DOOR
- ❏ Garage door tested (button on wall)
- ❏ Garage door tested (remote control)
- ❏ Reverse on garage door works (with/ without sensor)

EXTERIOR
- ❏ Roof maintenance completed, pipe boots replaced, nail pops repaired
- ❏ Chimney cap in good shape (no rust or damage)
- ❏ Gutters attached, sloped correctly, and look good
- ❏ Downspouts extended to ground and splash blocks in place
- ❏ No rotted/ missing siding
- ❏ No rotted/ missing trim
- ❏ No rotted/ missing fascia or soffit
- ❏ No holes in siding (including where utilities come into house)
- ❏ Exterior outlets are covered
- ❏ Porch/ deck railings secure
- ❏ Bushes/ trees cut back from house

OTHER

❏ Fireplace tested (gas key available)
❏ Handrails installed and secure on all stairs
❏ Paint touch-ups completed
❏ All bathroom/ kitchen caulking done (showers, tubs, sinks, etc.)

Dealing with Inspection Issues

No matter how well you perform your renovation and pre-inspection inspections, the inspector will invariably find some minor issues with the property. Remember, this is his job, and if he can't find anything wrong, it will appear that he's not doing his job very well. He won't let that happen.

In fact, on houses where I'm concerned that the inspector will have difficulty finding any issues, I may even leave a few minor things incomplete to help him out! For example, disconnecting a gutter downspout near the ground, miswiring an outlet or two, or misaligning a door so it doesn't open or close properly. That said, it's rare that a rehab will be so complete that a good inspector can't find a few issues. And when he does, you can bet that 90 percent of the time, the buyers will be asking you to complete some or all of the identified repairs.

I expect that on every house I'll be asked to complete a handful of repairs, and I always budget some money for this, around $500 to $1,000. If the list of repairs that the buyer requests is small or inexpensive, I'll usually agree to complete all of them. If the list of repairs is more comprehensive or expensive, I'll negotiate with the buyers on which repairs to complete.

In general, I look at repair issues from an inspection to fall into one of three categories:

1. Safety issues
2. Functional issues
3. Cosmetic issues

I will always fix safety issues, as not only do they risk holding up the deal (most lenders will not lend on properties that have safety issues), but they also risk giving me a bad reputation. Safety issues often include electrical repairs, fireproofing concerns, HVAC/gas issues, and water pressure issues.

I will fix functional issues, especially if they are things that should have been addressed during the rehab. Functional issues include things like improperly sloped gutters, cabinet drawers not operating smoothly, or doors and windows not working properly. These are things that we take pride in doing correctly during the rehab, so I will generally agree to fix them when identified by the buyer's inspector.

I will typically not agree to fix cosmetic issues after a buyer's inspection. For example, things like mismatched siding, poor kitchen design or layout, or lack of shelving in closets. While I always want my houses to look good, these are things that the buyer should have noticed during the initial walk-through(s) of the house, and they were aware of these issues prior to the inspection. If these issues didn't dissuade the buyer from putting in an offer on the property, they shouldn't dissuade the buyer from moving forward after the inspection.

Handling Appraisals

One of the biggest areas where flippers often get beaten is in their property appraisals. They buy right, do a great renovation, find buyers happy to pay their asking price, and then find that the property doesn't appraise at a value high enough to complete the sale! Remember, a lender performs an appraisal prior to lending on a property because they want to ensure that the house they are lending against is worth the amount they are lending.

A lender *will not* lend more than what their appraisal indicates the house is worth. If a buyer offers you $200,000 for your house, and the appraisal indicates that the house is only worth $175,000, the lender will only lend up to $175,000, meaning either the buyer will have to come up with the additional $25,000 to buy the house, or you'll need to drop the price to $175,000 to complete the sale!

This is why appraisals are so important and why you should do everything ethically and legally in your power to ensure that any appraisals the buyer or his lender perform on your property come in as high as possible. Obviously, you'd like your property's value to stand on its own without any help from you, but—especially in down markets—anything extra you can do to ensure your property hits its target appraisal price is important.

Appraisals are just as much an art as a science. Oftentimes, there is a lot of information that the appraiser is not privy to, such as what the interior of a comparable property looks like, the circumstances surrounding the sale of a comparable property, or the circumstances surrounding the motivation of the seller of other comparable properties. So, while two appraisers may be equally experienced and skilled, they may select different comps, make different adjustments, and come to different values of your property.

While I will assume rehab is top-quality in all respects (visually, functionally, price-to-value), **the key to ensuring consistently successful appraisals is to focus on your interaction with the appraiser himself.** Because the appraiser does have leeway in making decisions on comps and adjustments, his attitude while preparing the appraisal—towards you and the property—may very well impact the result.

Specifically, when dealing with the appraiser, you should strive to do three things:

1. Provide information
2. Build rapport
3. Build trust

By doing these three things, you can go a long way towards getting appraisers to err on the side of trying to help your appraisals come in at your target price. Let's look at each of these in more detail...

1. From a standpoint of providing information, remember that appraisers have a tough job. They need to make a lot of people on different sides of the table happy. Helping them do their job effectively and efficiently will make their lives easier—especially when the underwriter comes back and asks for more details to substantiate the number—and in return, will make your life easier. It's not uncommon for an appraiser to be performing an appraisal in an area that he isn't very familiar with, so if you are intimately familiar with your farm area, you may be more knowledgeable then they would be about which comps are best and other factors that may influence the property's value.

2. For building rapport, if someone knows you and likes you, they are going to want to help you. Ask the appraiser about his family, ask about his business, ask him questions that allow him to feel like you appreciate his "help," and (if it's true) insinuate that you may want to use his services in the future. We don't like to let our friends down, so the goal is to get the appraiser to feel as if you're a friend in the short time you're together.

3. In building trust, remember that many appraisers (and others) are leery of flippers, simply because a few of them give the rest of us a bad name with shoddy work, lying about repairs, etc. Oftentimes, when appraisers walk into a rehabbed property, they assume that the value is *lower* than an equivalent house that isn't being flipped. By proving

to the appraiser that you're in the group of flippers who take pride in their work and do things the right way, you'll get him to appreciate your work and efforts and to trust that your house is probably *more* valuable than an equivalent house that isn't being flipped.

With that background, here are my concrete suggestions on how best to work with appraisers:

- Always ensure that you know when the appraiser is coming to your property. We make sure that our properties are on an agent lockbox and are alarmed. We then tell the lender/broker that the appraiser needs to call us to get access to the property. Nine out of ten times we'll get a call the day before the appraisal, but occasionally the appraiser will call while standing outside the house when he sees the "alarm" sign on the door. When that happens, we tell him how to disable the alarm, but now that we know he's at the property, we can rush right over or send our project manager over to meet him.
- Always make sure you are present when the appraiser is doing his walk-through. This is your opportunity to build rapport, provide information about what work you did, brag about the fact that you pulled all required permits and only used licensed contractors, and to take credit for the great rehab your team has done.
- At the end of the walk-through, you have an opportunity to provide information to the appraiser that he can take back to the office and review. This is the information that will help with the appraisal and justify the final appraised number in case anyone asks.

Here are the things I provide, nicely organized in a folder:

- **Renovation overview.** This is a Microsoft Word document listing all the renovation that was done on the property. It is basically my SOW but written in plain English for the appraiser.
- **Rehab cost breakdown.** This is a Microsoft Excel spreadsheet that contains the breakdown of renovation costs for the property by task. It is basically my project budget using the actual costs from the project.
- **Before/after pictures.** These are before and after pictures of the project to give the appraiser an idea of the amount of work that was completed to justify the increase in price after rehab.
- **Comps:** When possible, I will provide the appraiser comps that I'm familiar with that support the contract price of the property.

Of course, while most appraisers are happy to have you around during the inspection and happy to take the information you have, don't just assume this. I will always ask upfront, "Do you mind if I stick around during your walk-through?" Before I hand over the folder, I will always say, "I certainly don't want to do your job for you, but I have some documents here that will give you more information about the rehab I did, the money I spent, and some of the comps I know about in the neighborhood... Would you like them?"

I've never had an appraiser who seemed bothered by the fact that I stuck around during the walk-through (most of them are talkers and like the company); and I've never had an appraiser who didn't want my extra information. (Again, most of them were very appreciative of anything I had.)

Do these things and you can be sure that the appraiser will see your point of view and hopefully use the leeway inherent in the process to your advantage.

Beware of Buyer Financing Traps

Especially in down markets where lending is tight, and lenders are creating a lot of restrictions, there are many things you need to be aware of when selling to a homeowner who is getting a loan on the property. Specifically, buyers who are getting FHA or conventional loans will deal with extra scrutiny during the loan underwriting process. While there is no way around the extra scrutiny, you should be aware of the rules so that when issues come up—or more importantly, *before* they come up—you can deal with them as effectively as possible.

FHA 90-Day Rule

FHA loans have specific rules that prohibited flippers from purchasing a property, fixing it up, and then reselling it to a homeowner in less than 90 days from the date they originally purchased it (the FHA 90-Day Rule). In other words, if you purchase a property on July 1, complete the renovations quickly and then get it under contract with a buyer who is getting an FHA loan, that buyer would not be allowed to close on the purchase of the property until at least October 1.

In fact, for many FHA lenders, the buyer will not even be allowed to put your property under contract until October 1, which means they likely won't be able to close until November, extending your holding time on the property by several weeks.

In addition, many FHA lenders will take extra steps to ensure that a renovation was completed properly and that the flipper didn't cut corners. This may include a second appraisal or a full FHA inspection.

When dealing with an FHA buyer, I will always assume that the lender is going to ask for a list of repairs and an itemization of the repair costs. Not all lenders will ask for this, but I expect that they will, and I always have that information ready to be provided. To be safe, I will often include a list of renovation details, invoices, and receipts—anything to substantiate the work I've done and to support the resale value.

In some cases, if I'm concerned about the timelines of reselling to an FHA buyer—for example, the property is listed for resale within three months of my purchase—I will either put in the listing that I'm not willing to accept an FHA buyer, or I will try to convince any FHA buyers that come along that they should consider another type of loan instead. Because conventional loans these days have pretty much the same down payment and credit requirements as an FHA loan, convincing an FHA buyer to switch to a conventional loan is often not very difficult.

Conventional Loans

While your buyers getting conventional loans won't have the same restrictions and underwriting standards that FHA buyers will have, you'll find that many conventional lenders will require you to justify the increase in price from when you purchased the property. Lenders will want to see a list of repairs and may even ask to see receipts for those repairs. If the lender doesn't feel that you've done enough work on the property to justify the price increase, they can refuse to lend.

I've seen this happen several times on deals where I have tried to resell a property to another investor (usually a landlord) after doing a very minor renovation. The other investor attempts to get a conventional loan, and the lender refuses to fund the deal because they don't feel that the small amount of money I put into repairs justifies the $5,000 to $10,000 I'll make in profit on the resale. I don't know of any specific formula the conventional lenders use to determine if a price increase is justified or not but be aware of this general restriction any time you plan to resell a property to a buyer who is getting a conventional loan.

CHAPTER 20
THE CLOSING

For someone who is going through a first-time purchase or sale, the process can be daunting. Not only is there a lot to get done, but the order and timing of the process is very important. While you will hopefully have an agent to help you through this process, it's important that you have a good understanding of it so that you can protect your own interests in the deal.

And not only is it important to understand the process, it's important to understand what steps you can take to be proactive about ensuring that the sale gets completed in a timely fashion and without you risking your time or money during the process.

The rest of this chapter will focus on those two things.

The Closing Process

Here is the abbreviated process for a typical retail closing (meaning a typical private buyer and typical private seller):

1. Buyer and seller sign the contract. The contract is now called "executed" (or more accurately "executory") and the closing process starts.

2. One of the agents will at this point send the contract to a closing agent—either a title company or an attorney, depending on your state. This is referred to as "opening escrow."

3. The closing agent will at some point—hopefully pretty quickly—do a title search or order a title search from another company that specializes in doing them.

4. The buyer will at this point get their inspection. They may also get a termite inspection (or ask the seller to provide a clear termite letter), they may get a survey, they may get mold tests, radon tests—whatever they feel is necessary to be comfortable with the condition of the property. This time period is somewhere between 7 and 14 days but can be anything the buyer and seller agree upon.

5. If the buyer is getting a loan, the buyer at this point will fill out a formal application and get the loan process started. If getting a loan, the buyer will have a contingency in the contract where they have a period of time during which they can back out if they determine they can't get the loan. This is somewhere in the range of 21 to 30 days, but again, can be anything the buyer and seller agree upon.

6. The inspection results come back, and the buyer will ask the seller to make some repairs based on the results. Some of the requests may be necessary to get the loan approved (lenders will often see the inspection report and require certain repairs to ensure the house is in good shape), and if the property is being sold as-is, the buyer can still ask the seller to drop the price in lieu of making repairs. This is done using a contract amendment called a "repair amendment" or something similar.

7. Buyer and seller negotiate these repairs, and assuming they come to agreement, the buyer will generally agree that the "inspection period" or "due diligence period" is now officially over, even if all the time hasn't elapsed in the period.

8. Once the repairs are agreed upon, and after the lender/broker has a reasonable expectation that the buyer can qualify for the loan, the lender will order an appraisal. This is to verify that the property is worth at least the purchase price, so that the bank isn't lending more money than the property is worth. The appraiser will go to the house within a couple of days of the appraisal being ordered, do a walk-through, and then return the appraisal results within a couple days after that. The whole process takes three to seven days.

9. If the buyer is getting a loan, there is almost always an "appraisal contingency" in the contract. This says something along the lines of, "If the appraisal indicates that the property isn't worth what the buyer and seller have agreed upon, the buyer can walk away from the deal." In reality, the other options are that the seller reduces the selling price to whatever the appraisal value is, the buyer figures

out a way to pay the difference out of his own pocket, or a combination of both. But one way or the other, until the sales price and the appraisal value are reconciled, the deal can't go through and the buyer will generally have the option to walk away.

10. Before the end of the financing period, the buyer should determine if they can get their loan (the appraisal is one part of this determination), and by the end of that period, the buyer (or the lender) should provide a "commitment letter" to the seller indicating that the loan is pretty much approved. Once past the financing and inspection periods, if the buyer hasn't backed out with the appropriate reasons, they now either need to complete the deal or lose their earnest money.

11. There could be lots of other contingencies in the contract as well that need to be cleared. For example, the buyer may have a contingency that says they need to sell their house before buying the seller's house. If the buyer can't sell their house, they can back out of the deal based on whatever the terms are in that contingency. There are all kinds of potential contingencies (anything you can imagine), and as long as the buyer and seller agree, it's part of the contract and those need to be cleared before both parties are obligated to go through with the sale.

12. During this time, the closing agent is working on items needed for closing. They include ensuring that there are no title issues (and if there are, working with the seller to resolve them), contacting the HOA to get payment info, and finding out tax information.

13. At some point before closing, the seller makes the agreed upon repairs. The buyer will do a walk-through a few days before the closing to verify any requested repairs have been completed. The lender may send an inspector back to the property as well to verify the repairs if they are required for the loan.

14. The last week or two of the process is generally where the contract, loan information, the inspection report, the appraisal, and all other pertinent documents go to the underwriter. This person works for the lender and makes the final decision on whether the loan gets approved. During this time, the buyer may need to provide some extra documents, as might the seller or the closing agent. Every time the underwriter needs information, the process stalls for a couple days (underwriters are busy, and it can take two or three

days to review everything new that comes in). So, you may think you're a couple of days from closing, but the date keeps getting pushed back; this may be because the underwriter keeps asking for more and more information.

15. The last step the underwriter takes is to verify the buyer's employment. If the buyer lost their job in the past few weeks or lied about their employment, this may not be found out until nearly the end of the process and the whole thing can fall apart.

16. Once the underwriter verifies everything and gives the okay on the loan (called "clear to close"), they will send a closing package, which includes all the documents they need signed, along with a set of instructions, over to the closing agent. Generally speaking, the closing agent is representing the bank, not the buyer or seller, and the closing agent will follow the instructions the underwriter provides on what needs to be signed and taken care of.

17. The closing package contains all the financials of the transaction, including all the costs to the buyer for the loan. The closing agent will take all these numbers, along with all the payment information they gathered from the HOA, tax authority, etc. and create a detailed statement that itemizes how much each side (the buyer and the seller) need to pay and/or receive. This statement (the "HUD-1 or "Settlement Statement") is standard across the country, so it always has the same format wherever you may be.

18. A few days before close, the closing agent should send a copy of the HUD-1 to all parties to review. In reality this often happens the day before or even the day of. When dealing with a bad closing agent, it might happen while you're sitting in the closing office waiting to close.

19. The day of closing, the seller comes to the closing office with the house keys, the buyer comes to the closing office with a certified check for the amount he owes (or he can wire the funds), the bank wires the loan money, and lots of documents are signed.

Now, all that being said, here's a disclaimer:

Some areas may have other steps that I didn't mention; I may have missed some stuff; I may have glossed over some important stuff; some steps may not happen for some reason; sometimes things are done in a different way or by different parties; and, sometimes the process is much longer/shorter/complex/simple/etc. So, don't rely on this to pass any real estate exams—but it should give you a basic idea of the process for your next closing.

10 Tips to Improve Your Closing Success

I can't tell you how often I hear horror stories about how investors are able to get their flip under contract with a buyer, but then are not able to get it closed. The worst part is when I hear about situations where the investor is dragged along for months on end by the buyer and their agents, only to have the transactions eventually fall apart and the investor having to start all over, with nothing to show for it.

With our flips, we don't usually have this issue. About 95 percent of the time, our deals close, and close either on schedule or shortly thereafter. This hasn't always been the case. We've had our situations early on where we've been duped by buyers into long, drawn-out deals that never close—and we've learned from them!

Here are the rules we follow. I highly recommend you follow them as well, and I promise you that your deals will close more often, faster, and with less hassle:

1. The absolute best thing you can do is to have the buyer use a mortgage broker that you know and trust. When potential buyers use our mortgage broker, we know upfront if the buyer is qualified and whether we should even accept the contract. If our broker tells us he can get a loan done for our buyer, it will close 100 percent of the time and almost always on schedule. Our broker is that good, and you need to find yourself a broker who is that good—and get your buyers to use him. At the very least, require your buyers to get pre-qualified with your broker. And if the buyer doesn't use your broker to get the loan, call the buyer's mortgage broker to chat with them to make sure they are familiar with any flip rules that might be applicable and ask about the buyer's qualifications and biggest concerns about getting the loan done. If it's not the broker you recommended, they probably won't tell you anything worthwhile, but you may be able to pick up something from asking the right questions.

2. Get *as much* earnest money as you can. While everyone likes to be optimistic about the deal the day the contract is signed, I can't count the number of times I've looked back a few weeks later and

wished I had required a lot more earnest money.

3. Limit the buyer's financing contingency to 21 days. There is no reason it should take longer to get a loan commitment letter for the buyer (regardless if it's FHA, VA, or conventional). If the broker balks at the 21 days for financing contingency, make the buyer use another broker—there is either an issue with the buyer's finances or the broker isn't very good.

4. Keep the closing date to 30 days or less. Unless you live in a state where a 30-day closing is really tough (like New York), there's no reason it should take longer than that to get a loan funded and a deal closed. Good mortgage brokers can get FHA, conventional, and VA loans done in three weeks (four weeks tops), and that's even when two appraisals are needed. At the very most, give five weeks to close the contract if there is a good reason for the long wait.

5. Did the broker order an appraisal quickly? A sure sign that there is going to be an issue is when the broker drags their feet on ordering an appraisal. Buyers don't want to spend money until they're confident they'll close. Put in the contract that the broker will agree to order the appraisal within 48 hours of the inspection contingency being cleared. This will force the broker to keep the process moving.

6. The day the financing contingency is up, you should receive a loan commitment letter from the broker. No commitment letter, no deal—unless the buyer is willing to put up more earnest money. Put this contingency in the contract if it's not already there (it's standard in my state contract).

7. If the buyer requests an extension of the closing for any reason, ask the agent and broker how confident they are that the extension will be long enough to get the deal closed. Nine out of ten times, they'll tell you that they are certain or near-certain the extension will be enough time to conclude the deal. Reply with, "If you're certain the extension will be sufficient to get this deal closed, I'll grant the extension if the buyer puts up additional non-refundable earnest money. Since they'll need the money for the down payment at closing anyway and since you are certain the deal will close, there's no reason the buyer can't put the money in escrow today, right?" How much extra earnest money to ask for is up to you, but anything up to the entire down payment is reasonable, especially if the agent/broker tells you they are "certain" it will close.

8. Try not to give more than seven extra days in the first extension. (By the way, this is the best way to find out if the broker is really "certain" about the deal—if the buyer refuses to put up more earnest money, you can be pretty sure the deal isn't going to close and the broker already knows it, which is why they won't suggest the buyer put up more money.)

9. If the buyer requests a second extension, do it under the following two conditions (and don't give more than an additional seven extra days):

   a. The buyer puts up the entire down payment as non-refundable earnest money (if they haven't already); and

   b. You get a "kick-out clause" added to the contract, where you can start marketing the house again, and if you find another buyer you'd like to go with, the current buyer has 48 hours to get a clear to close, or you can go with the new buyer and keep any earnest money.

10. If the buyer requests a third extension, you have two choices:

   a. With the kick-out clause, you can extend as long as you want, as you always have the option to go with another buyer if one comes along. The only drawback is that you don't get the earnest money until you terminate the contract (though that shouldn't be your goal); or

   b. The other option is to terminate the contract and tell the buyer that if they figure out their financing issue and can get things resolved, you're happy to sign a new contract and apply the earnest money from the original contract, but you'll have a right to renegotiate terms and ask for additional earnest money for the new contract.

Throughout the process, call the mortgage broker (get the seller's written permission to contact the broker as part of the contract) once per week (Tuesday or Thursdays tend to be the best) and get a status on the loan. Ask what has been done, what the next steps are, if there are any issues that have come up, and when the broker thinks the loan will go to underwriting. In addition, once the loan is in underwriting, have the broker tell you every time the underwriter comes back with conditions, and what *specifically* those conditions are. This will keep you updated on exactly how close you are to the closing and what is holding it up.

FINAL THOUGHTS

Working on the second edition of this text forced me to sit down and re-read the entire book cover-to-cover—something I haven't done since I finished writing it over a half decade ago. It was as if I was reading the book for the first time and made me realize that there was one aspect of this business that I didn't delve into as thoroughly as I would have liked, mostly because there wasn't a natural place to include this information.

I'm including it here.

When I started flipping houses during the 2008 recession, it didn't take long before I started to feel like I understood all the moving parts required to flip houses and create a successful flipping business. I quickly came to understand which aspects of the business required brute force problem solving, which required a more nuanced approach, and which areas of the business we simply couldn't control no matter how we approached it.

I thought I had it all figured out. But, in retrospect, I was incredibly naive.

Over the past ten years, the market has evolved from one of tight credit and buyers having the bulk of the negotiating leverage to one of easy flowing money and sellers controlling the price and pace of sales. The skills required to be successful back when I wrote the first edition of this book, including the ability to raise capital and to stage and market properties, are vastly different from the skills needed as of the time of this writing: the ability to find deals, negotiate with sellers, and effectively manage difficult contractors.

The market has evolved in other ways as well. New forms of financing—

crowdfunding is the first to come to mind—are available today that were never available in the past. Marketing for property has evolved from primarily taking place in the physical world to now requiring internet marketing and online search skills. Thanks to brokerages now putting all their inventory on their websites, homebuyers are more informed and have access to more data than ever before, creating new challenges when trying to outcompete other sellers. And contracting is no longer primarily a word-of-mouth business; most contractors can achieve a level playing field for their marketing simply by listing themselves on popular websites that help them generate leads.

The big takeaway for me has been that real estate is ever-changing, and to be a successful investor over the long term requires a wide array of skills. But even more so than that, successful investors need flexibility and the mindset of continual learning. What worked last year is unlikely to work as well next year; and what will work next year may never have worked in the past. And while some of the tools and techniques being created today may just be passing fads, some may end up transforming the industry.

To be a successful real estate investor, you must constantly ask yourself:

"Where is the market heading?"

"What tools are available to give me a leg up on the competition?"

"What strategies should I be focusing on to grow my business next year?"

"What is my competition doing that I'm not?"

Real estate investing is a vibrant and ever-changing business, and if you're not in the lead, you will quickly find yourself falling behind.

ACKNOWLEDGEMENTS

A book like this is never written in a vaccum. It requires the support, dedication, and input of dozens of people, and I'd like to take a moment to thank those who have helped to make this book possible.

First and foremost, a neverending thank you to my amazingly supportive wife, Carol—you make everything I do easier and more fun, and without you, we never would have started on the journey that led to me writing to this book.

To the tens of thousands of people who have spent their hard-earned money to buy my books and the many thousands of people who have travelled to hear me speak, thank you, thank you, thank you. It is each of you who have given me the motivation to keep writing and creating.

To the dozen or so people who have provided me unsolicited (but very much appreciated!) detailed feedback and critique on the first edition of this book, thank you. The fact that you were willing to take the time to help me make this book better for future readers is a testament to your dedication to helping improve everyone's education.

A special thanks to Josh Dorkin, Scott Trench, Katie Askew, Brandon Turner, and everyone at BiggerPockets and BiggerPockets Publishing. A lot of time, effort, and patience went into building a great partnership that has led to this book, and each of you was instrumental in fostering that partnership. I look forward to working with each of you many times over.

Finally, thank you to the editors, designers and proofreaders who made this book worth reading: Thomas Hauck (Line Editing), Katie Golownia (Proofreading), Wendy Dunning (Layout), Jarrod Jemison (Cover Design), and Kaylee Pratt, who worked hard on the marketing to get this book into your hands.

ABOUT THE AUTHOR

J Scott (he goes by "J") is a full-time real estate investor and rehabber living in the suburbs of Washington, D.C. He is originally from the East Coast, and until spring of 2008, he resided in Silicon Valley, California, where he spent many years in management at several Fortune 500 companies.

In 2008, J and his wife decided to leave the 80-hour workweeks and the constant business travel behind. They quit their corporate jobs, moved back East, started a family, and decided to try something new. That something new ended up being real estate, and a decade later, they've built a successful business buying, rehabbing, and reselling single-family homes.

Since 2008, J and his wife have rehabbed over 150 of their own houses for millions in profits and have partnered with, mentored, and assisted other investors in rehabbing hundreds more properties. These days, the team has branched out, now flipping houses in different parts of the country and focusing on larger new construction projects.

J has detailed his real estate adventure on his blog: www.123flip.com, where he discusses all his team's triumphs, failures, and results—including all the nitty-gritty financial details of the business.

J can be reached at questions@123flip.com.

More from
BiggerPockets Publishing

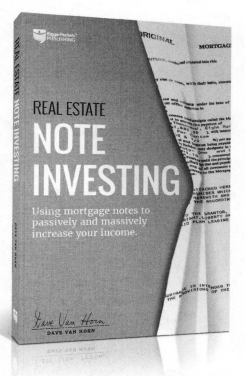

Real Estate Note Investing

Are you a wholesaler, a rehabber, a landlord, or even a turnkey investor? *Real Estate Note Investing* will help you turn your focus to the "other side" of real estate investing, allowing you to make money without tenants, toilets, and termites! Investing in notes is the easiest strategy to make passive income. Learn the ins-and-outs of notes as investor Dave Van Horn shows you how to get started—and find huge success—in the powerful world of real estate notes!

If you enjoyed this book, we hope you'll take a moment to check out some of the other great material BiggerPockets offers. BiggerPockets is the real estate investing social network, marketplace, and information hub, designed to help make you a smarter real estate investor through podcasts, books, blog posts, videos, forums, and more. Sign up today—it's free! **Visit www.BiggerPockets.com.**

The Book on Rental Property Investing

The Book on Rental Property Investing, written by Brandon Turner, a real estate investor and cohost of the *BiggerPockets Podcast*, contains nearly 400 pages of in-depth advice and strategies for building wealth through rental properties. You'll learn how to build an achievable plan, find incredible deals, pay for your rentals, and much more! If you've ever thought of using rental properties to build wealth or obtain financial freedom, this book is for you.

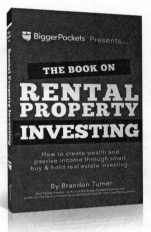

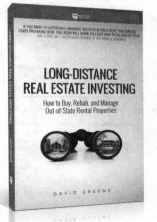

Long-Distance Real Estate Investing

Don't let your location dictate your financial freedom: Live where you want, and invest anywhere it makes sense! The rules, technology, and markets have changed: No longer are you forced to invest only in your backyard. In *Long-Distance Real Estate Investing*, learn an in-depth strategy to build profitable rental portfolios through buying, managing, and flipping out-of-state properties from real estate investor and agent David Greene.

More from
BiggerPockets Publishing

The Book on Investing in Real Estate with No (and Low) Money Down

Lack of money holding you back from real estate success? It doesn't have to! In this groundbreaking book from Brandon Turner, author of *The Book on Rental Property Investing*, you'll discover numerous strategies investors can use to buy real estate using other people's money. You'll learn the top strategies that savvy investors are using to buy, rent, flip, or wholesale properties at scale!

The Book on Tax Strategies for the Savvy Real Estate Investor

Taxes! Boring and irritating, right? Perhaps. But if you want to succeed in real estate, your tax strategy will play a huge role in how fast you grow. A great tax strategy can save you thousands of dollars a year. A bad strategy could land you in legal trouble. That's why BiggerPockets is excited to offer *The Book on Tax Strategies for the Savvy Real Estate Investor*! You'll find ways to deduct more, invest smarter, and pay far less to the IRS!

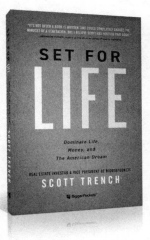

Set for Life: Dominate Life, Money, and the American Dream

Looking for a plan to achieve financial freedom in just five to ten years? *Set for Life* is a detailed fiscal plan targeted at the median-income earner starting with few or no assets. It will walk you through three stages of finance, guiding you to your first $25,000 in tangible net worth, then to your first $100,000, and then to financial freedom. *Set for Life* will teach you how to build a lifestyle, career, and investment portfolio capable of supporting financial freedom to let you live the life of your dreams.

Raising Private Capital

Are you ready to help other investors build their wealth while you build your real estate empire? The road map outlined in *Raising Private Capital* helps investors looking to inject more private capital into their business—the most effective strategy for growth! Author and investor Matt Faircloth helps you learn how to develop long-term wealth from his valuable lessons and experiences in real estate: Get the truth behind the wins and losses from someone who has experienced it all.

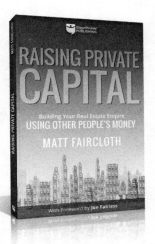

CONNECT WITH BIGGERPOCKETS

and Become Successful in Your Real Estate Business Today!

Facebook
/BiggerPockets

Instagram
@BiggerPockets

Twitter
@BiggerPockets

LinkedIn
/company/Bigger
Pockets

Website
BiggerPockets.com